OLD TESTAMENT STORIES
WITH A FREUDIAN TWIST

The Bible. What a book! Great and wide like the world, rooted in the gulfs of creation and reaching up to the blue sequence of the heavens. Sunrise and sunset, promise and fulfilment, birth and death, the whole drama of mankind, everything is in this book. It is the book of books, "Biblia". The Jews should easily console themselves to having lost Jerusalem and the Temple and the Ark of the Covenant and Solomon's implements and gems. Such a loss is small compared with the Bible, the indestructible treasure that they saved. If I am not mistaken, it was Mohammed who called the Jews "The People of the Book", a name that has remained among the Orient until the present day and that has a deep significance. A book is their Fatherland, their possession, their ruler, their fortune, and their misfortune. They live in the enclosed borderlands of this book; here they exercise their inalienable citizenship, here they cannot be chased away or held in contempt, here they are strong and admirable. Absorbed in the reading of this book, they noticed few of the changes that took place in the real world around them: nations arose and disappeared, saints blossomed, and expired, revelations swarmed over the earth, but they, the Jews, lay bent over their book and noticed nothing of the wild hunt of time that marched over their heads!

Heinrich Heine
(*Ludwig Börne: A Memorial*, 1830)

OLD TESTAMENT STORIES WITH A FREUDIAN TWIST

Leo Abse

KARNAC

First published in 2011 by
Karnac Books Ltd
118 Finchley Road
London NW3 5HT

Copyright © 2011 by Leo Abse
Illustrations © 2011 Martin Rowson

The right of Leo Abse to be identified as the author of this work has been asserted in accordance with §§ 77 and 78 of the Copyright Design and Patents Act 1988.

All rights reserved. No part of this publication may be reproduced, stored in a retrieval system, or transmitted, in any form or by any means, electronic, mechanical, photocopying, recording, or otherwise, without the prior written permission of the publisher.

British Library Cataloguing in Publication Data

A C.I.P. for this book is available from the British Library

ISBN-13: 978-1-85575-832-2

Typeset by Vikatan Publishing Solutions (P) Ltd., Chennai, India

Printed in Great Britain

www.karnacbooks.com

*Dedicated to
the memory of
Leo Abse
(1917–2008)*

CONTENTS

ACKNOWLEDGEMENTS ix

INTRODUCTION
Leo and I xiii
Ania Abse

CHAPTER ONE
Jubal: A discursive meditation
  on music and its origins 1

CHAPTER TWO
Jacob's wrestling match 63

CHAPTER THREE
The judgment of solomon 91

CHAPTER FOUR
Abishag: The lure of incest 127

CHAPTER FIVE
The nakedness of Noah 165

INDEX 207

ACKNOWLEDGEMENTS

I am greatly indebted to three of Leo's closest friends: the late Rabbi Dr Sidney Brichto, Martin Rowson, writer and *Guardian* cartoonist, and Oliver Rathbone, Leo's publisher at Karnac Books, without whom this posthumous collection would not have been published. Those three men promised Leo they would see his final work published and, out of loyalty and friendship, saw the book through to its final form.

In all his books Leo acknowledged the debt he owed to the Labour Party and to those who elected him to Parliament and consequently gave him 30 years of stimulating life as what he himself called "the child of the Mother of Parliaments".

I would like to thank the members of the Savile Club who provided many years of stimulating discussion at 69 Brook Street reflected in this work.

Frances Hawkins, Leo's long term secretary and amanuensis, made significant contributions to these essays.

Leo had two children, Toby and Sheba, to whom he was devoted. He had many talks with them about many of the matters discussed in this book. Leo's younger brother Dannie gave him much stimulus and support.

Leo would have wanted me to acknowledge the support of Dr Stephen Hirst, his ever reliable (to use Leo's own words) physician. Leo was empowered to complete this work due to the professional medical skills of: Helen Anastasion-Scanell, first ward sister; Dr Devinder Singh Bansi, gastroenterologist; Elizabeth J. Duffy, audiologist; Dr Peter Evans, consultant pain specialist; Elizabeth Gould, vision consultant; Dr George Lewith, professor of health research and physician; Dr Vidurath Mayadunne, geriatrician; Dr J. G. Owen, dental surgeon; Dr Panagiotis Vlavianos, gastroenterologist; Prof Ray Playford, warden of school of medicine and dentistry; Christine Pease, reception manager and colleagues of Western GPs surgery; Roger Pope & Partners, opticians; Rosemary Watts, vision consultant; Catherine Wallace, theatre nurse and practice manager; and Richard Wormald, optometrist of McPherson Optician.

Leo consulted widely on these essays. He sent drafts of the text to those who had particular expertise in many different disciplines. The discussions, arguments and redrafting that came from these consultations affected the final form of the book. I would like to acknowledge again on behalf of my late husband: Anda Anastasescu, pianist; Michael Bloch, biographer; R. Alan Cameron, managing director, W.W. Norton, publishers; John Gritten, biographer; Brett Kahr, psychotherapist and composer; the late Chris Phillips, banker; Elizabeth Phillips, biochemist and business consultant; Sally Roe, lawyer; Tony Scotland, biographer and broadcaster; Peter Soar, solicitor, writer and carpenter; and Brian Thompson, writer and educationalist.

This work could not have been completed without the aid and immense encouragement from Leo's close friends and neighbours. On behalf of Leo I would like to make a special acknowledgement to: David Andrews, schoolmaster and clock repairer; Gillon Aitken, literary agent; Dame Eileen Atkins, actress and screenwriter; Gordon Barnes, banker and bee keeper; Karen Barnes, private banker and confidante; Dr Reva Berstoc, psychoanalyst; Colin Bodman, antiques dealer; Michael Boulton, stylist; Ann Brown, antiques dealer; Henry Brown, architect; Nicholas Burden, heating engineer; Stuart Cameron, administrator; Lucy Carter, painter; the late Simon Carter, actor; Laura Coy, marketing consultant; Peter Coy, entrepreneur; Professor Dr Stephen Cretney, of All Souls College, Oxford; Tam Dalyell, former Father of the House of Commons; Richard Dance, garden designer; the late Rt Hon Michael Foot MP; Dr Hywel Francis MP, chairman, Welsh Affairs Select Committee; Richard J. Frank, professor of classics and history at the University of California; Tony Georgion, garage proprietor; Frank Glanville, ambulance officer; Maureen Glanville, dental practice manager; Geoffrey Goodman, editor and biographer; Paul Griffin, stylist; Kenneth Hammond, butcher; the late Patrick Hannan, MBE, journalist and broadcaster; Norman Hawley, decorator; John Haycock, travel tour operator; Sue Haycock, film editor; Richard Herner, art dealer; Anthony Howard, journalist and biographer; David Hughes, political editor of *The Daily Telegraph*; Rt Hon The Lord Johns, PC; Hardy Jones, educationalist; Daksha Joshi, postmistress and philosopher; Milan Joshi, lawyer; Rt Hon Lord Kinnock; Julia Langdon, biographer; the late Charles Leeming, solicitor; Professor Marie Lienard-Yeterin, maitre de conferences at l'Ecole Polytechnique in Paris; Brenda Maddox, biographer and journalist; the late Sir John Maddox, editor of *Nature*; Richard Martin, economist; Professor Eric Moonman, OBE, FRSA, City University, London and Potomac Institute, Washington; Rt Hon Paul Murphy MP, former Secretary of State for Wales/ Northern Ireland; Peter Oborne, political commentator and writer; David Parfitt, painter; Sara Parfitt, archaeologist; Matthew Parris, journalist and writer; Dacre Punt, designer; Conchita San Pedro; Jeremy Robson, publisher of J R Books; Andrew Ross, botanist; Ivan Sadka, solicitor and musician; Bill Shepherd, film producer; Peter Skea, constructor; Mike Steel, lobby correspondent; James Stewart, journalist and broadcaster; Baron Temple-Morris of Llandaff; Lord Touhig of Islwyn and of Glansychan; and George Warburg, banker.

INTRODUCTION

Leo and I

> Life is long if you know how to use it
>
> Seneca, c.5 BCE—AD 65
> *On the Shortness of Life*

Leo Abse lived his life to the full. He may have been small in stature, but he had a larger than life personality. Leo helped many people professionally and privately. His political achievements were immense and he made a profound impact in humanizing the law. He played the leading role in reforming divorce law as well as the law governing adoption and children; he was instrumental in securing reforms that finally decriminalized homosexual activity between consenting adults. He was always kind and helpful to those individuals who sought his advice. Publicly and privately he changed many people's lives for the better.

Leo understood and derived great pleasure from modern social trends, including fashion. He won an award as "the best dressed man in Britain".

He had an extraordinary ability to see through people. I was always amazed at how accurately he could perceive the character of those he had just met. His sound judgment was helped by an uncanny ability to understand people and the future ramifications of contemporary decisions. He predicted the current economic crisis, while many of his friends were still imagining a perfect world with no end.

It was sheer luck that Leo and I met 12 years ago. He had been an unhappy widower for four years. Close friends and neighbours told me how he had boasted that at last he had learned to do his shopping, though he confessed he had not yet mastered the art of using the oven. His elder brother, psychoanalyst Dr Wilfred Abse, had advised him that he "needed a younger woman". It was some sort of serendipity that brought us together.

My own life was greatly enhanced by this remarkable man. We had, intellectually and emotionally, a wonderful ten years together. I had to learn a lot in a very short time; just imagine being suddenly thrown into the deep waters of the world of the great and famous, when you can hardly swim. I had many challenges, some easy and some more difficult, but they were more than offset by the way Leo opened new worlds for me.

This collection of Leo's last essays are writings that he was working on from 2006 up to and during his final illness. They take as their starting point stories from the Old Testament. For Leo, the Bible provided a great inspiration for analysis, reflection, speculation. His own distinctive voice is evident in every essay.

Ania Abse
March 2010

JUBAL

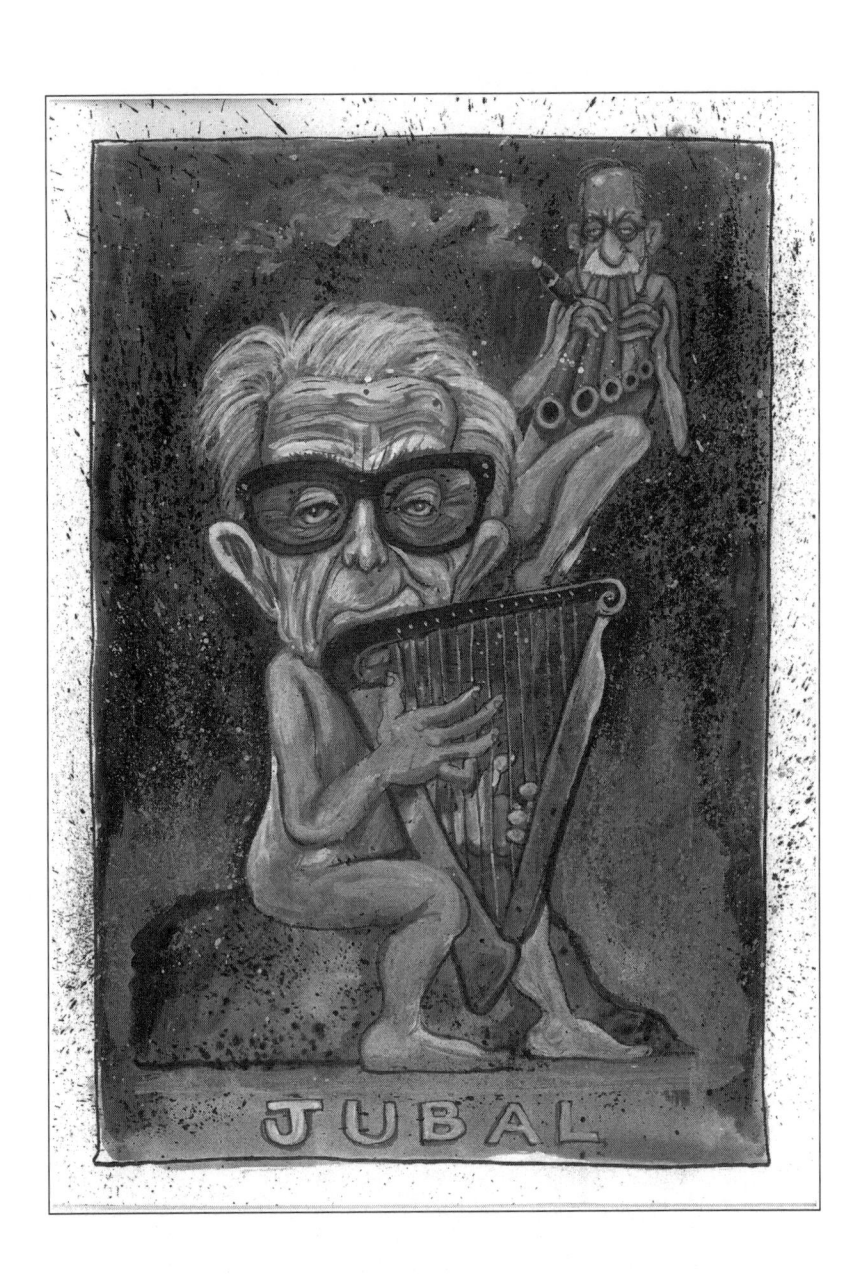

CHAPTER ONE

Jubal: A discursive meditation on music and its origins

As a little boy I would sit at the knee of my Talmudic grandfather and there he would spell out to me enchanting tales from the *Midrash Haggadah*, that roving rabbinical commentary beginning five centuries before Christ on the anecdotal and legendary portions of the Scriptures. And, sometimes, although rarely, to illustrate the stories, he would gravely unwrap the one icon permitted in his austere home where otherwise, in accordance with the Commandments, no hint of a graven image was to be found. No Catholic viewing the reliquaries in the shrines of Christendom could have gazed more reverentially at the bones of saints than did my grandfather and I when, with the containing silver box opened and the purple velvet covering removed, the treasure, a polished gleaming white ram's horn, came into view. This was the sacred *shofar*, to be blown in the synagogue only on the most solemn days of the Jewish religious calendar.

Such a *shofar*, I was instructed, at the time of the great Sinai theophany, was heard by my ancestors heralding the Covenant between God and the Hebrews who, in return for their affirmation that God was One, that gods were worthless idols, would be forever the Chosen People. And I heard too the less forbidding, more magical,

2   OLD TESTAMENT STORIES WITH A FREUDIAN TWIST

tales of the powers of the *shofars*: how, when blown, the enemies of my forebears suffered defeats, their sounds bringing down even the mighty walls of beleaguered Jericho. And how, when heard with a clean heart, their notes would bring hope of the fulfilment of Isaiah's vision of the in-gathering of all of us, my grandfather and I, exiled in the diaspora:[1]

> And it shall come to pass in that day, that the great trumpet shall be blown, and they shall come which were ready to perish in the land of Assyria, and the outcasts in the land of Egypt, and shall worship the Lord in the holy mount at Jerusalem.

But my protective grandfather shielded me from the knowledge of the potential awesome punitive power of the *shofar*: that sometimes it was not a white or fawn ram's horn but a black one, named *Cheres Shofar*. Such an occasion was the great excommunication, when, on 27th July 1656, in solemn ceremony, accompanied by terrible curses, the *shofar* was sounded at the Amsterdam synagogue proclaiming Spinoza, one of the greatest minds Jewry has given the world, to be an apostate, a heretic and outlaw.

There was, however, another date much more awesome that my grandfather, far from concealing, vividly impressed upon me: 9th Ap—17th August AD 70. This was the date the Temple was destroyed, the day when the fate of Jewry was decided for 2,000 years: from thereon they were to be dispersed, homeless among the nations. Until that date, in the Temple, apart from the original and simple ram's horn, more sophisticated musical ensembles had evolved: flutes and zithers, cymbals and triangles, and many percussive wind and string instruments were sounded at the great feasts of the Ancient Jews to enhance the solemn mood of the assembled congregation. But from the day the Temple fell there were to be no musical rejoicings in the synagogues of the diaspora. There the silence was to be broken only by the sound of the oldest wind instrument known: the sound of the prehistoric *shofar*; each year, and still today, on the fast-day the ram's horn is blown and the loss of Solomon's rebuilt Temple is mourned.

The renunciation henceforth of all musical instruments save the *shofar* reveals how profoundly Ancient Jewry experienced their loss; they were castigating themselves for the sins which had brought down upon them the wrath of the Lord who had found them no longer worthy of His Temple. To expiate their wrongdoing, to regain their Father's love, they were ready to give up their most precious possessions, even to end a musical tradition that had lasted for most of a recorded history of almost 4,000 years. No people, musical scholars assert,[2] have a history where music is more mentioned than that of the Jews. The Bible tells us that under King David, out of the tribe of 38,000 Levites, 4,000 were appointed as musicians. Josephus in the first century BCE, in his *History of the Jews*, is no doubt exaggerating when he refers to there being 500,000 musicians in Palestine prior to the dispersal, but that citation indicates how persistent had been, over thousands of years, the importance of the contribution of music to the enrichment and stabilization of ancient Israelite culture.

When the time came for me, in the years leading up to my *bar mitzvah*, to go regularly to *chedar* classes, the Hebrew classes where I would be taught to translate the Pentateuch, I discovered more about the *shofar* and about its inventor. In *Genesis*[3] the "father of all such as handle the harp and organ" is named as Jubal, a name that comes from the same Hebrew root as *jôbél* which signifies ram's horn or trumpet; the man whom the Bible names as the inventor of music, as soon as he is revealed to us, is identified with the *shofar*. The reference to Jubal is laconic, too laconic not to arouse suspicion of some concealment: such reticence is notably absent in the elaborate recitals of the discovery of music and the invention of musical instruments contained in the myths of the Chinese, Indian, the Egyptian and Greek cultures. And, alone among the nations, the originator in the Hebrew legend is declared to be a mere mortal, not, as in all other cultures, a god or demi-god.

The Greek version is more conventional and well illustrates the general portrayal of the antics of the gods that accompanied the birth of music. It is Hermes, the boy wonder, son of Zeus and Maia, born in a cave in Arcadia, who is credited with the invention of the lyre. The mischievous boy, on a nocturnal adventure, found a tortoise in his path. He picked it up and with a bright chisel emptied the shell. Around it he stretched oxhide with the aid of reeds and arranged over a bridge seven strings made from sheep gut which then gave out harmonious sounds. It was the first lyre. The boy had upset the god Apollo by stealing his heifers. To effect a reconciliation, he first played the lyre to calm and seduce the irate Apollo and then, as a gift, gave the lyre to the charmed Apollo. From then on, the two gods became locked in an intense and never-broken friendship, and Apollo became the god of music. The homoerotic elements of the tale are emphasized by an addendum: subsequently, Apollo used his musical endowments to seduce Daphnis, son of a nymph by Hermes, a tale of paedophilia that can be found exquisitely portrayed in Perugino's painting in the Louvre.

These transgressive, erotic, and incestuous tales are of gods—and gods, unlike men, know few constraints. In the Hebrew story, the inventor of music is a man and notably placed under the constraint of his inheritance. Jubal's mortality is stressed: his genealogy is painstakingly set out. He is no god but a man burdened with a tainted ancestry, a direct descendant of the most notorious murderer in history: the man upon whom God had embossed a mark, never to be erased, Cain, Jubal's progenitor. The family tradition was well maintained by Jubal's sibling, Tubal-Cain, the first armament manufacturer, the inventor of edged iron blades "and instructor of every artificer in brass and iron".[4] Jubal had a half-sister too, Naamah, whose name, the Mishnah tells us, refers to song. This was a family well-equipped to render, with vocal accompaniment, the most stirring of martial tunes. It was the talented trio of this family who bequeathed to their descendants the vividly descriptive Song of Moses to be sung by the Children of Israel to the accompaniment of Miriam's dancing and cymbal-playing on the shores of the Red Sea as they revelled in the drowning of Pharaoh's hosts. The bloodthirsty libretto spells out the message of the Song: "The Lord is a Man of War".[5]

The inventor of music thus emerges as coming from a family of terrifying violence, a family who worshipped that belligerent God. Jubal is not presented as a man of peace. Pulsating behind the two short, bland sentences revealing the identities of the authors of music and of arms, one hears a menacing beat; the chronicler hesitates to tell us more directly what is the source of the threatening sound, but etymology reveals all. Jubilation is the emotional component of triumphalism, the celebration of ruthless, homicidal victory over an enemy.

It is therefore not a disconcerting interpretative irrelevance that the two Biblical paragraphs naming Jubal and Tubal are immediately followed by the recording of a violent outburst by their father Lamech who triumphantly declaims to his wives his prowess as a killer:[6]

> ... Oh hearken my wives,
> You wives of Lamech give ear to my speech.
> For a man have I slain for my wound,
> a boy for my bruising.
> For sevenfold Cain is avenged,
> and Lamech seventy and seven.

Jubal comes from a criminal family, quick to take offence, whose hands are dripping with blood.

No wonder that as a little boy, when, on the Day of Atonement I heard the horn of Jubal sounded in my grandfather's synagogue, I trembled: there was murder in the air. I would feel the fear of the silent adults standing around me as, at the culmination of the fast-day, the *shofar*, in three sets of sounds, long, fearsome, mourning, and intimidatory, was blown by the cantor. All in the congregation were desperately hoping that he would not falter, that, despite the difficulty of playing such a crude instrument, the sounds would nevertheless emerge clear and strong for then the evil within themselves would be held at bay, that, as the cabbala has it,[7] Satan would be humiliated. Only then could they hope that they would benefit from the absolution contained within the benediction bestowed upon them before the *shofar* had been blown by the presiding rabbi:

> Praise be the Lord our God, the King of the Universe, Who sanctified us with His precepts and commanded us to hear the sound of the shofar.

And then, having observed the commandment and been granted the privilege of hearing, unmuffled and pristine, the sound of God's trumpet, thus temporarily sanctified, both young and old relaxed. As the final note of the *shofar* faded away, the eerie tension that had enveloped everyone in my grandfather's provincial synagogue dissipated.

Our supplications had been heard and answered. Our abnegations had not been in vain; in our prayers commencing the evening before and continuing during the long day of fasting, we had begged that our estrangement from God should end. I too, in my pre-pubertal unbroken voice, had added my pleas and had recited with the whole congregation the libretto the psalmist had required should accompany the compositions of Jeduthun, the chief musician of the Temple:[8]

> Hear my prayer, O Lord, and give ear unto my cry; hold not Thy peace at my tears; for I am a stranger with Thee and a sojourner, as all my fathers were. O spare me, that I may recover strength, before I go hence, and be no more.

And I too had followed the example of my elders and beat my breast six times as I had read the confessional *Al chate* prayer categorizing the sins my people had committed; at ten years of age I did not understand the nature of those sins but still it was as a penitent that I pleaded for forgiveness:

> For the sins which we have committed against Thee by compulsion; for the sins which we have committed against Thee wilfully; for the sins which we have committed against Thee secretly; for the sins which we have committed against Thee publicly; for the sins which we have committed against Thee through ignorance; for the sins which we have committed against Thee presumptuously.

I did not then know, as I do now, that a euphemistic quality pervades that categorization of our transgressions, that by appearing to present an all-embracing compendium of our sins, the specific and most serious of Israel's crime could be hidden beneath the generalizations: it is the crime so guilt-ridden that a recall would be too onerous to be borne by the individual. The *Al chate* prayer, therefore, is not to be read silently: it is to be proclaimed, not whispered in a confessional booth. It is not a private prayer, it is a collective response, an acknowledgement of a collective guilt. Even a hint of personal unshared responsibility would induce so crushing a sense of guilt that it could not be borne by an individual. The group had committed the crime, the group must carry all the blame. And on the Day of Atonement by group flagellation, by breast-beating, by ostentatious acceptance that their dispersal throughout the nations was punishment well-deserved, for they and their fathers had turned away from the Lord's goodly precepts and ordinances, they vainly hoped to expiate their terrible crime while leaving it unnamed.

These stratagems failed. The acknowledgements of guilt are too qualified, too tentative, to ever earn them total absolution. The cunning early Jewish Christians tried an avoidance tactic to achieve that end: they displaced the crime by crucifying the son. But stubborn mainstream Jewry scorned the camouflage: they knew the true name of the victim even although they could not utter it. By that omission the confession fell short of full disclosure. Only a remission, not an absolution, was to be available to those who had held back their complicity. Each year, and every year, they were to be summoned by Jubal's frightening *shofar* to return to the synagogue on the Day of Atonement to beg forgiveness again and again for the unmentionable crime that could never be erased from their history and from the history of all mankind. They were irredeemably guilty of parricide, the murder of the father.

***

Until the early 20th century that murder had been an unsolved crime. By then, thanks to the inspired surmises of Charles Darwin[9] and in response to the findings of the remarkable William Robertson-Smith,[10] physicist, philologist, Bible critic and archaeologist, and thanks also to the innovative Scot J.F. McLennan,[11] who discovered totemism and exogamy for the world, and to the publications of J.G. Frazer,[12] clues became available to Freud, encouraging him to overcome his hesitations and to publish in 1913 his *Totem and Taboo*,[13] so illuminating the mystery.

Adopting Darwin's hypothesis that the original structure of human society consisted of a group dominated by a primal father who reserved the women for himself and kept the potent sons in subjection, Freud claimed that the original source of man's guilt lay in that prehistoric rebellion of the sons who eventually joined forces to murder the father and to divide the women among themselves. To check the sexual rivalries that would otherwise have arisen among the sons, the rules of exogamy emerged, ensuring the sons could only take as wives women outside their own particular group. But such a neat evolutionary advance was not to be made by an amnesiac ploy. Mankind could not move on by blotting out the past. The body of the murdered father could never be simply abandoned, forgotten by his assailants. The memory of the crime was to haunt them and all their descendants—that is us—forever.

How that guilt-inducing memory was transmitted is problematic. Freud, who despite so much contrary evidence, was never to relinquish entirely the Lamarckian view that acquired characteristics could be inherited, continued to the end to insist that modern man's neurotic sense of guilt could be attributed to ancestral crimes committed in prehistoric times. Others, eschewing biological determinism, have preferred to find an explanation by drawing on Freud's own tentative emphases in his *Totem and Taboo* when he canvassed the possibility that each generation might intuit the unconscious of its parents:[14]

> An unconscious understanding such as this of all customs, ceremonies and dogmas left behind by the original relations to the father may have made it possible for later generations to take over their heritage of emotions.

Yet again there are those following the researches of the psychoanalyst-anthropologist Géza Róneim,[15] who had visited the Australian Aborigines and other primitive tribes, and found the memory of the primal murder was perpetuated by the initiation ceremonies in totemistic societies, rituals which can only be understood as re-enactments of the original parricide and subsequent guilty memory. Dissatisfied with all these explanations and finding themselves in an impasse when they seek the precipitates which brought about the changes taking mankind out of the primal horde into the totemistic society, "many anthropologists have renounced the search for psychological or historical explanations, and confine themselves to the search for the functions of institutions".[16]

The anthropologists' caution can act as a necessary *caveat* but it can also be a dangerous encouragement to a defeatism that would banish attempts of exploration into the prehistorical, and would confine us to a scrutiny of the remnants of totemistic societies presently, or recently, extant in remote areas of the world. Only the timid, however, will be wilfully deaf to the echoes from the prehistoric world reverberating in the Book of Genesis. When the chroniclers, probably in the eighth or ninth century before Christ,[17] recounted the genealogy of the murderous Cain family, they were nearer the time when the primal horde, by an act of parricide, heralded the totemistic society. Echoes of the awful event then perhaps were less muffled and the chroniclers, in giving the name of the ram's horn to Jubal, had felt impelled to give in semaphore code some intimation of the cause of the distant uproar.

Nowadays, with so many of the riddles of totemism solved, the chroniclers, by endowing the music originator with his ram's name, have enabled us, taking aboard the chroniclers' hints, to assert more overtly that the ram was once one of the many gods that the Ancient Israelites worshipped. That the animal totems they set up and which are sometimes hidden in the original Hebrew nomenclature of the 12 tribes of Israel are made almost explicit in what was probably the oldest extended text in the Bible,[18] Jacob's beautiful and powerful testament.[19] There, Judah is associated with the lion, Dan with the serpent, Napthali with a hind, Benjamin with a wolf—all allusions recalling the times when Israel did not believe in the existence of only one god, when the religion practised was essentially henotheistic or monolatrous.[20] Monolatry, the worship of a single high god, recognizes the existence of other deities and sometimes incorporates some of them into the pantheon as lower gods; there is ample evidence in Israelite literature of sacrifices to other gods who were understood to be subordinate in Yahweh's pantheon.

Our first anticipation is that the ram god would have had a high place in such a pantheon, but suspicions arise. Are we being deceived by the chronicler? Is what we are reading in Genesis a mere palimpsest? Has the original older record been erased in an attempt to bury the more dangerous memory of the worship not of a sheep but of a raging powerful bull? We recall that at Sinai, as soon as Moses turned his back, the Israelites, too immature to sustain the monotheistic belief in an invisible god, regressed and danced ecstatically around not a ram but a golden calf, an act that was to earn them the punishment of 40 years of wandering in the desert. And today the memory of that relapse is still so painful that, lest it be evoked, the *shofar* may be a horn of any animal other than a ram—except that it must never, never be the horn of a bull. Yet, betraying its aetiology, when the *shofar* is blown, the sounds issuing have not the slightest resemblance to the bleating of a ram: what we hear is the roaring of a bull in pain. The scene that is conjured up is that of a powerful animal being overcome and slaughtered: the totem bull, symbolizing the primal father, was being murdered as rebellious sons combined to end his mastery of the primal horde. No wonder, as a little boy, when I heard the *shofar* being blown in the synagogue I was terrified.

No one has more exhaustively revealed how the Bible's advertisement of Jubal as the originator of music is a ruse to discourage further investigation than Theodor Reik, one of Freud's earliest and most brilliant pupils. He put forward the hypothesis[21] that the testimonies of the Jewish cult of the bull are so numerous that one must conclude that it is highly probable that Jews worshipped the bull before they emigrated to Canaan. The ram's horn is a relic of a later totem animal but the very choice of a horn as a relic reveals the failure to obliterate the memory of the earlier totem animal, for it is a bull's horn, treated as a relic, that is particularly replete with sexual associations—and especially with the erect penis—an association made explicit today in the demotic use of "horny" to describe the emotional condition of an aroused man. It was such a condition, it can surely be presumed, that prompted the sexual envy of the sons as they combined to commit parricide in the primitive horde. The *shofar* is not primarily a vestigial symbol of a mere ram roaming among placid flocks of sheet: rather, it is a vestigial symbol of the rampant and powerful bull that we find playing so significant a rôle in so many mythologies.

In all religions of the Ancient Orient there was a time when, elevated to a god, the father, metamorphosed as a bull, was actually worshipped in that form. The Egyptians had the bull Apis, the incarnation of Ptah; the Babylonian gods were given the surname bull (Buru), with Marduk indeed represented as a bull, as was the weather god Adad who was called the "Great Bull". Zeus, father of the Greek gods, approached Europa and Io in the form of a bull and, as the discovery at Mycenae revealed, was worshipped in the form of a silver-horned bull's head with a double-headed axe symbolizing domination between the horns. The Jews were no exception in their early worship of a bull god; but in their attachment to the *shofar*, a memorial of that time, they show they still will not forget the primal father they loved, feared, and slew, and with whom they seek a passionate reconciliation.

In the synagogue the crushing guilt felt by the worshippers on the Day of Atonement comes from their identification with their murderous ancestors. All their ambivalences expressed in their fear of, and reverence towards, the *shofar* tell us that their handling and blowing of the horn "corresponds to the breaking through of the unconscious wish to get possession of the great penis of the father, to appropriate his sexual powers".[22] The Day of Atonement is the day of the great blow job. On that day father and son are conjoined. By fellatio, absolution has been sought.

***

In rationalist mode, dismissing as farrago the Biblical assertion that Jubal was the inventor of music, there have been many theories canvassed over the last two centuries claiming to identify the precipitates that brought music to mankind. Some have proposed that it arose as primitive man imitated Nature's sounds, the sounds of running water, of babbling brooks, of waterfalls, and of leaves played on by a rustling wind. Surveys of sound preferences in Canada, New Zealand, Jamaica, and Switzerland show these as registering the greatest pleasure to be gained from listening to Nature's sounds; the romantics would have us believe that that result provides corroboration of their theory[23] but musicologists and composers are dismissive of such fanciful notions, although for differing reasons. They emphasize that the sounds of which music is composed and which are referred to as "tones" are separable units with constant auditory waveforms which can be repeated and reproduced, but that Nature's sounds are irregular noises rather than the sustained notes of definable pitch which go to form music.

Another charming but unsustainable speculation is that music began with man's imitation of birdsong. Encouraging us to listen to the wood thrush which has a repertoire of as many as nine songs, Charles Hartshorne, the American ornithologist and philosopher, claimed that birdsong shows variations of both pitch and tempo:[24] accelerando, crescendo, diminuendo, change of key, and variations on a theme. He argued:

> Bird songs resemble human music both in the sound patterns and in the behaviour setting. Songs illustrate the aesthetic mean between chaotic irregularity and monotonous regularity ... The essential difference from human music is in the brief temporal span of the bird's repeatable patterns, commonly three seconds or less, with an upper limit of about fifteen seconds. This limitation conforms to the concept of primitive musicality. Every

simple musical device, even transposition and simultaneous harmony, occurs in bird music.

Claiming birds sing far more than is biologically necessary, he wishes us to believe birdsong is engaged in for its own sake. It would indeed be delightful to believe that music began with man simulating avian *joie de vivre* but, alas, this belief has been cruelly subverted, not least by Géza Révész,[25] psychologist friend of the composer Bartók. He has persuasively shown that if human music really began in this way we should be able to point to examples of music resembling birdsong in isolated pre-literate communities. Instead, we find complex rhythmic patterns bearing no resemblance to avian music. More, no primitive man could have easily imitated birdsong. Slowing down modern recorded birdsongs demonstrates that they are even more complicated than previously supposed. Technical difficulties in the realization of an imitation of a song of a thrush are enormous; no early primitive man could possibly have achieved such an imitation.

Some investigators, renouncing abortive attempts to link the birth of music to man's imitation of the sounds of the animal world, have focused their attention on pre-verbal neonates, on babes newly initiated into the world, and have brought forward a theory that music emerges from childish utterances, from the lalling of infants. According to the Harvard psychologist Howard Gardner,[26] who has conducted research into the musical development of small children:

> The first melodic fragments produced by children around the age of a year or fifteen months have no strong musical identity; their undulating patterns, going up and down over the very brief interval or ambitus, are more reminiscent of waves than of a particular pitch attacks. Indeed, a quantum leap, in an almost literal sense, occurs at about the age of a year and a half when for the first time children can intentionally produce discrete pitches. It is as if this diffused *babbling had been supplanted by stressed words*.

Then, Gardner instructs us, in the following year the child makes habitual use of those discrete pitches, chiefly using seconds, minor thirds, and major thirds; thus, he claimed, by the age of two or two-and-a-half, the child was beginning to notice songs sung by others. As an explanation of music's origins this at first seems persuasive. Closer scrutiny, however, reveals the argument to be fatally flawed. Révész, among others, has credibly asserted that the lalling melodies produced by children in the second year are already conditioned by songs which they have picked up from the environment or by other music to which they have been exposed. If lalling melodies are in fact dependent upon musical input from the environment, it is obviously inadmissible to suggest that music itself developed from infant lalling.

Many other hypotheses, equally unconvincing, have been advanced to identify the origin of music. One, based on the perception that the singing voice has greater carrying powers than the speaking voice, has led to the claim that early man, wishing to communicate with his fellows at a distance, discovered that he could do so more effectively by using a singing voice rather than a speaking voice. Proponents of this view assume that such calls can pass over into song quite easily. They ask us to believe, in short, that all music is derived from the yodel.

A more sophisticated but similarly incredible guess has been put forward by those who, following the precepts of linguistic analysts, distinguished prosodic features of speech from syntactic; stress, pitch, comma, volume, emphasis and any other features convey emotional significance, as opposed to grammatical structure or literal meaning. Implicitly this is the perspective of William Powell who wrote in *The Philosophy of Music*:[27]

> The earliest forms of music probably arose out of the natural inflections of the voice in speaking. It would be very easy to sustain the sound of the voice on one particular note, and to follow this by another of the same note at a higher or lower pitch. This, however rude, would constitute music.
>
> We may further easily conceive that several persons might be led to join in a rude chant of this kind. If one accidentally does, others, guided by the natural instinct of their ears, would imitate him, and thus you might get a combined unison song.

Today Powell's contention has been savaged by musicologists and anthropologists: his viewpoint is justifiably seen as that of a Victorian patronizing the savages; he shows little appreciation of the established fact that music among pre-literate peoples is often as complex as our own. And, of course, his theorizing is totally at odds with Darwin's romantic conclusion that music preceded speech:[28]

> The suspicion does not appear improbable that the progenitors of man, either the males or the females, or both sexes, before they had acquired the power of expressing their mutual love in articulate language, endeavoured to charm each other with musical notes and rhythms. The impassioned orator, bard or musician, when with his various tones and cadences he excites the strongest emotions in his hearers, little suspects that he uses the same means by which, at an extremely remote period, his half-human ancestors aroused each other's ardent passions during their mutual courtship and rivalry.

Darwin is here beguilingly presenting us with a most persuasive account of a function of music, not of its origin. In like vein we find two of our most distinguished authors, Bruce Chatwin and W.G. Sebold, both of whom, to our loss, died prematurely, using their distinctive sensibilities to divine other functions of music. Their arresting contributions have told us much of the various functions of music but they always stopped short of making hubristic claims to have identified its original source.

Bruce Chatwin drew upon T.A. Jones' study of the Australian Aborigines:[29]

> Since all their knowledge, beliefs, and customs, upon whose strict preservation through exact ritual observance the constant renewal of nature (and hence their own survival) was held to depend, were enshrined in and transmitted by their sacred song cycles, it is reasonable to think that theirs is the oldest extant, still practised music in the world. Since they had no form of writing or notation, oral tradition was the only means of retaining and inculcating their lore, and music therefore provided the essential mnemonic medium. As such it was invested with the utmost power, secrecy, and value.

In his enchanting book *The Songlines*,[30] Chatwin purported to demonstrate how songs served to divide up the land and constituted title deeds to territory. Each totemic ancestor was believed to have sung as he walked and to have defined the features of the landscape in so doing. Song was the means by which the different aspects of the world were brought into consciousness and therefore remembered; each individual inherited some verses of the ancestral song which also determined the limits of a particular area. The contour of the melody of the song described the contour of the land with which it was associated; when the tribe met to sing their own song-cycle on ritual occasions, song owners had to sing their particular verses in the right order.[31] As Chatwin's informant told him, "Music is a memory bank for finding one's way about the world."

W.G. Sebold, paraphrasing a comment of Freud, in his posthumously published *Moments Musicaux*,[32] proposes another function of music, one that could have been of particular use to primitive man anxious to be shielded from a fearsome and hostile environment. Sebold suggests that a deeper secret of music is that it is a gesture warding off paranoia, that we make music to defend ourselves against being overwhelmed by the terrors of reality.

When Donald Winnicott, paediatrician and psychoanalyst, was asked by a distracted mother what she could do about her two-year-old son who reacted to every loud noise with great distress, he suggested what proved to be a successful solution. That solution was perhaps analogous to that deployed by primitive man who, in paranoid mode, may have responded to noises interpreted as threatening: the child was given a spoon and a tin tray and encouraged to bang away so that he could retort to any loud noise that disturbed him; likewise, the primitive may have resorted to retaliatory noise that eventually was perhaps akin to music sounds. If there is validity in such a hypothesis, then one of the functions that it could be said music possesses is to abolish a sense of helplessness and restore a sense of competence, and this is what Sebold appears to be suggesting.

However, Sebold's Freudian quote, or indeed any other psychoanalytical contribution, is likely to be unsympathetically received by most of the cognitive archaeologists, evolutionary psychologists, geneticists, palaeontologists, and professors of prehistory who are currently so fiercely debating among themselves theories on the origin of music. In their academic world, battle lines appear to have been drawn between those who, with varying degrees of support, uphold either the view that music is a technological and not an evolutionary adaptation, that it should be seen as an accident, functionless, a mere by-product with no evolutionary value in itself, an inconsequential epiphenomenon of the evolution of language[33] or, on the other hand, those who argue that the human capacity for music arises from an ancient "musi-language" based on the transmission of messages rather than words, more akin to singing than a primitive lexicon. And, in a fundamentalist Darwinian flourish, they affirm that the evolution 1.8 million years ago of the first bipedal hominid (homo ergaster) precipitated a musical revolution, since the need for finer muscular control to walk on two legs led to an increased brain size, an enhanced capacity for rhythm, and a larynx sitting much deeper in the throat enabling production of a much wider range of sounds.[34]

Weary of their conflicted theorizing and evidently believing all the disputing parties are engaged in a fruitless task unbecoming to their disciplines, the distinguished American cognitive archaeologist Huron in 1999 pronounced:[35]

> Most scholars have wisely steered clear of the issue of music's origins, since clearly the enterprise is patently speculative. At its worst, proposals concerning music's origins are fictions masquerading as scholarship.

Fortunately his over-cautious advice is proving to be unacceptable and some working in this field boldly persist in their quest, insisting that even if music is, as so often, a nebulous concept, that does not mean that the capacities underling musical behaviour are in any way nebulous, or that investigation regarding their development and inter-relationships needs to be any more speculative than any other investigation into human origins. Dr Iain Morley, a Cambridge research fellow, has, in 2007, provided us, in a weighty work,[36] with evidential ethnographic insights, not least those telling us of how, in the society of our hunter-gatherer forefathers, when men considered themselves to have come from the land akin with other fauna present in the environment, music was used in an attempt to influence the world around them; and no less illuminating is his foray into evolutionary rationales for music. He proposes that developed musical behaviours had potential selective advantages:

> They could confer an advantage on individuals in terms of sexual selection—because of their foundations in the capacities

to communicate emotionally and effectively, to empathise, bond and elicit loyalty, musical abilities have the potential to be a proxy for an individual's likelihood of having strong social networks and loyalties, and of contributing to a group. Physical behaviour also has the potential for being a mechanism for actually stimulating and maintaining those networks and loyalties; because of the stimulation of shared emotional experience as a consequence of participation in musical activities, it has the potential to engender strong feelings of empathic association and group membership.

Despite stimulating work like that of Iain Morley, and despite all the panoply of forensic evidence from linguists, paleoanthropologists, archaeologists, and neuro-scientists that the conflicting protagonists have marshalled to advance their differing and often extravagant speculations, one wonders how much further they have brought us to a recognition of the origin of music than that provided more than two centuries ago by the revolutionary social theorist Jean-Jacques Rousseau in his essay *Essai surs l'origine des langues*. Rousseau, who was an accomplished composer, turned his focus on man's passions and put the view that music was a derivative of those ungovernable emotions; his biographer[37] has spelled out his argument:

> Men first spoke to each other in order to express their passions, and that at the early stages of human society there was no distinct speech apart from song. Earliest languages, he suggests, were chanted; they were melodic and poetic rather than prosaic and practical. He also claimed that it was men's passions rather than their needs which prompted their first utterances, for passions would drive men towards others where the necessities of life would impel each to seek his satisfaction alone: "It is not hunger or thirst, but love, hatred, pity and anger which drew from men their first vocal utterances." Primitive men sing to one another in order to express their feelings before they begin to speak to one another in order to express their thoughts.

Rousseau's perspective is far removed from that of most of our contemporary quarrelling academics, all claiming they have found the route map to music's origins. They focus on brain size, on the larynx, on our ancestors' gymnastic skills. Rousseau, however, wisely focused on the human heart, a notoriously irrational prompter: the heart's desires and anguishes cannot, like a larynx, be measured with a slide-rule. To explore the psycho-dynamics of the emotions which Rousseau names—love, hate, pity, and anger—requires a willingness to acknowledge the unconscious forces that moved primitive man as they do us, seeking always to find answers to the origins and development of music in man's responses to changes in his visible external world is surely to stake all on an inadequate ecological methodology. Such an approach may allow the investigator to feel in control and comfortable: he avoids the suffering of painful insights that have to be faced through the calibration by introspective work into personal resources that must accompany any genuine investigation into man's arcane unconscious world in all its unfathomable complexities which defy rational control and programmability and yet incessantly generate meanings.[38] With their sights fixed on the external world, too many of today's academics, in their theorizing on music aetiology, scotomatized to the interior life of man, an interior life that with so little modification is shared by primitive and contemporary man. Their marked resistance in their scholarship to any serious impingement on the findings of psychoanalysis is symptomatic, an illustration of the syndrome which Freud in his 1929 letter to Einstein[39] bitterly identified:

> All our attention is directed to the outside, from whence danger threatens and satisfactions beckon. From the inside, we want only to be left in peace. So if someone tries to turn our awareness inward ... then our whole organisation resists—just as, for example, the oesophagus and the urethra resist any attempt to reverse their normal direction of passage.

Freud's diagnosis, that the "unnatural" practice of turning the attention inward is bound to provoke resistances, retains all its validity today and certainly finds corroboration in the widespread avoidance of psychoanalytical applications by those academics who claim that they, not Jubal, have uncovered the secret of the genesis of music.

There does indeed appear to be a tradition among philologists generally to resist psychological approaches to the scientific exploration of language.[40] The work in 1885 of Phillip Wegener,[41] a scholar well versed in comparative philology of the Indo-European languages who attempted a profoundly psychological approach to the study of language, was largely ignored. And when, a few years later at the turn of the century, Wilhelm Wundt, the renowned German philosopher and psychologist, gave his lectures on the Mind of Man and Animal, his psychological emphases enraged most philologists. The intense opposition those lectures provoked caused the early rift separating linguistics from psychology, one that, despite the establishment more recently of psycho-linguistics as a separate discipline, has never been bridged and which in some respects has widened. One man, above all, who until his death in 1985 strove to bridge that gap between music and psychology was the remarkable Hans Keller, string-player, psychologically-oriented social worker, university lecturer on music theory, editor of the most combative music journals, arguably Britain's leading—and most certainly most controversial—music critic. Keller, from his position in the music department of the BBC and by his publications, sought to educate Britain's musical world into acceptance, for its own benefit, of psychoanalytical insights. He was a difficult man with whom I found it impossible to have a relaxed conversation but who, to my gain, was always eager to enter into an argument. Yet all his proselytizing was of little avail. When, in 2003, a distinguished musicologist valiantly presented, as editor, a collection of Keller's writings, he wryly and accurately commented:[42]

> ... readers may yet wonder whether the blissful dawn of Keller's Freudian exploration ... yielded to the glorious day that so many had anticipated. For, it cannot be denied that British musical criticism at the beginning of the new century is not in general orientated towards psychoanalysis. On the contrary, resistance is now widespread. There may be various reasons for this; as Keller often noted, the English are happier with a description of externals than analysis of internals, ...

The consequence of this rift is to be seen in the current controversies between academics on music's origins where depth-psychology has been elbowed out to the periphery of their internal debate; this is well illustrated when we note the expositions of the relationship of music to religion made by Steven Mithen,[43] the cognitive archaeologist and professor of early prehistory, who is at the centre of the current academic controversies. He has opined that as primitive man evolved, the music within his "musi-language" became superfluous and language itself became the principal communication system. As a result, he claims, man was "left with the question of who to communicate with through music .... So the human propensity to communicate through music came to focus on the supernatural ...." Music, therefore, "is used to communicate with, glorify and/or serve the divinities ...".

His premise, that man originally communicated in "musi-language", is not as innovative as he seems to suggest. He is not a plagiarist, but insulated as are so many in his discipline from the contribution made by psychoanalysis, he is apparently unaware that his premise is but a variant of the view I first heard in a lecture given more than 50 years ago by the much undervalued art critic, lawyer, and psychoanalyst, and himself an accomplished musician, Anton Ehrenzweig. In 1953 he wrote:[44]

> It is not unreasonable to speculate that speech and music have descended from a common origin in a primitive language which was neither speaking nor singing, but something of both. Later this primeval language would have split into different branches; music would have retained the articulation mainly by pitch (scale) and duration (rhythm), while language chose the articulation mainly by tone colour (vowels and consonants). Language moreover happened to become the vehicle of rational thought and so underwent further influences. Music has become a symbolic language of the unconscious mind whose symbolism we shall never be able to fathom.

Ehrenzweig, ever aware of the impenetrable unconscious forces at work in all musical composition, would never allow his premise to lead him to such a simplistic and jejune conclusion as that proffered by Mithen. As we have learned from Reik, the enmeshment of music in religious ritual with all the innuendos of lurking murderous and sexual violences that accompany such an amalgam cannot be explained away merely as an assuagement of primitive man's need to find a use for a musical facility surplus to his material requirements: it has no such innocence. It is no exuberant hallelujah, a convenient vehicle to communicate and praise a divinity as, in his

Procrustean exercise to squeeze it into his theorizing, Mithen would have us believe. Indeed, if his acquaintance with mediæval history matched that of his knowledge of early prehistory, he surely would have entered *caveats* to his theorizing, for not a few of those theologians regarded music not as a means of communication with God but rather as a dangerous obstacle to that achievement.

Augustine speaks in one breath of "*concupiscentia carnis, concupiscentia ocolorum et ambitio saeculi*"—"the greed of the flesh, the greed of the eyes, and secular ambition".[45] To the greed of the eyes, he added the greed of the ears. Augustine revealed that he was so entranced by the sensuous pleasures of sound that he feared his intellect was sometimes paralyzed by the gratification of his senses:[46] "... when I find the singing itself more moving than the truth which it conveys, I confess that this is a grievous sin, and at those times I would prefer not to hear the singer".[47] Augustine was evidently as aware as any present-day psychoanalyst that music could act as a magnet, pulling the listener towards the transgressive and the sensuous, and towards a reminiscent re-enactment of the original sin. Anodyne and simplistic interpretations of the relationship between music and religion blot out what Reik uncovered: that the original musical jubilations were the ambivalent rejoicings of the sons as they danced round the totem animal god, the surrogate of the father they had slain.

By endowing a mortal, Jubal, with the facility to invent music, giving him the name of "Ram's horn", thus hinting at but not making explicit the gruesome events from which music had emerged, the scribes sought to place an estoppel against further enquiry which would have occasioned conflict with a highly developed concept of God that obtained among the Israelites at the period of the composition of the Bible.

All other civilized people at that time, deficient as they were of any belief in monotheism, did not need to show such circumspection: they, absolving themselves of any personal responsibility for the initial determinant parricide, projected the invention and development of music onto their gods. Their myths shamelessly tell stories of how the inventors of music were young gods rebelling against authoritarian older gods. The invention of the flute and shepherd's pipe is ascribed to Marsyas and Midas who rebelled against Apollo and fought with him; and similar reflections of the primal episode can repetitively be found in their tales of the challenges made by rebellious heroes—such as Orpheus, Osiris, and Attis.

In all these myths we find two gods, the offended father-god and the son who has committed a crime against the father and must severely atone for it. Only the courageous monotheist Israelites accepted that they were complicit in the crime and must pay the price. All other people sought to cowardly assert that the crime was committed in the heavens, and there, not on earth, the consequent expiation must be endured.

But by nomenclature, by naming not a god but the mortal Jubal, he of the ram's horn, as music's inventor, the Bible reveals to us the historic truth: there are no other gods on whom blame for the primal parricide can be placed. There is only one God and only by acknowledgement of His pre-eminence and solitariness, confessing its guilt, can humanity find redemption. As a Jewish child I was taught to chant every day the declamatory *shema*: "Hear O Israel, the Lord our God, the Lord is One!" and I am required on my deathbed to intone the same affirmation. The scribes, by re-affirming the appointment of Jubal as the cantor to accompany that holy libretto, ensured that the vitality within the clamour of primitive man as he danced around the totem animal was transmuted into a propitious hymn to the one and only God. Music can be found to emerge and develop in polytheistic societies, but our Western music's evolution is inextricably bound to man's graduation to monotheism.

The Jews, confident of their austere monotheistic belief, welcomed music into their Temple. The dangerous intimations it brought of its dark, earliest parricidal associations could not subvert their stubborn Mosaic insistence on one God and one God only. In accordance with the psalmist's ordinance,[48] He was to be praised with the sound of the trumpet, the psaltery, the harp, the timbrel, stringed instruments and the pipe, the loud cymbals and also the high sounding cymbals. And thus it was until the Temple was destroyed. Then, silence fell upon the synagogues of the world. Christendom, however, with its belief in the Trinity, was not possessed of the same high confidence that it could resist the sensuous temptations of which Augustine wrote. The relaxed polytheistic world, successor to the totemistic society from which it had emerged, beckoned alluringly. Evocations within music of the orgiastic rites of primitive man's celebration of the slaying of the father were too attractive and too fearsome for some: they were the Christians who, anticipating Cromwell's Puritans, fought to ban from the Church Jubal and all his works.

In the history of Western Christianity none of the anti-Jubal brigade was more zealous than Luther's irreconcilable rival, the Protestant firebrand of Zurich,[49] Huldreich Zwingli. His famous falling-out with Luther arose out of their dispute on the nature of the Eucharist: whether the bread and wine became the body and blood of Christ or merely represented and symbolized them. Zwingli was ever acutely sensitive to the sources of religious ritual; he wanted to repress all doubts, and all memory of the sacrificial rites of totemistic clans regarded as anticipatory of the Christ story. It follows that, for him, music was a threat carrying intimations of a past which he wished to bury. Music, he ruled, must not be used in worship, and the canton of Zurich obeyed him.

But Zwingli over-reached himself. Now he demanded militant action against those cantons that still subscribed to Catholicism. In 1531 the Catholic cantons launched a pre-emptive attack on Zurich and the forces of Zurich were overwhelmed. One of those who fell on the battlefield of Kappel was Zwingli. It was a fortunate day for the future of music in Protestant Europe. Jubal's compositions in organ and song continue to be heard in our cathedrals.

That despite his bad and concupiscent name Jubal has triumphed over the ascetic kill-joys is due, not least, to his negotiating skills. He was a member of a dysfunctional family, descendant of murderous Cain, fathered by the terrifying Lamech, a family bereft of love but replete with aggression. Within such families the child must learn to manipulate: only thus can he avoid beatings, only thus can he survive. At Westminster I lived for decades with many such men who brought from their loveless childhoods manipulative skills which served them well in their politicking: at best it equipped them to be subtle negotiators, diplomatic reconcilers of quarrelsome partisans. Such a mortal was Jubal. The *terribilata* within his music was present but disguised, the menace was morphed into thrilling seduction; and thus masked, the threatening sounds bring us infinite masochistic pleasures, enjoyed without guilt, as we praise the Lord and welcome duplicitous Jubal into our churches and concert halls.

***

Those philosophers and anthropologists who naively tried to find the origins of music in primitive man's imitations of Nature's sounds or birdsong would have gained greater credibility if they had cast off their gentility and directed attention to a sound which in primitive times, as now, is possessed of far greater significance—the sound which every man and woman hears with relief for it heralds the expulsion of their inner badness, the self-created sound which reveals everyone's aspiration to be a musician, the sound of the fart. This association of the flatus with music has been well depicted by uninhibited artists throughout the centuries. We can find it in Hieronymus Bosch's 15th-century phantasmagoria where, with pipes or flutes up their anuses, naked fallen angels play the instruments by releasing intermittent farts and, in like manner, we find trumpets being blown in the well-known witty illustrations to the recently-published diaries of the 20th-century Australian artist Donald Friend.[50] In playgrounds everywhere little boys compete in their soundings of staccato or prolonged farts, ever taking much pride in their talents as embryonic composers. When they graduate to high school, they probably still recite, as I did, the old doggerel:

>There was a young lady named Cager
>Who, as the result of a wager,
>Consented to fart
>The whole oboe part
>Of Mozart's Quartet in F Major.

Only the prim, outlawing their early infantile coprophilous yearnings, fail to hear the farts behind the renderings of a Casals or Jacqueline du Pré. And when we hear a triumphant trumpet in an orchestra, who, familiar with Dante's *Inferno*, will not recall the March of the Demons led by Barbariccia:[51]

>Along the embankment to the left they started
>but first each one has stuck his tongue between
>his teeth, as a salute to their leader,
>And he promptly made a trumpet of his arse.

It is in the anality of man we find one of the sources of music. This should not surprise us. We ourselves were created by God out of shit or, as it has been more euphemistically told in *Genesis*, "The Lord God formed Man from the dust of the ground".

The ram's horn, the name given to the Biblical inventor of music, is not only a phallic symbol; it is a symbol too of the faeces to whose shape it conforms. The process which psychoanalysis has described as condensation is one whereby two or more images combine to form a composite image that is invested with meaning and energy derived from both; it is one of the characteristics of unconscious thinking and so we find it incessantly at work in our dreams. Jubal's talents are charged with such faecal energy and it is possible to persuasively urge that this has played a significant part in the initiating and development of music from the time that the first bipedal hominid walked on two legs.

The conjectures of Mithen that this evolutionary link, necessarily accompanied by an increased brain size able to assist the maintenance of finer muscle control which led to an enhanced capacity for rhythm and a deeper larynx, may indeed all have substance. But when man first stood erect, from his anality there came into place even far more compelling imperatives.

The adoption of an erect gait by the human race must have created a most severe sexual crisis: the female genitalia had disappeared from sight and with them the chief source of excitation leading to the sexual act. Now other parts of the female body were emphasized and made more visible: the flaunting breasts, the buttocks luring the male to an alternative sterile orifice. In nascent form the era of the tits, bum and wriggling lap dancing had begun. The non-genital parts of the body must have exercised the maximum excitation previously reserved for the genitals; the future of the human race was endangered. A total aberration of the sexual urge from the genitals to the new sources of excitement would have been fatal: the perverse, the fetishistic practice, could have supplanted copulation.

Ehrenzweig has powerfully argued that it was the resurgence of aesthetic enjoyment which prevented this fatal turn of events. He posited that by deflecting some of the sexual excitement, so perilously attractive, away from non-genital body parts and putting it at the service of aesthetic pleasure, genital sex was, as a consequence, gaining the right to retain its priority:[52]

> The genitals retain the maximum exciting faculty because they did not form aesthetic feelings, while the other non-genital

parts of the body have reduced exciting faculty because they did in fact form aesthetic feelings.

It is a subtle and some would say an over-sophisticated hypothesis but a scrutiny of the nature of our own enjoyment of art and music lends it credibility. Kenneth Clark, when commenting in his seminal study of the nude in art on the mixture of memories and sensations aroused by the nudes of Reubens or Renoir wrote:[53]

> ... it is necessary to labour the obvious and say that no nude, however abstract, should fail to arouse in the spectator some vestige of erotic feeling, even although it be only the faintest shadow—and if it does not do so, it is bad art and false morals.

De-sexualization in true art is never complete;[54] painting and sculpture are bathed in eroticism inspired by excitations aroused by the sight of non-genital body parts. And we find the same process at work in music, often indeed no less explicit than in the seductive paintings of a Boucher or Cranach.

Mozart in his scatological letters has provided us with a grandstand view of its workings. Reading the affectionate and startlingly obscene letters he sent to his mother and girl-cousin leads us to more than the world of scatology. We see that this genius is possessed of a faecal energy; it charges his compositions. Here he hears passing wind, the flatus, in every concerto. The fart so excites him that he burst repeatedly into verse to praise its wondrous qualities. He writes to his mother:

> Yesterday, though, we heard the king of farts,
> It smelled as sweet as honey tarts,
> While it wasn't in the strongest of voice,
> It still came on as a powerful noise.

Mozart revels in recounting his farting feats, delights in tracing them to their source. To his cousin he writes:

> Now I must tell you of a sad thing which has happened just this very moment. As I was doing my best to write this letter, I heard something in the street. I stopped writing—I got up—went to

the window and the sound ceased. I sat down again, started off again to write but I had hardly written ten words when again I heard something. I got up again—as I did, I again heard a sound, this time quite faint—but I seemed to smell something slightly burned—and wherever I went, it smelt. When I looked out at the window, the smell disappeared. When I looked back into the room, I again noticed it. In the end Mamma said to me: "I bet you have let one off." "I don't think so, Mamma," I replied. "Well, I am certain that you have," she insisted. "Well," I thought, "let's see." Put my finger to my arse and then to my nose and—*Ecce, provatum est*. Mamma was right after all. Well, farewell. I kiss you a thousand times ....

For Mozart, shit was the ultimate love token. He wooed his cousin Maria Anna with unusual delicacy: "*Oui*, by the love of my skin, I shit on your nose, so it runs down your chin".

In these scatological letters Mozart is providing us with an exotic and corroborative recall of the time when primitive man, adopting an erect gait, very reluctantly renounced some of the excitements of the anal zone and accepted the compensatory pleasures of aesthetic feelings. Mozart's overt nostalgia for his and everyone's infantile coprophilous delights was to our good advantage displaced onto his compositions. Yet even then he was not satiated but must needs, in pornographic wordplay, seek his satisfactions. The faecal symbolism of his name had determined the Biblical scribes' choice of Jubal as the inventor of music. They had divined, as had Mozart, that the origins of music must not be sought in the stars nor in the flirtations of gods in the heavens but deep down, buried in the shit of mankind.

Today we live in a society which is well able to appreciate how serious a biological threat was the lure of the anus to early erect man. Within our more permissive society, inhibitions that for so long, often at the cost of grim distortions of the human spirit, were in place, are being cast aside and we now see insouciantly acted out transgressions previously severely inhibited by law and by the tenets of religious upbringing.

De-sensitized, we have lost much of our capacity to be disgusted. It has been disgust that hitherto kept us from adoring the anus and, like Mozart, revelling in its products. But the defences which psychoanalysis calls reaction-formations are crumbling; the process by which an unacceptable impulse is mastered by exaggeration, by hypertrophy of the opposing tendency, is often no longer functioning. Anal intercourse is no longer the undisputed prerogative of the homosexual. Women columnists in the quality newspapers, unabashed, do not hesitate to recommend its practice and pleasures within heterosexual relationships. Tunbridge Wells has been wiped off the map: the anus is no longer resistible. We are presently witnessing how powerful can be the ebb-tide carrying us away from genitality to anality. When, therefore, Ehrenzweig posits that it is aesthetic feelings that helped to save primitive man from being swept away to extinction, we fully understand how necessary was that raft to rescue him.

But no alchemy can transmute a borrowed anality into aesthetic pleasure without it still bearing traces of its tainted source. Striated in the greatest of musical compositions is the sadism that is a concomitant of the inescapable anal phase which every infant, as a rite of passage, must endure. The bi-phasic functioning of the anal sphincter, exercising control over the retention and evacuation of the faeces, has its correspondences: the anal erotic zone is the site where mastery is sadistically displayed and enjoyed by evacuation or retention. In the infant's defecation the behaviour patterns within adult relationships of possessive control or cruel abandonment are all anticipated. And in music the faecal energy charging the composition ensures that sadistic elements are never totally absent.

Sometimes they will envelop a score, as in Britten's *Billy Budd* and *Peter Grimes*, yet usually they are muted, but not necessarily less bestirring or disturbing, as they operate to destroy the over-familiar, the stale, and sweep us along into strange territory. In denial, fearful of their powers and frightened that the precarious control of their own sadism will be breached, there are some who will treat music as a holy anodyne, a spiritual unguent. From their ranks are the arrangers of Musak where, in the service of contemporary capitalism, they re-compose classical music by expurgating irregular metres or rhythms occasioned by the assaults of a beneficent sadism, and so ensure that the consumer in the supermarket will be undisturbed, never startled. Such debased music is calculated to act as a soporific, soothing customers who, suitably drugged, will in a trance purchase more and yet more goods. Music of this order, going perhaps a little beyond temporal regularity and Musak simplifications, may have its therapeutic uses in the treatment of some mentally disturbed patients, but purged of its sadism, limpid music is a poor thing.

We are indebted to Jubal, that menacing scion of a murderous family to whom the stench of ordure always clings. Without his disturbing presence profound music is not possible. For some listeners he may be an unwelcome intruder: they want pap, a baby's comforter, a dummy, not the turbulences and tensions he brings. Jubal's music is disruptive, challenging: he is the carrier of the darkest tides of music. Jonathan Kramer, professor of music at Columbia university, recently pungently inveighed against those who would overvalue the tranquilizing music that by its soothing regularity claims to bring us immediate stability;[55] rather, profound music has within it "instability, discontinuity, unexpectedness, or irrationality"; with his authority as a composer, musician, and renowned music theorist, he instructs us: "challenging music, unusual music, may force us beyond our selves. It may help us to form new selves. It may provoke us with disunion rather than welcome us with union." It is not still or placid: it is replete with tension, with imbalances. And to ensure that we fully understand his instruction Kramer, by way of illustration, generously provides us with a list of the music that has moved and changed him most: Beethoven's A-minor string quartet, opus 132; Mahler's ninth symphony; Schubert's C-major's string quintet; Sibelius' Tapiola; Bach's B-minor mass; Brahms' clarinet quintet; Mozart's G-minor quintet; Ives' trio; Bartok's music for strings, percussion, and Celeste; Stravinsky's symphonies of wind instruments; Messiaen's Chronocromie; Xenakis' Eonta.

In all these glorious compositions, violent and sadistic Jubal is present not as a silent observer but as an iconoclast contemptuously breaking up anachronistic configurations that have long since lost meaning and vitality. We, composer and listener, together pick up the fragments; defiantly we use them to re-assemble a new pristine configuration.

***

We would, however, be dupes if we unquestioningly accepted the claim of Jubal—a member of an unscrupulous family that was to become notorious for its thefts of the birthrights of others—as being the sole inventor of music. Our acknowledgement of his considerable contribution should not lead us to dismiss any other claimant to the title the Biblical scribes so determinedly but abruptly bestowed upon him. Christendom's belated patron saint of music, sweet Saint Cecilia, the fastidious lady who retained her virginity within her unconsummated marriage, may be unfashionable and can be regarded in these unsentimental and promiscuous times as quaint and cloying. And it must be conceded that the asphyxiating music of which Kramer legitimately complains is under her aegis.

Yet, are we giving Jubal more than his due when, patronizingly, we acknowledge but relegate the music where Jubal's clamour and provocations play little part, which lacks challenge, that gives us a welcome hiatus in our hurried and harassed lives? Not all possess the stoicism to renounce the solace that music can bring; many too lack ambitions to engage in the palingenetic endeavours which Kramer recommends spurring us to wrest from music "new selves". There is more than a hint of condescension in the didacticism of the maestros towards those enchanted and relaxed by gentle Cecilia's dulcet notes. In his 2006 Reith Lectures for the BBC, Daniel Barenboim told us that music:

> gives us formidable weapons to forget our existence and the chores of daily life. My contention is that this is of course possible, and is practised by millions of people who like to come home after a long day at the office, put their feet up, if possible have the luxury of somebody giving them a drink while they do that, and put on the record and forget all the problems of the day. But my contention is that music has another weapon that it delivers to us, if we want to take it, and that is one through which we can learn a lot about ourselves, about our society, about the human being, about politics, about society, about anything that you choose to do.

Barenboim is here assigning to music an ennobling rôle, a weapon to be used in political engagement and unceasing self-analysis; there is a faint but distinct note of disapproval of those who put their feet up to find a little peace away from their troubled selves and from a troubled world. When Cecilia gives us that peace, we should feel no shame: in a world enveloped in anomie, alienated man yielding to her charms is not necessarily a coward retreating from reality. In her arms loneliness is being overcome and when, after a little while, we relinquish her embrace and put our feet down, we stand firmly on the ground more confidently facing the world. Such a developmental process was poignantly depicted by one who had endured the suffering of the Nazi-created Lodz ghetto when she told how listening to herself singing helped her to feel less isolated:[56]

> Only singing could help. When one sings, even when he sings a sad song, his loneliness disappears, he listens to his own voice. He and his voice become two people ... and afterwards you feel free.

Drawing comfort from being both singer and listener—single but not "alone"—evokes memories of the safety experienced when babe and mother were as one. In that dual unity mutual responsive cooing and expressive vocalization between the two partners long antedated verbalization and being able to distinguish oneself from a loving Other. But an exploration of our nostalgic attraction to music would not be complete if we went no further than remarking on the responses of the babe: we should remind ourselves of the hearing of the foetus, a hearing known to be fully developed from the fourth month of pregnancy. It is the first fully developed sensory organ and by registering the mother's voice it perhaps brings us our first intimation of the presence or absence of our mother and thus shapes our earliest experiences of security and loss. And it is not only his mother's voice that the foetus is registering: it also registers her pulse, her breathing rhythms, and her movements as she walks around. The unborn child's acoustic environment, resulting from these biological conditions, reveals astonishing parallels with ordering patterns in music. There are correspondences between the mother's cardiac and respiratory rhythms and those of musical metre and phrasal structuring, between the experience of tension and relaxation and the course of melody, as well as the tension-curve of harmonics.[57] Music, therefore, adopts the parameter of the bodily unity that is experienced with the mother and inscribes it in a quasi-linguistic system. The music which comforts us in our adult life is often one that, adopting the parameters of the bodily unity, we once enjoyed within our mothers: it recalls or imagines the paradisiacal environment within the womb. The music is our mourning, mitigating the pain of our loss.

For many youngsters too, at an age-appropriate time, rock music can sometimes be singularly therapeutic: the worldwide appeal of much of its thumping beat originates in unconscious pre-natal memories of the maternal heartbeat. Most rock tempos fall into the 60–80 bpm range, about the same as the human heart at rest: the rhythmic model of much rock music is a heartbeat. It has been persuasively affirmed:[58]

> Many bands devise (consciously or otherwise) ingenious rhythmic echoes of the heartbeat sound—for example, three or four quick beats followed by a pause (often played on higher pitch drums, but also by unison guitars or keyboards). The effect simulates an actual pulsing heart. These various heart-pulse rhythmic patterns not only support ... birth/rock music co-relations ... but they also imply that the sonic honorary presence of the maternal heartbeat is more significant that its bpms. Remember that foetal ears are a mere four—six inches from the booming maternal rock beat for most of their first nine months of life—all but a few hours of which pulse along 60–80 times a minute.

In their rock sessions, the adolescents are wailing, crying over their loss of the reassuring heartbeat of the Mama. Their renderings, extraordinary regressive imaginative fantasies, can sometimes act as a catharsis easing their anguishes.[59] It is a catharsis that is the prototype of that which Saint Cecilia provides when encountering a mourner: afflicted by the premonition of our own inevitable death, we are struck dumb. My poet brother, in his threnody *The Origin of Music*,[60] has told of her gentle aid:

> When I was a medical student
> I stole two femurs of a baby
> from The Pathology Specimen Room.
> Now I keep them in my pocket,
> the right femur and the left femur.
> Like a boy scout, I am prepared.
> For what can one say to a neighbour
> when his wife dies? 'Sorry'?
> Or when a friend's sweet child
> suffers leukaemia? 'Condolences'?
> No, if I should meet either friend

> or stricken neighbour in the street
> and he should tell me, whisper to me,
> his woeful, intimate news,
> wordless I take the two small femurs
> from out of my pocket sadly
> and play them like castanets.

By their contrast Jubal's music and that of consoling Cecilia define each other. Responding to Jubal's challenging clamour, Saint Cecilia tremulously, in the interstices of profound music, insinuates herself and gently she counsels resignation, reconciling us to mortality. She may be muted in the compositions Kramer, encouraging boldness, has categorized and promoted,[61] but her music is neither saccharine nor banal as she brings us rare quietude and serenity. When we hear Bach's Air on a G-String, Beethoven's Moonlight Sonata, Mozart's Concerto 21 K467, Pachebel's Canon, Handel's Water Music, Albinoni's Adagio, Schubert's Trout Quintet, Fauré's Requiem, Satie's Gymnopedie, Tchaikovsky's Swan Lake, Mendelssohn's Fingal's Cave Overture, Samuel Barber's Adagio, or any of the countless other works issued on compilation CDs as "Easy Listening", we applaud Christendom's apotheosis of Cecilia.

Without Cecilia's contribution, the Platonic ideal of music, so sought by the Greeks, could certainly never be attained. Plato wrote in his *Timaeus*:

> All audible musical sound is given us for the sake of harmony, which as motions akin to the orbits in our soul, and which, as anyone who makes intelligent use of the arts knows, is not to be used, as is commonly thought, to give irrational pleasure, but as a heaven-sent ally in reducing to order and harmony any disharmony in the revolutions within us.

Plato's reference to music as a "heaven-sent ally" was not accidental. It was derived from the "Music of the Spheres":[62]

> The single harmony produced by all the heavenly bodies singing and dancing together springs from one source and ends by achieving one purpose, and rightly bestowed the name not of "disordered" but of "ordered universe" upon the whole.

Among the Greek philosophers there was much dispute as to what modes of music could or should relieve us of our disharmonies.[63] Plato himself, ever conservative and severe, praised its use in battle but wanted to banish the sorrowful or plaintive from state-style music, associating as he did these qualities with indolence and drunkenness. And between Aristotle and Socrates there were disagreements as to how permissive music should be—Aristotle always fearing the imbalances destroying harmony that could arise if the orgiastic and emotional accompaniments of fifth-century BCE Dionysian rites were allowed to infiltrate a composition. In their idiom, the responses of these Greek protagonists to music are our own as we too, in making our evaluations, find we are bestirred by Jubal or becalmed by Cecilia.

Sensitive to music's components, our poets, by temperament soothsayers not rabble-rousers, make their obeisances to Saint Cecilia, and all others, Ancient Israelites or Greeks, claiming to be originators of music are demoted, granted only subsidiary rôles. John Dryden in his wondrous paean to music, *Song for Saint Cecilia's Day, 1687*, firmly places Jubal with his trumpet and Orpheus with his lyre as players within the domain governed by the inspired organist Saint Cecilia. Jubal with:

> The trumpet's loud clangor
> Excites us to arms,
> With shrill notes of anger
> And mortal alarms.
> The double double double beat
> Of the thundering drum
> Cries "Hark! the foes come;
> Charge, charge, 'tis too late to retreat!"

And although:

> Orpheus could lead the savage race,
> And trees uprooted left their place
> Sequacious of the lyre;

he is nevertheless trumped:

> But bright Cecilia raised the wonder higher:
> When to her Organ vocal breath was given

> An Angel heard, and straight appear'd -
> Mistaking Earth for Heaven!

It is she, it is claimed, who can capture for earth-dwellers heaven's harmony:

> From harmony, from heavenly harmony
> This universal frame began:
> From harmony to harmony
> Through all the compass of the notes it ran,
> The diapason closing full in Man.

Yet in these sceptical seasons when so many regard absolute faith as over-compensated doubt, we want to know more about the credentials of this angelic lady. With so many large claims persuasively made on her behalf we are surely entitled to ask what are her origins, why there are strange gaps in her CV and why knowledge of her musical talents remained concealed for 1500 years after her martyrdom. Our curiosity is not assuaged by the legend that her patronage of music arose because of her singing hymns while being unsuccessfully martyred in boiling water. If that well-peddled tale were true, it would certainly have been one of the earliest and most dramatic consequences of singing in the bath. It may be discourteous of us to reject the story—and her endowments have been so generous it may be regarded as an act of ingratitude to so invade her privacy—but these are cruel days and even saints are not granted immunity.

***

Music's earliest function, Darwin brilliantly intuited, was to act as a sexual arousal mechanism; with music our "half-human ancestors aroused each other's ardent passions during their mutual courtship ..."[64] How then has it come about that Christendom has chosen as the patron saint of music the most determinedly virginal of women, one who secured her martyrdom and canonization by the most dramatic of renunciations of all carnal desires? If we accord to Darwin the respect that his surmise deserves, then positing Cecilia as the patron saint of music is indeed to be regarded as a monumental act of denial, a repudiation of a past unexcelled in the history of Christendom, an extraordinary over-determined distancing of music from its original rôle as foreplay to copulation. Given that the legend of Cecilia has had this extraordinary consequence, it certainly requires no less scrutiny than that afforded to the Bible story of Jubal.

Once during the war, in Rome, when I was serving in Italy, I called upon her at her church in the Trastevere. I found her there lying on her side in a singularly curious pose under the high altar. It was claimed in the inscription by Stefano Maderno who had sculpted this marble statue that he himself, when she had been disinterred, had seen the uncorrupted body of the "most holy virgin" and that he had in the marble depicted the saint in the very same posture as that body. Be that as it may, certainly the awkward posture became the saint; she was a very awkward lady.

Since it is said that she lived in Sicily in the second century and her story appears to have remained unrecorded until the fifth, unsurprisingly there are many variations in the stories of her original sufferings and anguishes. But, if we are not distracted by the attendant gory details of the martyrdom, a careful reading of the stories reveals that she died, above all else, for her unflinching attachment to the one true God and for her refusal to be contaminated by the pagan world. In her pubertal years she had avowed her virginity to God. When, against her will, she was married to the pagan Valerian, she resisted intercourse, telling him that an angel of God had told her He wished her to retain her virginity. Treating this as an unlikely yarn, Valerian ironically told her he would respect her wish only if he could meet this angel. She thereupon produced the angelic emissary and, convinced, Valerian quit his polytheism, converted to the religion of one God and, after many vicissitudes, he, as an apostate, was slain for his Christian belief, while she, unsullied, was tortured to death.

Severe prohibitions are needed only if there are strong temptations: Cecilia's extravagant response to the lure of polytheism tells us how dangerously attractive she had found its practices. If, as we have suggested, Jubal had been created as an estoppel, as a barrier holding back further enquiries into the gruesome events from which music had emerged, so, too, there is in place an abortive attempt by the Bible scribes to conceal the bacchanals in which the forebears of Jubal's sister, Naamah, would have participated. Her nomenclature, like her brother's, betrays its totemistic origins: anticipating Cecilia's rôle millennia later, bearing a name whose Hebrew root means song, the Bible dare not make more explicit the identification which would align her, like her siblings, as a founder of a basic activity of human culture. The scribes draw back, as part of the original epic roll-call, from declaring her the first singer, the woman who would have had as an accompanist the inventor of music. That indeed would have been a seductive and dangerous ensemble, for their melodies could well have evoked nostalgic memories of the relaxed polytheistic world, a world so less demanding than one governed by an austere monotheistic creed.

But there were more and other reasons for the diffidence of the redactors of the Hebrew Bible that explain their failure to elaborate on the musical capacities of Naamah. The scribes were aware that soon they would in Exodus be required to tell of another sister, of Miriam, of her misconduct when her brother Moses left for Mount Sinai to receive the Ten Commandments. She was the diva who had led, with timbrel in hand, the Israelite women when in dance and song they rejoiced as the pursuing Egyptians were drowned in the Red Sea; and she was a participant later, when they, in her younger brother's absence, lapsed to create and worship the golden calf in the accompanying bacchanalian revelries. She is described as a "prophetess", the Hebrew term for which is an "ecstatic"—one who typically employs songs and dance to induce prophetic frenzies.[65] With their foreknowledge of the association of music with such vibrant temptresses who by sinuous dance and lascivious song attempted to woo Israel away from prohibitory monotheism to the permissive promiscuity of polytheism, it is unsurprising that the scribes feared to give Naamah her full due as the first songster.

Their prejudice was more than misogyny: music was a dangerous drug. It could be used therapeutically as when David played his lyre to soothe and dissipate the madness of Saul, but when abused, it could have catastrophic consequences. Jezebel, the notorious wife of Ahab the king of Israel was, like her father, a king of the Zidonians, a worshipper of the goddess Ashraroth. With 400 priests and musicians at her disposal, she sought to stupefy Israel and so achieve her objective of exterminating all the prophets of God, thus ridding the kingdom of any trace of monotheism. She almost succeeded. Redactors of the Hebrew Bible had good reason to be wary of the wiles of those women who used music as a ploy to subvert belief in an exclusive one incorporeal God.

The Jezebel tale[66] is indeed a paradigm telling of the continuous struggle of the Hebrews who had quit Egypt to maintain in Canaan their monotheistic tenets and withstand the assaults and seductions of the gods of the indigenous tribes with whom they now consorted. The prophet Elijah is depicted in a confrontation with Ahab who is told that equivocation must end and he must choose between allegiance to the incorporeal Hebrew god or the god worshipped by his wife Jezebel: the Hebrew god was a jealous god who would permit no rival and Ahab could not maintain fealty to two gods. To resolve the issue, a grand barbecue was set up on Mount Carmel attended by all Israel. There, two separate piles of wood, the one regarded as Elijah's and the other as that of Jezebel's "prophets", were set up and a steak laid upon each. Neither pile of wood was lit. Then the protagonists were told by Elijah: "And call ye on the name of your gods, and I will call on the name of the Lord; and the God that answers by fire, let him be God. And all the people answered and said, 'It is well spoken'". Needless to say this fateful cookery contest had a happy ending: Jezebel's priests were outclassed. They drew a blank: all their frenzied beseechments to their gods brought no response. But, in response to his prayer, the fire of the Lord fell upon Elijah's wooden pile and ensured his steak was well-done. "And when all the people saw *it*, they fell on their faces; and they said, 'The Lord, he *is* the God; the Lord, he *is* the God'". The people of Israel, enraged at the deceptions the meretricious priests had practised upon them, turned upon Jezebel's prophets and slaughtered all of them.

The story is, of course, a wish-fulfilment and not a historical reading. The reality was that the unadulterated pure monotheism of the followers of the original Moses was always under threat from the moment the Hebrews quit Egypt, and continued to be so even until and beyond the time of the Fall of the Temple and the ultimate dispersal of the Jews. The suspicion always was in place that music could be used as a beguiling ally of the anti-monotheistic brigade.

With considerable success, within the massive walls of the temples built on solid and spiritual foundations, music was contained and put to the service of the one true God. But its suspect history and capriciousness, its past association with totemistic revels, meant it was far too explosive to be placed within the frail peripatetic synagogues of the dispersal. There, faint echoes of Naamah the songstress could be heard in the lamentations of the cantor but all other musical forms were prohibited. Music misapplied could dangerously adulterate the monotheistic creed. Its upholders would give no ground. Music potentially could so insinuate itself as to challenge the inviolability of the fundamental tenet, that the Lord is God and that God is One. Only when we grasp the significance of this resistance can we begin to understand why Cecilia, despite her impeccable credentials as an anti-pagan, was not initially accorded the accolade of music's patron: she had to await centuries after her martyrdom before Christianity would dare to breach the Jewish prejudice and, hesitatingly, pronounce Cecilia as the guardian saint of music.

The rigidity with which the Jews held the monotheist belief which so influenced and restrained Christianity from acclaiming Cecilia's musical powers was the legacy of the man who some, including myself, consider the greatest man who has ever lived, Akhenaton, King Amenophis IV, who ruled Egypt for 17 years in the middle of the 14th century BCE.[67] He was the first founder of a monotheist counter-religion to polytheism. The monotheistic revolution he ruthlessly imposed upon his kingdom was the most radical and violent eruption of counter-religion in the history of mankind.[68] Temples were closed, the images of the Egyptian gods were destroyed, their names were erased and their cults were discontinued. No derogation from Akhenaton's form of monotheism was permitted expression. This history is familiar to many modern music lovers who have been entranced by Philip Glass's 1984 opera *Akhnaten*. When, after Akhenaton's death, the inevitable reactionary counter-revolution occurred, bringing back the gods, a Hebrew group living in Egypt, inspired and led by Moses, himself probably an Egyptian prince who had remained loyal to the Akhenaton ideal,[69] quit the land for Canaan and were to become the Israelites who, eccentrically, in a Middle Eastern region throughout which polytheism prevailed, insisted that God was incorporeal, invisible and One. Although some compromises had to be made by the migrants to accommodate the idol worship of the indigenous tribes with whom they were intermingling, notably to Yahweh the volcanic god, they nevertheless continued to hold fast to the essential tenets of the Akhenaton creed.

It was not an easy feat. It is probable that it was not until the late sixth century BCE that belief in the exclusiveness of the incorporeal invisible God became Israel's unchallengeable orthodoxy. Before that syncretized views had widely prevailed and monolatrous forms of worship, where other gods were worshipped along with the God that the migrants had brought with them from Egypt, were tolerated. Indeed, some of the Israelites conflated Yahweh, whom they named as the Hebrew God, with his spouse the goddess Ashraroth. But in the end Israel proved herself a worthy keeper of the Covenant deserving to be the Chosen People. Morning, noon and night all Israel united in prayer to affirm the oneness of the non-corporeal God. Not until the first century AD did anyone among the Jews dispute that assumption: then a small sect broke ranks and, outraging all their co-religionists, propagandized that God had a son born to a virgin mother. This, for most Jews, was a blasphemous assertion, a ploy to drag them back to the polytheistic world where anthropomorphic gods had sported and begat. It mattered not that this sect claimed that the unity of God was not challenged. At that time and ever since in one form or another Christians have sought to explain that the doctrine of the Trinity in no way subverts monotheistic belief. Reflecting the view of Jesus' earliest followers, the doctrine is now authoritatively expressed[70] in the words:

> The Father himself is God, the Son is God, and the Holy Ghost is God and yet they are not three Gods but one God ... for like as we are compelled by the Christian verity to acknowledge every Person by himself to be God and Lord, so we are forbidden by the Catholic religion to say that there be three Gods or three Lords.

But at the time of Jesus and ever since, stubborn Jewry has rejected the claim that belief in the Trinity is compatible with a belief in one God. They have paid dearly for that rejection.

In the playground of my primary school, I learned for the first time of Christ. I was forever involved in fights as I responded to taunts that I had crucified Him. My wise Welsh Nonconformist teachers who regarded me as a member of the Chosen People never interfered with the fisticuffs if I was gaining the advantage; if not, they would come out of their staff room, seize my tormentor, and give him a thrashing for breaking the rule that no fights were permitted in the playground. My experience as a little boy was indeed benign compared with the calamities that over thousands of years fell upon my ancestors as they faced the charge of deicide.

The zeal and extraordinary persuasive powers of the early Christian Jews were eventually to bring Christ as the Lord to all Europe excepting only to their own scattered one-time co-religionists, but the impress of that Judaic origin was nowhere more explicit than in their suspicion of musical instruments. Vulnerable as they were to the charge that the Trinitarian doctrine was a regressive exposition of polytheism, they could not afford to attach to their martyrs the odium of an association with an art that so recalled the revels and rites of the polytheistic world. For centuries, to ward off the accusation that Christianity was a heavy flirtation with polytheism, the Church approved only of the use of song to praise the Lord: hymns were not to be accompanied by musical instruments. There was a fierce determination to distance the Church from the snares and seductions music could initiate. In the fifth century AD we find St. Jerome writing that a Christian maiden ought not even to know what a lyre or flute was like, or to what usage they were put. At that time besmirching the memory of Cecilia by depicting the virginal martyr, as she is now identified, holding an organ or other suggestive instrument, would have been regarded as outrageous.

Christendom has still not entirely overcome such feelings of revulsion. The Greek Church continues to forbid all musical instruments. In 17th century England the influence of Presbyterians and Independents in the Commonwealth which resulted in organs and choirs being removed from the churches lingered on in Presbyterian Scotland where, until the mid-19th century, organs in churches were regarded as sinful, and today Nonconformists still show considerable restraint in the provision of music.

But it is not only churchmen who fear music's snares. Music is unruly, often corroborative but also often subversive. In our day we have seen the tyrant Stalin tremble as brave Shostakovich dared to create his operas and symphonies even as, in other days, in the early 15th century, the House of Commons quivered as Welsh minstrels beguiled their fellow countrymen. These minstrels were denounced by the legislators as instigators of rebellion:[71]

> No westours and rhymers, minstrels or vagabonds, be maintained in Wales to make kymorthas or quyllaghes on the common

people who by their divination, lies and exhortations, are partly the cause of the insurrection and rebellion now in Wales.

It requires a much more confident Establishment to leave music uncensored and free to roam, not afraid of its eroticism or its revolutionary incitements. Such a society was evidently in place in Rome in 1584 when, abandoning the inhibitions and ambiguities that had clung to the status of music in the Church, and feeling sufficiently politically secure, approval was given by the Vatican to the newly founded Academy of Music to choose Cecilia as its patroness: her iconic status as a saint was thereby enhanced, not defiled. A complete *volte-face* had taken place within a confident Roman Catholicism impervious to any charge of polytheism and indifferent to the wiles and the misbehaviour of women associated with music in the Hebrew Bible: a sweet and solicitous Cecilia had emerged to bless the music-makers and sanctify their compositions. This was occasioned not by serendipitous chance but by the gradual spread of Mariolatry and then by a profound cultural change wrought by the Renaissance. Mariolatry ensured that Cecilia, as a forgiving soothing pacifier, would be welcome to join the throng of women saints attendant upon the Virgin Mary. And the Renaissance, which had brought the despised pagan gods and goddesses of classical mythology into the midst of Christian Europe, relegated their status ensuring they were no longer perceived as awesome threats, no longer possessed of powers to regulate our fates. Galileo's time was approaching when the world would be seen to be revolving around the sun; the heavens were being emptied of the gods, and the Mother of God and her attendants would soon be given ample space to dwell untroubled in the Elysian Fields. And when, later, the Counter-Reformation came, the gods had been so domesticated, so trivialized and prettified, that they could adorn public places without causing any of the offence they once had brought to Savonarola. Mariolatry, now in place, was not the slightest bit challenged by the playful and erotic representations of the ancient gods.

That development of Marian devotion, the necessary prerequisite to the acceptance of Cecilia as a comforting lullaby saint, had been singularly tardy. The Gospels provide us with only sparse details of Mary's life. So low profile is her presentation that even interpreters who accept the snippets available as Biblical historical accounts have found it difficult to draw a portrait of Mary on the basis of what the Gospels niggardly provide. It is not by chance that this has been occasioned. The Jewish writers of the Gospels were well acquainted with the cunning, terrifying, and always ambiguous rôle assigned to so many of the outstanding women of the Old Testament: Eve, the disobedient temptress, Namaah, member of a violent family, the jealous and ruthless Sarah, ready to despatch her handmaiden's son to die in the desert, Rebecca, counselling her son in the deception of blind Isaac, Lot's reckless wife turned into a petrified monument to divine displeasure, Potiphar's adulterous spouse, the judgmental and military strategist Deborah, treacherous Delilah, adulterous Bathsheba, wicked Jezebel, the conspiratorial Naomi and Ruth engaged in trapping Boaz into marriage, Esther bringing about the hanging of Haman, heroines like Judith, engaged in the decapitation of Israel's enemy—the image of women of the Old Testament is wholly incompatible with that of Mary, the gentle, forgiving mediatress and Mother of God. Rather than risk evoking memories of the dangerous Old Testament women, the Gospels made Mary a shadowy figure and kept her firmly in the background.

But in the second century a more subtle effort was made to dissociate Mary from the scandalous women of the Old Testament. The Christian philosophers, Justin and Irenaeus, both later to be canonized, developed in their several ways the theme of Mary as a new Eve whose obedience cancelled the disobedience of the old Eve in Eden. It was a valiant effort to free Mary from the taint of the sins of her notorious predecessors. But the fear that she would relapse into their sinfulness remained; the need to assign Mary a rôle that would quench such apprehensions remained. It took a couple of centuries and much labyrinthine debate on issues such as whether Mary's virginity only arose in birth and after birth, or whether it was "perpetual" and whether or not she earned the title "Immaculate" free of all sins, including original sin, before, at the Council of Ephesus in 431, her status was authoritatively determined: there it was declared that she was *Theo Tokil*, Mother of God. Thus was Mary's significance enhanced by emphasizing the rôle she had in the Redemption; it was explained, tortuously, that the title given her was because of the hypostatic union of Divinity in the single person of Christ. By such a formulation the Church tempered its ambivalence to granting overmuch prominence to Mary. But, nevertheless, the fear of the feminine embodying Christianity, so fiercely displayed by Paul's antagonism to sexuality, was not entirely eliminated. Always it was feared that the shadow of Eve would fall upon the "Blessed Mary". Indeed, the immaculate assumption was not conceded to Mary for many centuries: it was not until 1854 that the doctrine of the Immaculate Conception was finally defined as Roman Catholic dogma. According to this dogma, Mary was not only pure in her life and in her birth but "at the first instant of her conception was preserved immaculate from all stain of original sin, a singular grace and privilege granted her by Almighty God, through the merits of Christ Jesus, Saviour of mankind". And it was not until 1960, after 8,000,000 people had petitioned the Vatican, that Pope Pius XII capitulated, making the dogma of the Assumption official, when he declaimed that the "Immaculate Mother of God, the ever Virgin Mary, when the course of her earthly life was run, was assumed in body and soul to heavenly glory".

From a Freudian perspective the profound esoteric arguments over the attributes of Mary that raged for so many centuries before the Catholic Church closed its internal debate can be seen as mere epiphenomena. The extirpation of all hints of Mary's sexuality and her ultimate disembodiment as she, sinless, floats into heaven where for ever she tenderly and forgivingly overlooks us, tells us of the fissure, sometimes fatal, within man's desire. The successful fusion of tenderness and lust, as in love, is so often unachievable. The resulting dichotomy can leave man resentful of the bondage which enslaves him to the woman for whom he lusts and whom he despises. And ashamed of his inadequacy with the woman he adores, he excuses himself, claiming that she is too wondrously virtuous to be despoiled. The madonna/whore syndrome, familiar to today's clinicians treating the impotence of husbands and lovers at ease only with prostitutes, is fully played out in the Bible. In the Old Testament woman is intemperately demonized; and in the early exegetical interpretation of the New Testament she was soon to be extravagantly idealized.

Long before it became orthodox Catholic dogma, boundless idealization in the form of devotion to "Our Lady" spread throughout Europe. The faithful were being required to know the "Hail Mary" as well as Our Father and the Creed. At the end of the eighth century in England there were only 20 churches dedicated to Mary but the number had risen to over 2,000 before the Reformation cried a halt. In Catholic Europe there were no such checks. There, stern

Jehovah, the God of Justice, could often barely hold His place as the merciful Lady of Pity with her intercessionary powers was increasingly invoked. Often, through the centuries, we witness this struggle of Christians fearful that the growing cult of the Virgin Mary would lead to idolatry. At the outset of the 16th century, the works of the greatest artist of the period tell us how fierce was the debate;[72] in one of Holbein's famous illustrations for Erasmus's *Encomium Moriae* a kneeling woman prays before the image of the Virgin to which she has offered various candles. The author uses the printed commentary in the margin to function as a title to this image: "*Suspitosus cultus imaginum*".

And, echoing Luther's insistence that religious imagery required to be purged of such vulgar superstitions, we find the most intellectual of all artists, Albrecht Dürer, infuriated by a cult damaging the pure imagery that he believed true worship demanded. His failed intervention in the notorious controversy around the Regensburg Pilgrimage well illustrates the tumultuous ambivalences in place as nascent humanist Protestantism joined battle with the papal exploitation of man's need to recapture the maternal solace he once received in his mother's arms; and it also, ironically, reminds us that the ultimate source of the whole controversy was to be found in the hatred inspired against the Jews because of their obdurate and total denial of the virgin birth of Christ. In 1519, at the instigation of an anti-Semitic master, the heavily indebted city council had decided to tear down the Regensburg synagogue and the adjacent Jewish quarter, and to expel the Jews from the city. One of the workers was seriously injured during the demolition of the synagogue but returned to work next day claiming the Virgin Mary had healed him. His explanation was interpreted as a divine endorsement of the pogrom.[73] A pilgrimage centre was founded there with the authorization of the Pope which, given the massive influx of faithful pilgrims, became a lucrative business for the church and the city. In a commentary, penned by his own hand, Dürer quoted the holy scriptures and railed against the improper use of the Virgin's image:

> This spectre arose in Regensburg against Holy Writ, and although it has been authorised by the Bishop, it was erected for earthly use. God help us that we should not so dishonour His Holy Mother but venerate her in Jesus Christ. Amen.

But despite the protests of Christian humanists like Dürer, and despite the growth and spread of Luther's Protestantism, the tide running in favour of Marian doctrine continued and continues. It could hardly be otherwise: the doctrine is safely ensconced and propagated in the greatest glories of our Western civilization. The displacement of God the Father in favour of the Blessed Virgin has given us some of Europe's most resplendent cathedrals. One of the most explicit of Marian basilicas, one dedicated to the Assumption of the Virgin, is to be found in Burgos. There, in the huge cathedral, one of the largest in Spain, it is difficult to find any representation of God the Father.

This is Mary's domain. No matter that she is there under an assumed name. In the original Greek manuscripts of the New Testament her name, phonetically, was given as "Miryam"; but carrying that name would have recalled the frenzied dancing of Miriam, sister of Moses, singer of bloody war-songs and a participant in the revels around the golden calf. In the greatest of Marian cathedrals, in Burgos, one finds however a far more orthodox and becoming recall: there, on the high altar of the entrancing Chapel of the Conception of St Anne, there stands the gorgeous reredos depicting the Tree of Jesse legitimizing the fateful embrace of Joachim and Anne, the parents of Mary. Nowhere has there been expressed a conception more expunged of sexuality.

And, too, in another chapel, so all-enveloping is the Mariolatry ethos that Christ Himself is stripped of his gender and scandalously feminized. In the Chapel of the Holy Christ of Burgos the image of the crucified Christ is an object of continued veneration by the politically reactionary citizens of Burgos and by millions of Catholics in South America, where it is known as "the Lord of Burgos". Here Jesus has lost his manhood. Made of wood covered in calf-skin, jointed and flexible to the touch, we have a vivid representation of a Christ wounded and dead on the cross. But here He lacks the usual loin-cloth covering His genitalia; here, as in other monasteries close to Burgos, we find a Christ with long hair, divided into many tresses and lingering on His shoulders, draped in a long embroidered woman's skirt, one that could earn the label of today's fashionable designers. He is not being depicted as gender-free: this is a Christ who is a woman. This is Mariolatry's affirmative reply to the question: "Was Jesus a woman?"—a question that has so often been put since Clement of Alexandria, in the second century, explored the feminine qualities of Christianity's Godhead. Clement spoke of the Father's "loving breast" and of the "milk of the Father". Similarly, and in even more explicit mode, in the 14th century the female mystic Julian of Norwich wrote: "And so Jesus is our true Mother in nature by our first creation, and He is our true Mother in grace by His taking our created nature." In the same tradition, Katherine Schori has compounded the "offence" of being the highest-ranking woman in the Anglican Church, by saying, in her first sermon since her election in 2006 as the 26th presiding bishop of the US Episcopal Church: "Mother Jesus gives birth to a new creation—and you and I are His children".[74]

At which point, in this long history of the development of Mariolatry, Cecilia was first permitted to be presented as the patron saint of music is not known. She tip-toes into that history, an imaginative creation of artists. The template they used in their depictions was that of the Virgin Mary: by extolling Cecilia, endowing her with the virtues and sinlessness of Mary, they dared to place a lyre or organ in her hands, confident that she was so pure that no-one could accuse her of being a siren using music, as it often had been in the past, to lure man into dangerous trespasses. When Raphael painted his altarpiece for the Church of San Giovanni near Bologna and depicted her with an organ, it would have prompted no frisson: it was already a convention. More perplexing is why the artists chose as the emblem of music a saint bearing a name that comes from the Latin word meaning blind. Perhaps they wanted no reprimanding saint gazing sternly down on them; perhaps they felt a forgiving saint, blind to their transgressions, would be more agreeable.

But whatever the motivation may have been behind the nomenclature, the artists' widespread advertisements of the lady assured her success in a market eager for a product tempering Jubal's abrasiveness. No monopoly was to be granted to the man fathered by the terrifying Lamech whose name in Hebrew means "The Wild Man, the Striker-Downer"; the qualities Jubal inherited from his sire needed containing. Only thus, to our continuing benefit, could music, free from imbalances, relieve us from what Plato had called the "disharmony in the revolutions within us".[75] According to our moods, temperaments, and predicaments, we variously respond to Jubal's stirring incitements and Cecilia's soothing emollients, but acoustics ensure that profound music will never be heard unless, when Cecilia plays her organ or plucks her lyre, Jubal's music also resounds in the background, however muted.

Matchlessly fused the sounds bring relief from the pains of the Ur-fracture which, Plato affirmed, man is fated to endure: in the beginning there was wholeness but now we are maimed. As we limp along, profound music has the capacity to help us maintain our balance. By its intimations we are given the courage to continue the vain but perpetual pursuit of the hermaphrodite ideal which Plato has taught us is our destiny. In Plato's *Symposium* we are instructed:

> First of all, you must learn the constitution of man and the modifications which it has undergone, for originally it was different from what it is now. In the first place there were three sexes, not, as with us, two, male and female; the third partook of the nature of both the others and has vanished, though its name survives. The hermaphrodite was a distinct sex in form as well as in name, with the characteristics of both male and female, but now the name alone remains, and that solely as a term of abuse. ... Each of us then is the mere broken tally of a man, the result of a bisection which has reduced us to a condition like that of a flatfish, and each of us is perpetually in search of a corresponding tally.

Nowhere was that yearning and that search made more explicit than when, hypnotized, men and women listened to the entrancing songs of the castrati.

***

Papal approval was given in 1562 to the selection of boys with exceptional musical ability for castration so that, for the greater glory of God, they could sing in church choirs; the Church condoned the often fatal emasculation because the children died in the service of God and by their death were saved from sin. With such absolution available the widespread demand for castrati was fully met. When, 100 years later, the castrati were employed in Italian opera, thousands of boys aged eight or nine years were taken by their parents to the barbers for castration. Since the larynx is a secondary sexual organ which undergoes decisive changes in puberty, the removal of the sex glands inhibits the growth of the larynx, and particularly of the vocal chords, but the chest diameter of the body will continue to grow. Sometimes, among those who survived the ordeal, the consequence was the endowment of a beautiful voice with an exceptional range. The voice of the castrated boy could span several octaves, covering the ranges of both male and female voices; his soprano singing was enhanced by the chest register and resonance: this combination resulted in a tone quality not obtainable by singers of either sex. Indeed, special instruction in breathing and chest expansion allowed the castrato's tone to be held longer than that of any instrument. The bisexual quality of the castrato's voice represented a blurring of boundaries between male and female, between young and old, sacred and profane.[76] The listener to the castrati was granted the joyous fantasy that boundaries which separate our wishes from reality could be erased, that the painful specificity of gender could be transcended. The castrato fulfilled vocally the longing for the hermaphroditic ideal.

Precipitating sexual arousal in men and women, they caused such jealousy among husbands that some (like the famed and threatened castrato singer, Caffarelli) needed bodyguards to protect them from their rage; others were kidnapped to be sodomized by their besotted admirers. Many accumulated fortunes in salaries and gifts, and some acquired great power in the service of princes or kings, such as Farinelli: he was invited in 1737 to the court of the Bourbons in Madrid to calm the schizophrenic Philip V and enable him to function for a few hours for governmental business.

It was the gifted otolaryngologist, Paul J. Moses, a specialist in voice pathology, who possessed empathic qualities which often enabled him to diagnose his patients' illnesses by the reverberations he could detect almost instantaneously in the voice. When he died in 1965 he left an unfinished manuscript[77] in which he was explicating the significance of the hermaphroditic ideal to those who had abandoned themselves to the charms of the singing of the castrati. And drawing on the phenomenon of that singing he was, up to his death, endeavouring to show how different proportions of maleness and femaleness can be expressed and combined in the voices of both men and women, and how different times and cultures leave in their vocal styles the testament of their particular hermaphroditic ideal. In both early and late opera he was certainly not lacking in illustrative material to substantiate his thesis.

All who enjoy opera are familiar with the stratagems deployed by composers to assuage the hermaphroditic yearnings of their audiences. The most obvious ploy is the use of the so-called "breeches" part. A rôle, usually that of an adolescent young man, is sung by a female soprano—as for the page Oscar in Verdi's *Un Ballo in Maschera*, and the young lover, Octavian, in Strauss' *Der Rosenkavalier*. But this bisexual representation in opera is certainly not confined to adolescent and breeches rôles; in so many operas intimations of hermaphroditism are provided by the hero who has a high voice which roams within the natural register of women. And, to add or provide alternatives to such a peregrination, we often find composers precipitating the required *frisson* by separating unequivocal male and female voice qualities according to the actual rôle gender and thenreuniting the two sexes by blending their voices in melting duets.

The vile Wagner in turn perfected another dodge to achieve the same effect: with characteristic sadism he brutally imposed a bisexual mixture of male and female headregister for singers of both sexes, and so forced the development of a new singing technique to equip women with the head and chest registers necessary for their more active aggressive rôles. He masculinized women, and his masochistic devotees submit and wallow in their abasement. That is one route, not necessarily the preferred or commendable one, to be rid of the specificity and burden of gender and to hallucinate the attainment of the hermaphrodite ideal. Wagner ensured that by a singing technique, one violating the usual mode, there would be no mismatch between the transgressive content of his operas and their form. A polymorphous perverse accompaniment was always made available corroborating his fantasized world, a world unconstrained by gender boundaries or consanguinity prohibitions. All this, typically, was played out as in *Die Walküre* where the incest between brother and sister, Siegmund and Sieglinde, is one of the main themes, and where Siegfried's belovèd Brünnhilde was fathered by Wotan, his own grandfather, and is thus his aunt as well as his mistress.

In Wagner's operas the taboos that civilized primitive man are all exploded and we are invited to join in the delusion that man can go beyond the irrevocable narrow limits of his condition, that confusion between sexes and generations is the prerequisite enabling us, free from the burdens individuation imposes, to push forward the frontiers of what is possible and unsettle reality. This, psychoanalytical clinicians have revealed, is the regressive sick dream of the perverts they have endeavoured to treat.[78] It was, of course, the dream that enveloped the enthusiastic Wagner worshipper, Adolf Hitler. It is the universe depicted by Sade who, throughout his works, regarded sexual intercourse as a group activity. The protagonists in his tales, men and women, children and old people, virgins and whores, nuns and bawds, mothers and sons, fathers and daughters, brothers and sisters, uncles and nephews, noblemen and rabble—all build up extremely complex positions which are then unmade and transformed: "All will be higgledypiggledy, all will wallow, all will mix, will commit incest, adultery and sodomy." Such is a precept to be found in the "Code of Laws" of his *120 Days*.

The temptation to lose oneself, to abandon individuation and gender, to be irresponsible, to let Fate take over one's destiny, to avoid the agonies of personal decision-making, to gain a respite from the increasing complexities of contemporary life—are all lures especially attractive to lonely, irreligious, faithless modern man. Many in the past and present have found temporary relief from the affliction of anomie by forgetting themselves and submitting to Wagner's imperious commands. But there are some significant figures, initially admirers of his works, who ended by finding his creations repellent; submitting to them had become demeaning. The incomparable Nietzsche first revelled in Siegfried "the man without fear who is destined to abolish old contracts, free the world from the tyrannies of laws, moralities and institutions, and usher in a new society".[79] But Nietzsche's admiration was not to be sustained and he was to become increasingly disenchanted. Defeatism was no part of Nietzsche's manifesto. He regarded Wagner's later operas, with their preoccupation with redemption and death, as an affront to his own optimistic and life-affirming philosophy. Wagner's incorporation of Christianity in his last opera, *Parsifal*, was, for Nietzsche, a betrayal of the heroic ideal in favour of renunciation and self-sacrifice. Nietzsche had no taste for the pleasures of humiliation, broke with Wagner and would take no bit part in any Wagner sado-masochistic idyll.

Similarly, Thomas Mann, although recognizing that great music may sometimes transcend the individual who composed it, could not forbear when movingly acknowledging his indebtedness to

Wagner to tell of his profound distaste for the personality so jarringly manifesting itself in Wagner's works. Mann wrote:[80]

> The man had so much ability, talent and interpretative skill—more than words can say. Yet so much affectation with it, such lordly pretension, self-aggrandisement and mystagogical self-dramatisation—again, more than words can say or patience can bear.

And Nietzsche certainly lost patience with Wagner; he would not tolerate the debasement of music by an ugly intrusion of personality distracting us from our search for "the primal unity", the name he so appositely gave to the hermaphroditic ideal. Neither the bombastic rhetoric of Wagner nor, indeed, the eloquence of lyric poetry, could bring us nearer to our goal than does music:[81]

> Language can never adequately render the cosmic symbolism of music, because music stands in symbolic relation to the primordial contradiction and primordial pain in the heart of the primal unity, and therefore symbolises a sphere which is beyond and prior to all phenomena. Rather, all phenomena, compared with it, are merely symbols; hence language, as the origin and symbol of phenomena, can never by any means disclose the innermost heart of music; language in its attempt to imitate it, can only be in superficial contact with music; while all the eloquence of lyric poetry cannot bring the deeper significance of the latter one step nearer.

Nietzsche disdained the signpost positioned on Wagner's polluted route to the hermaphroditic ideal. As an accomplished pianist and composer himself, he found his own way to a music which could bring him, and so many of us, intimations of "the primordial contradictions and primordial pain in the heart of the primal unity" which had finally occasioned its severance. Thus he declared his preference for Bizet to that of his former idol, Wagner; the contrast between Bizet and Wagner was "an ironic antithesis"[82] and in Bizet could be found "the divine frivolity of the dance".[83]

By postulating music as the medium which could give us a reminiscence of the primal unity, in place before we were "reduced to a condition like that of a flatfish",[84] Nietzsche was reiterating the Platonic view. That in primordial time there was such a primal unity is not, however, an exclusive Greek concept; it is implicit in the Biblical creation story. In Hebrew Adam is a generic term for human beings, not a proper noun suggesting maleness;[85] the traditional rendering of "man" is misleading. The feminist critics are fully justified in inviting us to imagine Adam as sexually undifferentiated until, from Adam's rib, woman was fashioned. God's anaesthetic had been administered, and Adam put to sleep, but the removal of the rib was a brutal piece of surgery. The pain and the trauma of that operation remains with us; we complain that we are unwell, suffering from an undiagnosed disease: we yearn for the wholeness and perfection that once was.

***

Perhaps no music more poignantly and explicitly seeks to provide a palliative for the pains of this irrevocable separateness of the human condition than that of the composer who suffered most from the affliction, the bachelor Johannes Brahms, the loneliest of men. For the contemporary composer and distinguished scholar Hugh Wood,[86] Brahms truly "was the most profoundly unhappy of all the great composers". Nietzsche's penetrating commentary on its yearnings described his music as the "melancholy of impotence". It was the tragic fate of Brahms that he was never, even fitfully as many of us do, to lose his aloneness in a physical merger with a loved one. His loss was to be our gain as his genius conjured up compensatory auditory images replete with intimations of the lost primal unity that in real life was ever denied to him.

He had been born into a poor but unusual family unit; his mother, plain and lame but of aristocratic lineage, was 17 years older than his father. The late arrival of her first-born son was wondrous for her, and she worshipped him. In turn he responded and his idealization of this "superior" woman was to be morbidly sustained throughout his life. But there were to be other women of a very different order who were also to determine the little boy's destiny; these were the whores who frequented the dock taverns of Hamburg where the 12-year-old, to relieve the poverty of the family, would play the cheapest of cheap music for the entertainment of visiting sailors and where "the ladies of the town who frequented the locale to ply their trade were not above making use of the boy pianist to kindle the ardour of their seafaring admirers".[87] The template of Brahms's adult private life was shaped by his vision as a child of an immaculate mother and of the predatory prostitutes of the taverns. For Brahms, women were either angels or despised whores. He could establish passionate asexual relationships with older women, as with Schumann's widow, but all his attempts to have flesh and blood loving relationships with women ended in disaster. Nietzsche had accurately diagnosed his predicament: to ease the anguish of his incompetence, Brahms vented his frustrations upon all womankind excepting only in his notorious misogyny the few chosen older mother surrogates whom he chastely adored. After a glass of champagne, his tongue loosened, he would shock company as in the coarsest of language he lashed out against the wiles of women:[88] they were all trash.

Yet withal, it was precisely because he was thus emptied of his anger, all bitterness released, that he could give us his final renowned Fourth Symphony, calm, balanced, logical, full of strength, restrained with no exaltation, with his "impotent melancholy" sad but not self-pitying, and expressed with stoical resignation. This most quarrelsome of men, ever insulting those with whom he consorted, a man who would leave social gatherings with the provocative taunt, "Is there anyone here whom I have not insulted?", would, with his aggression thus discharged, give us the magic music of post-coital stillness. In his compositions he achieved for himself, and for all of us fractured men and women, the healing reminiscence of the primal unity which was physically denied to him in real life.

To resolve his dilemma he courageously relied on himself alone. He rejected all props, unequivocally affirming his agnosticism and rejection of Christian belief. His great Requiem, Opus 45, the first piece to build his international reputation, was no death-bed testament; with deliberation his text refused to engage with the central requiem canon of the Catholic doctrine that Christ died for us. The text he chose demonstrates that this non-believer had a formidable command of biblical scholarship; his message was forward-looking, valuing and treasuring the achievements of our transitory lives. Even although he had no faith, still he preached hope. It is unsurprising that so many musicologists pronounce this work as the most optimistic of all requiems:[89] "Ye see for a little while I labour and toil, yet have I found rest",[90] and having found his peace in his lifetime in his creative work, he challengingly recites: "O death, where is thy sting?

O grave, where is thy victory?"[91] Brahms himself once pronounced the work a "human requiem". It was a just claim, for his aspiration and his constant awareness of the tragic brevity of life is not eccentric but is one shared by all but the purblind.

But there is one predominant feature of the music of this great lyricist that troubles all his biographers, one that is acknowledged as both his strength and weakness. Its quietude, its restraint, its freedom from extravagance, its eschewing of the pretentious rhetorical afflatus of Wagner and of the obtrusive *cri de coeur* of Tchaikovsky is achieved at a price: he takes no risks, he is cautious. Alike in music and in life the adventurous impulse was sternly repressed. His perceptive musicologist biographer tells us that "in his music, he would undertake no enterprise whose end he could not see, no course of action whose consequences he could not control".[92]

We find and respond to the dignity of the measured reserve of his compositions. In his social life his misanthropic conduct ensured that no-one would presume to intrude upon his privacy: all were thus distanced. And in his works the constraints he imposed upon himself meant no-one would find revelatory outbursts telling of the secrets of his inner life. His romanticism was not dead but it was "closely prisoned. He fortified himself behind barrier after barrier of reserves and precautions".[93]

Only rarely do we find any intimation of who was the enemy against whom he is erecting his defences, but we are put on enquiry by the Delphic content of the congratulatory letter he wrote on the occasion of the engagement of his close friend, the renowned violinist, Josef Joachim, when Brahms mused upon his own continuing bachelor condition. The letter could not have been written in more cryptic form or in phrases clothed in a more distorted and oblique manner:

> I have not ceased to wonder whether, since I must guard against dreams of another kind, I had better not experience and enjoy everything with one exception, or whether I should not be sure of one thing—that is, go home and let the rest lie.

This obscure utterance, full of hints and allusions, has bewildered musicology historians but if it is read with a full awareness of the ecology which so determined Brahms' emotional growth, it is surely capable of being deciphered.

We should remember the rôle reversals within the Brahms family were dramatic. The weak and feckless, but kindly and gentle, father was not in command: it was the very much older mother who dominated the household. She held it together and took all the decisions necessary to keep their poverty at bay. She was "the man" in the house; her husband, with his modest musical ability and his limited ambition of becoming a double-bass player in a local band, drifted passively in the wake of his formidable partner. The dominant passion in the family was not between husband and wife— that relationship was to come to grief—but was between the young Johannes and his belovèd mother. As subsequent events showed, Brahms was to remain irrevocably mother-bound, never to marry. The normative development of a boy who works through his Oedipal struggles and achieves his maleness by way of an identification with his father had not taken place; he remained enveloped in a hazardous feminine identification with his mother. When later, astonished at his irrational vituperative onslaughts on womankind, we cannot but compare them with those made by those unhappy homosexuals who, having never come to terms with their sexual orientation and, unconsciously blaming their mothers for the emasculation, so bitterly mock women and their vanities. The enemy Brahms feared, and against whom he so determinedly erected his defences within his music, was surely the homosexual component within his own nature: he feared his own femininity could overwhelm him.[94]

> His own high voice, the voice of the woman encapsulated within him, was too revealing; it had to be suppressed. Determinedly he decided to rid himself of the embarrassment by doing vocal exercises of his own devising, and to strengthen the vocal apparatus by the method of shouting above the din at his Singverein rehearsals. The result of this regimen, besides annoying his singers, was to give himself a voice permanently hoarse and barking, while still rather high. The good singing voice he had once possessed was ruined. From then on, in heated moments his voice would break like a pubescent teenager's. Given his disappointing vocal endowment and physical size, Brahms would be forced to rely on cigars, alcohol, gruffness, racy jokes, and eventually on beard and girth to furnish him with manliness.

So acutely aware of his vulnerability was he that he laid down within his music strictly defined boundaries. Away from the pitfalls in the surrounding territory and undisturbed, he found in music some peace from his private agonies. Because his dilemmas, albeit usually less acute, are endemic to the human condition, our turbulences too are stilled by his music: the soothing maternal element in his works comforts us. The many musicologists and critics who, while acknowledging the wonders of his compositions, complain that Brahms is, however, too cautious, too unadventurous, are greedy: they should be content and marvel at how Brahms' genius enabled him to transmute the consequence of his disadvantages, of his physical impotence, and of his repressed homosexuality.

He courageously, persistently, wrestled with his demons and often, as his music reflects, he won his battles. He did not externalize his travails, dramatize them, project them on to a stage. Not for him the rodomontade and histrionics of Wagner. It was within the privacy of his interior life, not in the theatre, that the resolution of his conflicts took place. He abjured Wagner's gaudy effects, even refusing to use the new valve horns and trumpets, and never using trombones in his concertos: in at least half of the movements of his symphonies they do not appear at all. He would not with meretricious asides ever compromise the essential austerity of his work. And, stoically, to maintain his authenticity, he walked alone, a godless man who despised those who, like Wagner and his ilk, strove to escape from themselves and unload their sicknesses upon the ancient German gods. Submitting to Wotan was cowardice; Brahms stood up to himself—a braver encounter.

By 1860 Brahms could no longer tolerate the pretentious claims made by the self-styled neo-German movement, led by Wagner; their pretentious assumption that their neo-German theories were shared by all musicians of consequence enraged Brahms. Together with the Hungarian-Jewish violinist Joachim he issued the manifesto that was to lead to the lifelong estrangement between Wagner and himself. Brahms declared the Wagner new theories "as contrary to the innermost spirit of music, strongly to be deplored and condemned". He clearly had no doubt in the rightness of his belief that the healing balm of music which fractured man sought could only be found after "innermost" internal painful struggles that should not be dodged: it was not to be found in staged pyrotechnics, however dazzling. A furious Wagner, his megalomania punctured, then made his infamous response in his venomous anti-Semitic *Das Judentum in der Musik*, a seminal work that was later to be so enthusiastically endorsed as part of the Nazi canon. With his sights on Joachim as well as Brahms, Wagner affirmed that the Jews in the musical world were debauching the purity of the Aryan renderings which he and the "revolutionary" neo-German movement were upholding.

Brahms never deigned to make a public reply. He had no need, for his response was to be found in his music where he now pruned even further the luxuriances to be found in his early work; even more sternly he rejected the picturesque, ruthlessly imposing an austerity on his works, freeing them from any hint of ostentatious vulgarity. In his "Handel Variations" we witness the dignity of his stance; increasingly he scorned the claims of the self-styled *avant garde* radicals of the neo-German faction and entrenched himself firmly behind the well-tried ramparts of classical design. And as he ages, we find neither defeatism nor tears. Instead there is superb resignation, a realistic recognition and acceptance of the limits earthbound man must endure: not for Brahms any indulging in escapist regressive Wagnerian fantasies where the omnipotence of thought over reality ensures the gods in Valhalla will, by their transgressions, relieve men of the necessity of scrutinizing their own trespasses. But Brahms in his music took full responsibility for himself, never in exculpatory mode projecting blameworthiness upon a persecutory fate. His courageous self-scrutiny gave him not only an especially acute awareness of his lonely condition, but also a resource from which he simultaneously could draw upon his creativity to ease his plight. If we too are aware of our own condition then, self-consciously, we are better equipped to ask and, without being left in nostalgic despair, answer the fundamental question that Nietzsche posed:[95]

> And so I ask myself: What is it that my whole body really expects of music? I believe, its own *ease*, as if all animal functions should be quickened by easy, bold, exuberant, self-assured rhythms; as if iron leaden life should be gilded by good golden and tender harmonies. My melancholy wants to rest in the hiding-places, and the abysses of *perfection*; that is why I need music.

And, thanks to the invention of Jubal, the intervention of Cecilia and to composers like Brahms, that need is met by music forever helping us on our tragic journey from birth to death.

***

Notes

1. *Isaiah*, ch. 27, V. 13.
2. Scholes, Percy A. *Oxford Companion to Music*, p. 538, OUP, 1991.
3. *Genesis*, ch. 4, V. 21.
4. *Genesis*, ch. 5, V. 22.
5. *Exodus*, ch. 13.
6. *Genesis*, ch. 4, V. 23–24.
7. *Shene Luhot ha-Berit*, 17b.
8. *Psalm* XXXIX.
9. Darwin, C. *Descent of Man*, 1871.
10. Robertson-Smith, W. *Lectures on the Religion of the Semites*, 1889.
11. McLellan, J.F. *Studies in Ancient History*, 2nd series, 1896.
12. Frazer, J.G. *The Golden Bough*, 1911.
13. Freud, S. *Totem and Taboo*, SE, Vol. xiii.
14. Freud, S. *Totem and Taboo*, SE, op cit.
15. Badcock, C. *Essential Freud*, Basil Blackwell, 1988.
16. *Encyclopaedia Britannica*, Vol. 22.
17. Alter, R. *The Five Books of Moses*, North, 2004.
18. Alter, R. *The Five Books of Moses*, op. cit.
19. *Genesis*, ch. 49, V. 1–29.
20. Eilberg-Schwartz, H. *God's Phallus*, Beacon Press, Boston, 2004.
21. Reik, T. *Ritual: Four Psychoanalytic Studies*, Grove Press, New York, 1962.
22. Reik, T. *Ritual: Four Psychoanalytic Studies*, op. cit.
23. Murray Schafer, R. *The Tuning of the World*, Knopf New York, 1977.
24. Hartshorne, C. *Born to Sing*, Bloomington Indiana University Press, 1973.
25. Révész, Géza, *Introduction to the Psychology of Music*, Longmans, London, 1953.
26. Gardner, H. *Art, Mind and Brain*, Basic Books, New York, 1982.
27. Powell, W. *The Philosophy of Music*, 6th edition, Routledge & Kegan Paul, London, 1924.
28. Darwin, C. *Descent of Man*, op. cit.
29. Jones, T.A. *The New Oxford Companion to Music*, Vol. I, Oxford University Press, 1983.
30. Chatwin, B. *The Songlines*, Jonathan Cape, 1987.
31. Storr, A. *Music and the Mind*, Harper Collins, 1992.
32. Sebold, W.G. *Moments Musicaux*, in *Campo Santo*, Penguin, 2006.
33. Spinger, S. *How the Mind Works*, New York, 1997.
34. Mithen, S. *The Singing Neanderthals*, Phoenix, 2006.
35. Huron, D. *Is Music an Evolutionary Adaptation?*, Annals of New York Academy of Science, Vol. 913, pp. 43–61, 2001.

36. Morley, I. *The Evolutionary Origins and Archaeology of Music: An Investigation into the Prehistory of Musical Capacities and Behaviours*, Ph.D. thesis, University of Cambridge, 2003.
37. Cranston, M. *Jean-Jacques*, Allen Lane, 1983.
38. Abse, L. book review in *Psychological Medicine*, Vol. 11, pp. 651–652, 1981; Grubrich-Simitis, I., *Early Freud and Late Freud*, Routledge, 1997.
39. Grubrich-Simitis, I. in *International Journal of Psychoanalysis*, Vol. 76, 1995.
40. Abse, D.W. *Language Disorder in Mental Disease*, John Wright, 1971.
41. Wegener, P. *The Life of Speech* (translation), John Wright, 1971.
42. Keller, H. *Music and Psychology*, ed. C. Wintle, Plombago Books, 2003.
43. Mithen, S. *The Singing Neanderthals*, op. cit.
44. Ehrenzweig, A. *The Psychoanalysis of Artistic Vision and Hearing*, Routledge & Kegan Paul, 1953.
45. Waelder, R. *Psychoanalytical Avenues to Art*, Hogarth, 1965.
46. Storr, A. *Music and the Mind*, op. cit.
47. St. Augustine, *Confessions*, trans. R.S. Pine-Coppins, Penguin, 1961.
48. *Psalms*, 150.
49. McKie, D. *Firebrand of Zurich*, in *The Guardian*, 13th April 2006.
50. Friend, D. *The Diaries of Donald Friend*. National Library of Australia, Canberra, 2003.
51. Dante, *Inferno Canto*, xxi, pp. 136–139.
52. Ehrenzweig, A. *The Psychoanalysis of Artistic Vision and Hearing*, op. cit.
53. Clark, K., *The Nude: A Study of Ideal Art*, New York, Pantheon, 1956.
54. Waelder, R. *Psychoanalytic Avenues to Art*, Hogarth, 1965.
55. Kramer, J. in *Foreword* to Rose, G.J., *Between Couch and Piano*, Brunner-Routledge, 2004.
56. Flam, G. *Singing for Survival: Songs of the Lodz Ghetto 1940–1945*, in *Urbana & Chicago*, University of Illinois, 1992.
57. Leikert, S. *Die Vergessene Kunst*, in *Psychosozciel-Verlag*, Giessen, 2005; Maiello, S. *The Sound Object; A Hypothesis about Pre-Natal Auditory Experience and Memory*, in *Journal of Psychotherapy*, 21, 1995.
58. Alvin & Lawson, *Journal of Psycho-History*, Vol. xxi, No. 3, Winter 1994.
59. Abse, L. *Rock*, in *The Man Behind the Smile: Tony Blair and the Politics of Perversion*, Robson, 1996.
60. Abse, D. *The Origin of Music*, in *New and Collected Poems*, Hutchinson, 2003.
61. See Kramer's list quoted p. 33.

62. Aristotle, *Metaphysics*.
63. Storr, A. *Music and the Mind, op. cit.*
64. See p. 14.
65. Alter, R. *The Five Books of Moses, op. cit.*
66. *First Book of Kings*, ch. 18.
67. Aldred, C. *Akhenaton, Pharaoh of Egypt*, Abacus, 1972.
68. Assmann, J. *Moses the Egyptian*, Harvard University Press, 1998.
69. Freud, S. *Moses and Monotheism*, SE, Vol. xxiii.
70. *Encyclopaedia Britannica*, 1960s, exact date not recorded.
71. Lang, P.H. *Music in Western Civilisation*, Dent, 1963.
72. Checa, F. *What Cannot Be Painted*, Museo Thyssen-Bornemisza.
73. Schoch, R. *Image and Images: Albrecht Dürer and Image Controversy*, Museo Thyssen-Bornemisza, 2007.
74. *The Guardian*, 23rd June 2006.
75. See p. 33.
76. Rollamn-Branch, H. & Moses, P.J. *The Hermaphroditic Ideal and the Voice*, in *Psychoanalytical Forum*, Vol. 4, 1972.
77. Moses, P.J. *The Voice of Neurosis*, Grune & Stratton, New York, 1954. Moses, P.J. *The Psychology of the Castrato Voice*, in *International Journal of Phoniatry*, 12(3), 1960.
78. Chasseguet-Smirgetl, J. *Creativity and Perversion*, Free Association Books, 1985.
79. Nietzsche, F. *The Case of Wagner*, Vintage Books, New York, 1967.
80. Mann, T. *The Sorrows and Grandeurs of Richard Wagner*, Faber & Faber, 1985.
81. Nietzsche, F. *The Birth of Tragedy*, Vintage Books, New York, 1967.
82. Nietzsche, F. *Beyond Good and Evil*, Penguin, 1973.
83. Nietzsche, F. *The Will to Power*, Weidenfeld & Nicolson, London, 1968.
84. See p. 48.
85. Alter, R. *The Five Books of Moses, op. cit.*
86. Wood, H. *Staking out the Territory*, Plumbago Books, 2007.
87. Latham, P. *Brahms*, J.M. Dent, 1948.
88. Latham, P. *Brahms, op cit.*
89. Peebles, C. Programme note, *Brahms German Requiem*, 2008.
90. *Ecclesiasticus*, 51: 27.
91. *I Corinthians*, ch. 15, V. 55.
92. Latham, P. *Brahms, op cit.*
93. Latham, P. *Brahms, op cit.*
94. Swafford, J. *Johannes Brahms*, Macmillan, 1997.
95. Nietzsche, F. *The Gay Science*, Vintage Books, New York, 1974.

JACOB

CHAPTER TWO

Jacob's wrestling match

In the Prado in Madrid there hangs the most terrifying painting in European art: it is the depiction by Goya of the Greek god Cronus devouring his new-born child. In the Greek cosmogony Cronus, initiator of the Creation, plays a primal rôle. Married to his sister Rhea, he fathered six children. Ever fearful that if they survived they would depose him, he swallowed them whole as they were born. By a ruse of Rhea, one son survived and Cronus was thus thwarted of his wish to leave no posterity; and when that son, the god Zeus, attained the strength of manhood, in revenge, he banished his father. By his might, after a struggle, he overcame Cronus who, vanquished, was driven from the sky and, enchained, was cast into the very depths of the universe.

This Greek myth is brazen. The struggle between father and son, endemic to the human condition, is overtly and unashamedly illustrated in this doom-laden tale. But there are other Greek myths which tell the story of every man's infanticidal and parricidal desires with more circumspection, where mitigation of murders and attempted murders by fathers and by sons is proffered to the protagonists, where the murderers are depicted as victims, haplessly spurred on to be killers by cruel and relentless fate. Such mitigation is to be found in the myth of King Laius who, warned by an oracle that his son would one day kill him, carried his newborn child to the wilderness, pierced the infant's feet with a nail and tied them together solidly hoping, in vain, thus to be rid of him. The child survived and, in turn, as an adult, now named Oedipus, was told by an oracle that he would kill his father and marry his mother, a scenario which he, not knowing his true parents, proceeded, with much aplomb but unwittingly, to enact. This was the tale which Freud deployed as corroboration of his clinical findings when he revealed to an unbelieving Western world the psycho-dynamics of the Oedipus complex.

These stories were unknown to me in my boyhood. In my underfunded, down-at-heel secondary school in impoverished south Wales, Greek was certainly no part of the curriculum; the teaching of the classics was a privilege reserved for the pupils of public schools. But I was not thereby deprived. I had the privilege of another resource. At my Talmudic grandfather's knee, and in the evenings in a *cheder* in a grubby ante-room of the local synagogue, I was taught to read Hebrew fluently and to translate, albeit clumsily, the inspired texts of the Pentateuch. There I discovered for the first time how the dramatic lives of the patriarchs were punctuated by awesome parricides and infanticides.

The Hebrew legends, like the Greek myths, tell of the terrible violences that once upon a time fathers and sons inflicted upon each other. Often, however, the Biblical stories are more subtle, disguising the rôle and the guilt of the biological father by shifting the responsibility for the decision to slay a newborn babe on to another father, a supreme father, a king or a god. Abraham himself, ancestral father of the Jews, as a babe barely survived the murderous hand of Nimrod, "the first man on earth to be a mighty man".[1] The mediaeval version of that Biblical tale in the *Sefr ha-Yashar*, the Book of the Righteous, recounts how Abraham's biological father, Terah, commander of King Nimrod's army, while celebrating the birth of his son, heard that Nimrod had been advised that the infant would grow up and overthrow the king. Fearful, Nimrod ordered the child to be handed over and killed but Terah deceived the king and handed over another hapless babe, and thus little Abraham survived.

This haunting infanticidal theme insistently continues in *Genesis*[2] with God ordering Abraham to kill Isaac, his only son:

> Take now thy son, thine only son Isaac, whom thou lovest, and get thee into the land of Moriah; and offer him there for a burnt offering upon one of the mountains which I will tell thee of.

But, at the last moment, even as the obedient Abraham was lifting his knife to slay the bound Isaac, God commanded him to desist. And, similarly, we learn that only a last-minute intervention by God saved the infant Ishmael, Abraham's son by the bondswoman Hagar, from dying of thirst in the wilderness to which, with Abraham's condonation, he and his mother had been ruthlessly expelled.

Such awesome legends spell out explicitly the uncomfortable truth we prefer to hide, that the birth of an infant son brings about an ambivalent dyadic relationship: love, pride, and devotion may be the father's manifest emotions but darker shadows can be felt by the father seeing his infant son's exuberant lust for life. Negative feelings, unacknowledged, unconscious, can drift into the relationship. Hostile emotions of envy, resentment and death wishes are not necessarily reduced to insignificance by the joy and elation evoked by paternity; often they are not so benignly neutralized. When the fifth century redactors composed the allegories of the patriarchs they boldly exposed the existence and strength of such hostile emotions. And, belatedly, they dared to confront us with the death wishes pervading every father and son relationship. But the scribes were no mere diagnosticians: they were the Temple priests, conscious of the didactic and pastoral duties requiring them to be reconcilers, healers able to apply balms to the wounds fathers and sons inflicted upon each other. And so, even as the redactors recited the attempted assassinations of their progeny by the early patriarchs, they told too, in a therapeutic legend, how the last of the patriarchs, Jacob, discovered how patriarchal and filial love could yet triumph over and transcend the deadly rivalry and hatreds between fathers and sons.

Intimations of that encoded message within the Jacob allegory came to me strangely, elliptically, and early, even as I was still within the period of my childhood which Freud has assigned as the time when Oedipal manifestations emerge, when they are governed by unconscious ideas and feelings centring on the wish to possess the parent of the opposite sex and eliminate that of the same sex. When I was four I complained to my mother that I had a pain in my thigh, and she, finding there a little lump, took me along to the doctor. Our usual GP was on holiday. The young locum and my mother soon found they came from the same Welsh-speaking south Wales valley and, as I was being examined, the two chatted, half in English, half in their vernacular Welsh. Then, in an aside to my mother, he, memorably for me, pronounced: "You know, Jews have weak thighs".

He had not learned that in his medical college; he had doubtless picked that tale up in his chapel Sunday school. As I was growing up I was to encounter many such myths about Jews abounding in the Bible-reading Nonconformist Wales. In the playground I was involved in many a fight when, to the deicide charge that I had killed Christ, would be added the taunt that as a Jew I could not spit. My response thereupon proving the contrary, spitting into the face of my tormentor, unsurprisingly always precipitated an exchange of blows. Even as a child I knew that the source of that particular tale lay in the story that Jews are classed with an inability to expectorate because, at Calvary, they had spat upon Christ. But the source of the thigh tale, which I was sometimes to encounter, remained perplexing, although in my *cheder* days, alerted by the well-intentioned remark of the Welsh doctor, I responded with an unsatisfied curiosity when I came across thigh stories in my Torah readings. I felt my *cheder* preacher was holding something back, perhaps from himself and certainly from his pupils, when he came to passages like those telling how Abraham had required his servant to solemnize an oath by placing his hand beneath Abraham's thigh,[3] or when Joseph was required to swear to keep a promise by putting his hand under Jacob's thigh.[4] It was not until I appreciated the centrality and solemnity of the thigh story within the Bible anecdote of the wrestling match between Jacob and the Man that I understood how loaded and significant were these tales of thigh-touching. A rereading of the wrestling story is a rewarding exercise.

***

The allegory of "Jacob and the Man" told in *Genesis* 32 is a marvellous story of how a son's determination, after decades of acceptance of his exploitation, tardily but effectively released his aggression, overcame his oppressive father figures, and became his own man; it is a rich illustration of one man's successful negotiation of that fateful rite of passage.

No tale of a man struggling with his aggression towards his father has a longer lineage than that recounted in the Biblical tale. Sometimes overtly, sometimes disguised, sometimes depicted by Renaissance painters or contemporary sculptors, always in every kosher restaurant, the story, slyly or brazenly, is told of the greatest unarmed struggle ever known, of a wrestling contest between two well-matched protagonists that lasted a whole night, leaving the victor wounded but in sufficient rude health to establish the state of Israel.

So awesome and explosive is the story that, unlike the initial chronicler, subsequent editors and interpreters of the Bible created a new title for the tale—"Jacob and the Angel"—in order to temper the combustibility of the original. But there is no angel, and never was; neither in the original Hebrew nor in the King James edition of the Bible does any angel appear. Jacob wrestled with the Man, and so terrifying was that Man that to avoid contemplating the vengefulness of this terminator, he has been metamorphosed by subsequent chroniclers into an angel. Thus garbed, it is hoped that the hint that he may be an avenging angel is well concealed within the drapery that always covers up well brought-up angels. The story is thus transmitted in Sunday schools, *cheders*—and doubtless in the *madrasas*—and, stripped of its homoerotic undertones, continues to reduce this stupendous wrestling match to a boisterous romp which ended in one of the participants suffering a little hurt.

Although attempts have thus been made to sanitize this tale of fierce aggressivity, the sinister Bible story remains. Thousands of years after the first telling of this tribal tale, the story resonates with everyman's continuing predicament, the Oedipal dilemma of the son who, to achieve his own individuation, must needs overcome his father and yet continue to love him and to be loved by him. For the Man with whom Jacob wrestles, and whom the chronicler is too careful to name, is the father, behind whom looms God, the father of us all. This is the story of the ambivalent incestuous love that exists between every father and every son.

Initially, the chronicler hesitated explicitly to recite this story so seductively redolent with fearful intimations of the ultimate taboo.

Jacob's Oedipal struggle is first cunningly displaced from one with his father to one with his oppressive father-in-law, Laban. To gain his beloved Rachel, Jacob was required to work for Laban for seven years. Then Laban cheated him and by a stratagem ensured that Leah, his elder daughter, was taken to Jacob's marriage-bed. To gain Rachel, therefore, Jacob had to work a further seven years. In all, Jacob's working life—and sexual life—were controlled by his father-in-law for 20 years; then he could suppress his resentments and aggressions no longer and, because he still could not dare a confrontation with Laban, he fled secretly with his wives and sheep to establish his own domain.

But the chronicler knows that thus recounted, the story is only half told and he finally summons up the courage to complete the tale. After sending his entourage ahead, leaving himself all alone, Jacob prepared for his real confrontation, a night-time demand to his progenitor that he should be granted his manumission and no longer submit to patriarchal commands. With the demand not heeded, the awesome power struggle ensued.

Jacob was not to have an easy victory. The castrating Man endeavoured to tear the balls off him but, missing the target, wrenched the hollow of Jacob's thigh, leaving Jacob limping. Every Jewish boy brought up in an observant home knows this detail, for *Genesis* commands that to ensure we remember the dangerous grappling, the veins of a cow's thigh must never be eaten. Since the costly procedure of removing the sciatic nerve and other tendons and arteries is the prerequisite of observance of that Biblical injunction, Orthodox Jews do not eat the hind-quarters of a cow. As a boy, filet mignon was denied to me in my mother's house and, as every gourmet knows, no good steak and chips is ever available at a kosher restaurant.

These are whimsical consequences of the myth; there are more sombre sequelae. When the dawn broke and the exhausted Man conceded defeat, the occasion was acknowledged by the Man accepting Jacob's contemptuous repudiation of the name given to him by his father: henceforth he was to be Israel, blessed with inheritance of lands promised by God to his grandfather Abraham. Nowadays, in the Middle Eastern Jewish state bearing Israel's name, rabid right-wing Jewish settlers, backed by American Pentecostals, draw on the myth to "prove" their title to land on the West Bank in occupied Palestine.

Withal, the myth has, however, grander and nobler themes. The Jewish Biblical myths are never entirely fanciful and are invariably didactic: the telling of this wrestlingmatch is a moral exhortation. It addresses the problem with which, as part of our maturation from dependency to adulthood, all must wrestle: how to dare to give up enjoying the shelter and security that masochistic submission affords, to break the chains of our bondage and, abandoning passivity, turn around our masochism into well-directed aggression, in the therapeutic rite of passage that destiny demands of mankind.

Peniel, the name in Hebrew of the place where the significant struggle occurred, tells us that Jacob stood up to face the Man direct and give his forceful but measured response in such a fashion that when he became Israel, his own man, he still retained the affection of the Man who then bountifully blessed him. The happy resolution of a man coming to terms with his own father-aggression was never better told.

***

Calvary, not many miles from Peniel, was the location of another historic attempt to resolve the love-hate dilemmas besetting father and son relationships. There, unlike on the occasion when God intervened to save Isaac, the son of Abraham, from his father's knife, there was no last minute reprieve for the son of God, no substitute sacrificial lamb was proffered. In vain did Jesus on the cross plead: "My God, my God, why hast Thou forsaken me?"

I did not read an account of this earth-shaking event until I was 25 years old. It was on the most disagreeable journey of my life, in a packed troopship, part of a convoy suffering grievous losses taking us around the Cape to reach the Middle East, that I first read the New Testament. On my embarkation leave I had managed to squeeze two books into my kitbag; one was the Bible and, with all mobility severely restricted on that hideously overcrowded boat, on the six-week journey, with a pristine eye I was for many hours almost mesmerized by the visions of the evangelists. I discovered that two of them, the Jew Matthew and the Gentile Luke, were, with deliberation, seeking by their nativity stories to subvert my Jewish credo.

My grandfather, to insulate me as a lad from what he regarded as the corrosive influences of the Christian ethos, had firmly taught me that Christ was a bastard, that, as told in the Talmud, Miriam, the mother of Jesus, was an adulterous hairdresser, the wife of a man called Stada, with a lover named Pandera. The only doubt my grandfather seemed to have about what some would hold to be a calumny was that the story may have become confused with a second-century pagan tale that Mary was divorced by her carpenter husband for having an affair with a Roman soldier called Panthera. But in any event, of Jesus' illegitimacy, there could, I was taught, be no doubt. It was the view, of course, held by a more doubtful authority, by Hitler who, in his after-dinner monologues as reported by Martin Bormann, repeatedly asserted that the father of Jesus was a Roman legionary. But it was my grandfather's confident assertion that became my prejudice, and only my readings during my involuntary confinement on the wartime troopship brought me nearer to understanding that disbelief in the miraculous nativity provided no justification for leaving the wondrous Gospels unread, to dismiss them all as fairy tales. Yet, withal, given the increasing dependency throughout the ages of Christian belief upon acceptance of their reality, the significance of the stories of the annunciation and incarnation cannot be minimized or treated as an irrelevancy, underpinning as they do the whole faith of today's Christian believers.

It was not ever thus. In the earliest of the Gospels, that of Mark, Jesus appears on the scene fully grown; the annunciation and virgin birth play no part in the original recounting of the Christ story. Nor can any hint or mention of the miracle of the nativity be found even in the miracle-strewn Gospel of John. It is in Matthew's Gospel, a work probably compiled by a Greek-speaking Judaeo-Christian towards the end of the first century of the Christian era, that we are first told of the virginal birth of Jesus. The imaginative compiler was a cunning propagandist, a missionary who set out to convert both his non-Jewish Greek readers and his fellow-Jews in the Diaspora by reassuring them that what he was telling them was not innovatory, that it had been foretold in the Septuagint, the Greek translation of the Hebrew Bible, where would be found, in Isaiah, a prophetic text proclaiming the coming of a miraculously-conceived Messiah, of Jesus Son of God.

The compiler's citation of Isaiah was profoundly misleading; in no way does the Hebrew text suggest that the Messiah would be conceived by a virgin. On the contrary, the context suggests that the favoured young woman who would give birth to the liberator,

Emmanuel, was to be already married. A mistranslation, accidental or deliberate, of the Hebrew word *almah*, which means a young woman, not necessarily a virgin, into the Greek word *parthenos*, a virgin, gave the Matthew collator his opportunity. On the basis of that mistranslation, he posited the claim that the conception of Jesus towered above all the other miraculous conceptions of the Old Testament.

It was a valid claim; there is a fundamental distinction between all the miraculous pregnancies reported in Old Testament narratives and that of Mary. Childless old Sarah, with Abraham a centenarian husband, barren Rebekah, distraught and frustrated Rachel, all, following the intervention of God who opened up their wombs, became pregnant by their husbands. But in the account of the nativity in the Gospels of Matthew and Luke, Joseph, young Mary's husband, is excluded: there is no participation; no coitus between the man and woman preceded the conception of Jesus. Matthew, in a few fateful passages,[5] expunged any hint of human agency. The Holy Ghost visited the espoused Mary "before they came together". Christ had no biological father. Joseph is marginalized. Jesus is the Son of God begat by a virgin.

The other evangelists did not pursue such a claim; as missionaries they would have known well that potential Jewish converts would be estranged, not persuaded, by attributing such carnal activities to a God whom they regarded as incorporeal. In vain did Matthew rail against stubborn Jews who then, as now, resisted his blandishments. He had, however, successes in the Greek-speaking world of the Diaspora, for there many unsophisticated Jews were partly assimilated and enveloped in the prevailing Hellenic culture, one moulded significantly by myths where gods regularly came to earth and besported themselves with women and men. Such Jews would not necessarily resist a legend that told of a god who entered a beautiful virgin. But the Christian Jews of Jerusalem, headed by James, "brother of the Lord",[6] had other memories warning them of the dire consequences of such liaisons. In the Jewish literature of the inter-Testamental age, the Genesis story of the Flood had been elaborated: the fable of heavenly beings and terrestrial women had emerged to explain why God had almost destroyed mankind. The Jews in Palestine were steeped in the amazing tale of the "sons of God" who fell for the charms of the "daughters of men" and, captivated by their beauty, they abandoned their comfortable heavenly abode and came down to earth bodily to enjoy female company. The adventure quickly went awry. Their offspring turned out to be giants whose depravity precipitated God's anger and brought on Noah's Flood.[7] With such apocalyptic forebodings, part of the memory bank of the Jews of Palestine, it is unsurprising that Matthew's importunings, as his vitriolic recriminatory attacks upon them reveal, had little success; and even when conversions to Christianity took place, as with the Christian Ebionite sects, the acceptance of the miraculous conception was specifically no part of their belief in the messianic Christ.

More, among the Jews in the Hellenic Diaspora there were sophisticates versed in Platonic philosophy who joined, or perhaps initiated, the Christian Gnostic sects distinguished in the epithet of Docetes: they most certainly would have no truck with Matthew's tale of the annunciation. These were the Christians whose heretical challenges to the nativity story still, in the 18th century, enraged Gibbon—as the great historian acerbically told of their ingenious formulations:[8]

> Educated in the School of Plato, accustomed to the sublime idea of the Logos, they regularly conceived that the brightest aeon, or Emanation of the Deity, might assume the outward shape and visible appearances of a mortal, but they vainly pretended, that the imperfections of matter are incompatible with the purity of a celestial substance. While the blood of Christ yet smoked on Mount Calvary, the Docetes invented the impious and extravagant hypothesis, that, instead of issuing from the womb of the Virgin, He had descended on the banks of the Jordan in the form of perfect manhood; that He had imposed on the senses of His enemies, and of His disciples, and that the ministers of Pilate had wasted their impotent rage on an airy phantom, who seemed to expire on the Cross, and, after three days, to rise from the dead.

But the missionaries preaching the miraculous virginal birth had not only to contend with dissident Christians like the Ebionites and Docetes; they also had to contend with texts within the Gospels themselves. Somehow the contradiction between a Messiah who, it had been prophesied, was to be a direct descendant of King David, and one who, without such lineage, was the Son of God, had to be smudged; and there were other serious obstacles. The most challenging to those committed to an *a priori* doctrine of divine Sonship or the supernatural birth of Jesus was the presence of James, of the actual brother of Jesus in the flesh. In the Gospel of Matthew itself, the dogma of perpetual virginity, as ultimately pronounced by Catholic and Eastern Orthodox Christianity, is subverted. While Matthew[9] tells us that Joseph accepted the miraculous nature of Mary's pregnancy, he further tells us that Joseph refrained from "knowing" her "until she had borne a son". To unprejudiced readers this signifies that, while in Matthew's account during the period of gestation Joseph had kept away from Mary, after the birth of Jesus they resumed normal life together, as man and wife. To overcome suspicions aroused by Matthew's comments, there are many and various dubious ripostes. One was that Joseph, when betrothed to Mary, was a widower and that James had been born to this earlier marriage. The Roman Catholic Church ultimately went even further to protect the dogma of perpetual virginity and asserted that James had both a different father and a different mother, that he was only a "cousin" of Jesus.

The leaders of the Hellenic Christian Jews of the Diaspora knew that the goal of their hidden agenda, that of making the doctrine of the perpetual virginity part of the dogma of the Christian Church, could not therefore be attained unless they were rid of the severe embarrassment of the existence of Jesus' blood brother; so, although James, in 40–60 CE, was in Jerusalem and head of the Christian Jews of Palestine, nevertheless they airbrushed him out of scripture. James was consigned to the scrapheap of history.

It was, the great Biblical scholar Robert Eisenmann commented, one of the most successful over-written enterprises ever accomplished.[10] When, in Acts ch. 12 v. 17, James suddenly emerges as a principal personality and leader of the Jerusalem Church, there is no introduction as to who he was or how he arrived; and in Acts there is subsequent silence about his fate. All we know of the historical James comes from extra-Biblical sources like those within the works of the first-century Josephus. The erasure and marginalization of James was a ruthless exercise; he was eliminated because he was guilty by association. His father was Joseph and since it could therefore be blasphemously asserted that he shared the same father as Jesus, he must be expunged from the record. But the assault was essentially a cowardly deflection, a circumlocution, a timid avoidance of the challenge to the real culprit, to the man who shared his bed with Mary. Fearful of releasing their anger against the perpetrator, it was displaced upon James. The relegation of James was a spiteful act by those who, like all men, cannot forget or forgive their own conception; at that fateful moment in the revel they had been excluded and betrayed. To acquit the mother, the impregnator must be made responsible and the rage of the son against his father is such that it endures in his unconscious unto death.

The nativity story is therefore to be seen, certainly from a Freudian perspective, as an imaginative allegorical resolution of the love-hate dilemmas, endemic to the human condition, that are posited by the son's rage against the usurping father. Matthew's Gospel affords an opportunity to dream our dream that our mother is unsullied, never possessed by our father, and we, the sons, are left free to fantasize, within a palingenetical[11] myth of spiritual rebirth away from the world of the flesh, that we were never fathered, The death-wish against the father is effortlessly fulfilled, without any such struggle like Jacob's engagement with the Man. We wipe him out. Joseph is an aged cuckold trumped by the Holy Ghost.

The phenomena of the ablation of parents, of the desire to suppress a biological past, of insistence upon being self-made with no fertilization by a father or any link to a mother's womb, has been well explored in clinical studies by psychoanalysts of character disorders.[12]

***

The analysts have learned, from the dreams of such patients, that, in ablative mode, they ended their allegiance to a biological parent. With the natural parent excluded, the patient acquires an illusion of choice about precisely those aspects of himself that are givens and unalterable, his parentage, his identity, his physical and mental constitutional endowment; he is no longer beholden to his father, his father's genes have not determined him, the father is slain, psychologically dead to him. This dream process of re-creation can sometimes be creatively acted out in real life: it can then sometimes be imaginatively liberating, but more often its essential falsity and dishonesty cannot be gainsaid. It can only be squared with the dreary truth by the suppression of facts, by the distortion of others, and by the subordination of memory to mythopoeisis. At its worst, I have seen the process at work in the impersonations assumed by the confidence tricksters whom I have professionally defended in the courts; claiming an aristocratic lineage, under false names, they would dupe the hoteliers and other victims into extending to them credit and advances which their assumed identities commanded.

But such aberrant pathological human behaviour is, as ever, but a caricature or exaggeration of the normative; what on the couch the psychoanalysts had found in the dreams of their disturbed patients, and what I discovered in the awareness of the fantasies of my criminal clients, lies dormant but present in every man. Every man, after puberty, must break through parental authority to become sexually mature, but to achieve such adulthood a revolt against the father is required. Each generation, in order to advance, has to escape from the domination of the last. In the Jacob allegory we see the patriarch ultimately facing up to his progenitor, confronting him, wrestling with him, body to body. In the Christ story there is no such confrontation: such a struggle is avoided by denying, as do pathological ablators, the very existence of a father. But the crime of parricide—for such is the killing by ablation of the father—cannot be concealed by such legerdemain; the murderers cannot escape from their own guilt by repressing the memory of their terrible crime. However, the Christ legend, elaborated with considerable artifice, has mercifully provided an indemnity to the perpetrators of the crime. The father is disposed of or depicted as a Joseph, an old impotent man, and yet there is to be no retribution. Christ will be their Saviour and take upon Himself their sin; for their sake He will be crucified. Belief in Him will give them redemption and they, as parricides, will receive no punishment. More, as a bonus, they will enjoy the exclusive love of an unsullied mother, a Virgin Mary forever tending them.

With such a persuasive prospectus, the wondrously eloquent early Christian Jewish missionaries brought their good tidings to the non-believers and made more and more converts. The conservative Christian Church in Jerusalem, the lack of corroboration in the Gospels of Mark and John, the contradictions in Matthew's Gospel, the upholders of absolute belief in an invisible non-corporeal God, all were obstacles swept aside by these passionate zealots. What they were offering was, and is, irresistible to many: relief from the anguish and ambivalence of a love-hatred relationship with the parent. A believer in Christ would no longer tremble under the accusing eye of a stern Jehovah, a God of Justice: his sin had been washed away in the blood of Jesus. Believe and all is forgiven. God is Love. The very presence, however, of James, the actual brother of Jesus, remained a challenge to the mysteries of an *a priori* doctrine of divine sonship or supernatural birth; his presence needed obfuscation. More, the missionaries had to counter the contradiction[13] which had carelessly remained uncorrected in the Gospel of Matthew itself, which undermines the dogma of perpetual virginity. These early missionaries were in fact offering more than could be claimed or delivered: the primal crime and accompanying guilt could not be so neatly expunged; the crucified Christ could not carry the full weight of the sins of the newly-converted Christians. Still many of them felt burdened: their unease stemmed from doubt whether Jesus was conceived miraculously, whether He was truly divine. The fierce debates over the doctrine of consubstantiality of the nature of the relationship between God the Father and the Son, which for centuries raged throughout early Christendom, reflected the doubt. From today's psychoanalytical perspective, these extraordinarily divisive debates, centring on the status of the Father, on the issue of whether the Son was subordinate, all tell of the unresolved Oedipal dilemmas afflicting the opinionated protagonists. Perhaps nowhere more than in the tumultuous debates which led, early in the fourth century, to the Council of Nicaea's condemnation of the teachings of the Alexandrian priest Arius, do we see those dilemmas overtly exposed.

Arius taught that Christ is not truly divine but a creature *ex nihilo*, who at one time did not exist. The fundamental premise of Arius was the uniqueness of God, who alone is self-existent and immutable. Because the Godhead is unique, it cannot be shared or communicated, so that the Son cannot be God. Because the Godhead is self-existent, the Son, who is not self-existent, cannot be God. Because the Godhead is immutable, the Son, who is mutable, being represented in the Gospels as subject to growth and change, cannot be God. The Son must therefore be deemed a creature who has been called into existence out of nothing, who had a beginning—"there was when he was not". Consequently the Son can have no direct knowledge of the Father, being finite and of a different order of existence.

At Nicaea the Council condemned such teaching as heresy and affirmed that the Son is *homoousion to patri* (of one substance with the Father) thus declaring Him to be all that the Father is; He is completely divine. Even as a surly adolescent rebels against the domination of a father and defiantly declares he is as good as his Dad, so did the bishops at Nicaea reaffirm that Christ was not subordinate to God the Father. Any Christian who suggested otherwise was to be anathematized. The bishops' view that if the incarnation, and all its implications, were disputed, the whole elaborate Christian edifice—constructed as it was to ensure mankind, saved by Christ's sacrifice, would be relieved of the guilt of parricide—could crumble. The anathemas were manifestly framed to completely exclude the Arian teaching that the Word is no true Son of the Father, but is a creature totally different from, and inferior to, Him in nature. The bishops were adamant that Christ the Son was not to be deemed inferior:

> But as for those who say, There was when he was not, and, Before being born he was not, and that he came into existence out of nothing, or who assert that the Son of God is of a different hypostasis or substance, or is created, or is subject to alteration or change—these the Catholic Church anathematises.

But the anathemas, although oft-times repeated over the centuries, have never succeeded in completely extinguishing the heresy; in one form or another it has continued to troublesomely simmer beneath the Church's orthodoxies. The emergence in the late fifth century of the Athanasian Creed, an exposition of the orthodox teaching on the Trinity and the Incarnation now regarded as authoritative by the Roman Catholic, Anglican and leading Protestant communions, betrays an extraordinary anxiety that any hint of Arianism should ever become part of Christian doctrine: the Creed begins and ends with stern warnings that unswerving adherence to the exposition within the Creed is indispensable to salvation. By denying there is any incompatibility between God the Father and God the Son, the Creed endeavours to impose a truce among those fiercely contesting the priority to be accorded to either. It is affirmed that the Trinity in no way divides the divine substance and that the substantial unity does not lessen the reality of the personal distinctions. Jesus Christ, while indissolubly one in person, is simultaneously fully divine and fully human, His humanity comprising a rational soul as well as a body. The unity of these two disparate elements, divinity and humanity, in a single person is as complete as the unity of body and soul in the human individual. Within its 40 verses the Creed, by emphasizing and re-emphasizing the doctrine of one God in Trinity and Trinity in Unity, the full divinity of Jesus is thereupon upheld without negating His humanity and without challenging God the Father.

Some may regard the Creed's sophisticated exposition as cunning sophistry but most practising Christians do not resent its coercive commands, and willingly recite its dogmas which they treat as peaceful resolutions of intemperate theological disputations which so plagued the Church in past ages.

It is, however, a precarious peace, one easily disturbed by any authoritarian churchman who, restless with an interpretation of the Trinity according no priority to the Father, breaks ranks when he finds he lacks the scriptural authority to tell sons that they should behave themselves and know their rank. In England in the early 18th century we had a droll illustration of such a manifestation when the Rector of St James, Westminster, no longer able to contain his indignation, in books and preaching, notoriously maintained that Jesus was divine only by the communicating of divinity to Him, being the Son of God rather than God the Son. The resultant vigorous riposte published by fellow-churchmen ensured that for a while the London Church was engulfed in controversy. In England resistances to the demotion of God the Father have, however, sometimes brought about more than individual dissidences of prominent churchmen: they have precipitated the founding and spreading of alternative Christian movements. The Unitarians are virtually Arians in that they are unwilling either to reduce Christ to a mere human being or to attribute to Him a divine nature identical with that of the Father. And anyone who has endured the representations of a proselytizing Jehovah's Witness is being subjected to the Arianism of C.T. Russell, the founder of the Christology Movement.

To treat all the doctrinaire controversies, past and present, as mere epiphenomena reflecting the Oedipal struggle of the protagonists may be regarded—given the oft-times subtle and sophisticated arguments advanced in the debates—as a secular impertinence, and excessively reductive. But what cannot be gainsaid, and what is highly suspect, is the extraordinary passion with which the theologians waged their arguments.

Gibbon, as a believer, shows, like some of today's Christians, some embarrassment over the intemperance with which the theologians conducted their campaigns, and, defensively, he unconvincingly tries to justify their "zeal". While he tells us "a chosen society of philosophers, men of a liberal education and curious disposition, might silently meditate, and temperately discuss, in the gardens of Athens or the library of Alexandria, the abstruse questions of metaphysical science", their "lofty speculations" are to be differentiated from those of the Christian theologians. Their Platonic speculations are "the amusement of a vacant hour". Contrariwise, the Christian theologians' speculations became:[14]

> ... the most serious business of the present, and the most useful preparations for a future life. A theology, which it was incumbent to believe, which it was impious to doubt, and which it might be dangerous and even fatal, to mistake. ... The cold indifference of philosophy was inflamed by the fervent spirit of devotion.

And then Gibbon praises the Christians "who abhorred the gross and impure generation of the Greek mythology" and resisted the temptation to:

> argue from the familiar analogy of the female and paternal relations. The character of Son seemed to imply a perpetual subordination to the voluntary author of His existence; but as the act of generation, in the most spiritual and abstracted sense, must be supposed to transmit the properties of a common nature, they durst not resume to circumscribe the powers of the duration of the Son of an eternal and omnipotent Father.

Gibbon is here at work vigorously affirming the basic tenets of the authorized Athanasian Creed. But even Gibbon, the great stylist, cannot conceal the bombast that lies behind his affirmation as that of the absolutist theologians he is defending and praising. Too often, as here, absolute certainty is over-compensated doubt. Any scintilla of doubt, any query of the reality of the singular miraculous conception of Jesus, could mean that Christ had died in vain, that He had lacked the strength to carry upon Himself the sins of parricide affecting mankind, that the attempt to oblate the father had been botched, and that Joseph lived on as the biological father of Jesus. With so much at stake, unsurprisingly, any hint of heresy derogating from Matthew's account of the Annunciation was savagely attacked.

But, even more provocative and infuriating than the heresies spelling out niceties differing from orthodox interpretations of the

Matthew story, was the refusal of stubborn Jewry to countenance any validity whatsoever to Matthew's account of the birth of Jesus. It is clear from the disapproval often expressed by the Church fathers that, for a while, it was not uncommon for the two communities, Jews and the Christian Jews, to participate in each other's activities, even in their houses of worship,[15] and it may have been possible that, if Jesus had remained a son of man, had remained simply a prophet, the great divide between Jewry and Christianity would not have taken place. But in the event, Matthew's presentation of the Annunciation increasingly enveloped Christian doctrine: with the Jews, then as now, regarding any attribution of corporeality or carnality to God as blasphemous, intellectually and morally demeaning, the conflagration ignited by Matthew was set to rage for millennia.

The inspiring Russian Jewish philosopher of the early 20th century, Ahad Ha-Am, has explicated anew that the nature of the religious divide between Jew and Christian is not occasioned by a trivial shibboleth; the gulf is wide and unbridgeable:[16]

> What essentially distinguishes Judaism from other religions is its absolute determination to make the religious and moral consciousness independent of any definite human form, and to attach it without any mediating term to an abstract incorporeal ideal ... . Christianity links up the religious and moral consciousness with the figure of a particular man, who is regarded as the ideal of absolute perfection, and belief in whom is an essential part of a religion inconceivable without it. Judaism, and Judaism alone, depends on no such human figure. For Judaism God is the only ideal of absolute perfection, and He only must be kept always before the eye of man's inner consciousness, in order that man may "cleave to His attributes". No man, not even the most perfect is free from shortcomings and sins; no man can serve as an ideal for the religious sentiment, which strives after union with the source of perfection. Moses died in his sin, like any other man ... his image is not an essential part of the very fabric of the religion.

Against such core belief, not even the most eloquent man that Jewry has ever produced, Paul of Tarsus, could make headway. According to *Acts*, Paul, when he preached in the coastal cities of the Mediterranean—Antioch, Ephesus, and Corinth—tried first to bring the message to the

Jews in each place. He failed; it was only then, full of anger against his disbelieving fellow-Jews, that he turned more successfully to the local Gentiles in each place.[17] His frustration and consequent rage, as dramatically illustrated in his diatribes against the "foolish" Galatians,[18] were to reverberate through the ages in the works of his followers. By the middle of the second century the ground was well prepared for thousands of years of Christian anti-Semitism. In his treatise, *The Dialogue with Trypho the Jew*, Saint Justin characterizes the Jews as "intransigently hard-hearted, carnal, stubborn, sinful and idolatrous".

The Jews were indeed to pay a heavy price for their refusal to collude with their deviant fellow countrymen in their ingenious attempt to exculpate mankind from guilt. The long dependence of man upon his first carers—longer than any other species—means that in the prolonged helplessness of his infancy, he fantasizes a world where he, not a carer, is totally in command, every wish fulfilled, every desire consummated; in adulthood, loath to shed these transgressive lusts and impossible desires, he strives to evade acknowledgement of the guilt his secret lingering desires bring. The essential difference between the Jesus myth and the allegory of Jacob and the Man is that in the one all guilt is projected upon a Christ who died to save men from the punishments they, as closet parricides, deserve—whereas, in the other, Jacob dares to take upon himself personal responsibility for the parricidal wishes he harbours, acts them out, confronts the father, engages in a fierce struggle and, although wounded in his thigh, succeeds in establishing a truce. Each year, however, on the appointed Day of Atonement, on Yom Kippur, to ensure the truce remains in place, he must publicly confess to his crime and so obtain his annual respite.

The truce is not an armed truce bristling with forebodings of renewed struggles; on the contrary, in the hiatus between one Yom Kippur and the next the protagonists are tenderly concerned with one another. The Book of the Jubilee, written by a Pharisee between 135–105 BCE, records the long tradition of associating the Day of Atonement with the anguish of Jacob when he was informed by his mendacious sons that his favourite son, Joseph, was dead. In an exquisite display of empathy with the afflicted father, and as penance for the sins of all wicked sons:[19]

> It is ordained for the children of Israel that they should afflict themselves on the tenth of the seventh month—on the day that

the news which made him weep for Joseph came to his father—that they should make atonement for themselves ... for they had grieved the affection of their father regarding Joseph his son. And this day has been ordained that they should grieve thereon for their sins and for all their transgressions, and for all their errors, so that they might cleanse themselves on that day once a year.

When, on that day, we find the children of Israel comforting the father, mourning together with him, not receiving from him punishment but taking upon themselves chastisement, we know that Yom Kippur is more than just another fast day in a religious calendar. It is a sombre celebration of the tempered resolution of every man's Oedipal struggle that had been symbolically represented in the unforgettable wrestling-match at Peniel: there, the Man knew when to yield to the courageous Jacob, and there also, when the thigh-wounded Jacob limped away, he was full of both respect and affection for the Man who, although potentially powerful enough to have inflicted a worse fate, mercifully desisted and spared him. Alone, Jacob had taken on his daring rebellion; his family and servants he had sent away before the struggle commenced: he personally wrested his manumission from the Man.

Not everyone has the capacity to embark on such a risk-taking confrontation. To the despairing and pusillanimous the Christian Jewish proselytizers offered, however, an escape route bypassing the fearful Peniel. On this route travellers would not, like Jacob, face a terrifying struggle; on this wondrous highway, if they believed, they would not be required to carry the weight of the austere, uncompromising Judaic doctrine: they would be relieved of their burden of guilt by a Saviour. The eloquent missionaries who preached this creed had mastered the art of scapegoat politics: Christ would be crucified, taking upon Himself the sins of all believers and they, redeemed—if they kept the faith and were thus exonerated—would gain entry to heaven. It has been recorded that I fought as a candidate more local and national elections, 17 in all, than any man in Britain in the 20th century; that experience well taught me how electorates resent painful confrontations with reality and how readily they are seduced by illusions and scapegoating. I doubt if it could be claimed that in world history there was ever a more politically successful group than the handful of poor, parlous, dissident Jews in first century Palestine; their millenarian manifesto, laced with its scapegoat declarations, had, by the fourth century, governed the world view of those who held power in Rome and hence the creation of Christian Europe. The phenomenon of the extraordinary success of Christianity in the Roman Empire can only be matched by the capture of Russia and China by the 19th century millenarian manifesto produced in London, in grubby committee rooms and shabby lodging houses, by the penniless emigré dissident Jew, Karl Marx.

The battle-lines between Jew and Christian had, according to chapter eight of the Gospel of John, been drawn up by Jesus Himself. In that Gospel we find the campaigning Jesus belligerently and provocatively walking into the Temple and shocking the Jewish worshippers by announcing that He was the Son of God. The disbelieving Pharisees present took up the challenge and a sophisticated argument escalated as they mocked His claims and as Jesus repeatedly warned them that if they persisted in their disbelief, they would die in their sins. And when, exasperated by their obstinacy, Jesus told them they were fathered by the devil they took up stones and Jesus fled and hid Himself to escape their rage.

But the retreat was only temporary. In the ensuing political contest of the early centuries between the anti-Christian Jews and the splinter group of Christian Jews, there was no doubt when the poll would be declared which party would have garnered the most souls. The Jewish manifesto was a loser with no popular appeal: it called for an allegiance to an invisible God that could not be named, seen or touched or, indeed, was permitted to be imagined in any form by humans; and, more, it was equivocal about the possibilities of its supporters gaining an afterlife. To this day, the Jewish traditional prayer for the dead, recited at the graveside—the *Kaddish*—says nothing about resurrection.

The austere manifesto was the unadorned Ten Commandments which, above all else, having ordered obedience to one God and to no other gods, demanded:[20]

> You shall not make yourself any sculpted image
> Or any physical representation of any body in the heavens above,
> On the earth beneath or in the waters under the earth.
> You shall neither bow down to them nor worship them.

If ever a political programme becomes a suicide note, in ancient times as now, it is one declaring its total commitment to the Ten Commandments. By refusing to jettison the prohibition against imagery, the Jews kept the Word but gave to the Christians the greatest propaganda weapon available to all proselytizers—art: what the Christian Jews imagined, they were to illustrate; the children of men, like all children, want pictures in their story-books. Seeing is believing. The babe sees long before he talks. Visual reality, as we well know in our television age, can usurp reality itself. Over the centuries in the West the Church became the monopolistic patron of the artist; at its command, every niche in the buildings of Christendom had portrayals of the nativity and the crucifixion. By a gaze, relief from tension and the shedding of guilt was available to the Christian believer at every street corner.

At the very time that, in the early 13th century, the father of modern Judaism, Maimonides, was re-asserting that there must be no corporeal dimension to be attributed to the Jewish invisible God, the Church, contrariwise, was building its most glorious Gothic cathedrals. Within and without, the edifice was sculptured and painted and blazoned into endless allegory, image, and personification. The glass, the frescoes, the oil paintings, the bosses and bronzes, the wrought iron, the carvings, and the tapestries were as books for the illiterate devout; these were, as St Augustine called them, the *libri idiotarum*. The Cathedral was an earthly story with a heavenly meaning: believe, and what is depicted here is an anticipation of the heaven which you will reach in after-life. Already, as the worshippers who entered through the West portal on the tympanum, the greatest sculptors of the age, of perhaps any age, like Gislebertus of Autun and Vezelay, had warned them, in depictions of the terrifying Last Judgement, of the grim consequences of disbelief. Choose hell or the heaven you will find within the Cathedral.

The Cathedral is a deliberate and stupendous act of defiance against the first and second Commandments; it asserts the Trinity against the One and sends its message in stone, the material of the idols which, the legend tells, were smashed by the Jewish ancestor-father Abraham. The Trinity everywhere is proclaimed and made visible:[21]

> Three portals under one arch—the Trinity. ... the buttresses are mystical in their number; and the finials, and the crockets too. Three bays, each with three arches, each arch surmounted by

three windows, each window itself triune; three portals, each with three doors; three aisles in each transept, three piers in each aisle—the Trinity is typified throughout.

Yet even as believers, choosing to relieve themselves of the guilt of their primal and other sins, made their pilgrimages and flocked to worship at the shrines of gorgeous and bejewelled icons in the resplendent cathedrals, Maimonides composed his anti-icon articles of faith. Within the unadorned walls of the synagogue the Orthodox, to this day, recite in their morning prayers Maimonides' declaration:

> I believe with perfect faith that the Creator, blessed be His name, is a Unity, and there is no Unity in any manner like unto His, and that He alone is our God, who was, is, and will be.
> I believe with perfect faith that to the Creator, blessed be His name, and to Him alone it is right to pray, and that it is not right to pray to any being besides him.
> I believe with perfect faith that the Creator, blessed be His name, is not a body, and that He is free from all the accidents of matter, and that He has not any form whatsoever.

The Jew through the ages denied himself the joys and solaces and inspiration of the Image; the magic imaginative super-reality of Christendom's myth is not for him. In the uncluttered sanctum of the Temple's Holy of Holies God was present, invisible, alone, never demeaned by any surrounding trifling iconic representations however beautiful, however pleasurable. Aesthetics are subordinated, not permitted to temper the pain and awfulness of reality: only thus can truth be known. When Freud postulated that our mental activity is governed by two principles, the pleasure principle innate and primitive, and the reality principle acquired only by a painful developmental process, he was walking in step with his rabbinical grandfather. That grandfather would have categorized the story of the miraculous birth of Jesus as a regressive retreat from reality, as a hallucinatory wish-fulfilment.

The imperfect Jacob and the perfect miraculously-born Jesus are each emblematic figures defining the profound differences between the believing Jew and the Christian Gentile. Jacob, unlike Jesus, was human, all too human: devious, pragmatic, a cheerful cheat, Jacob suggests a mythical trickster figure who can always squirm out of the traps his enemies have set for him. He is a Biblical Ulysses,[22] crafty but extraordinarily brave, determined to be his own man, not his father's meek and submissive son. It would be, of course, blasphemous to compare him with the incomparable Jesus, divine, faultless, able—if you come to Him—to relieve you of all your guilts and forgive you all your sins and trespasses, real and imagined. Nevertheless it would be a grave error to consider and to underestimate the significance of Jacob/Israel. Jews are correctly designated the "Children of Israel" and the Jew has willingly, with pride, accepted the nomenclature entitling him to claim his descent from the vigorous ancestral father siring the 12 sons who became the heads of the 12 tribes establishing the Jewish nation. In the telling of this tale, the physicality of Jacob, the champion wrestler, is ever emphasized; the potent ancestor is no mythological wraith. Unlike Jesus, he is not sexless or celibate. He is a man of this world, not of the next. His potency and that of all his descendants is, however, not promised unconditionally; it is dependent upon the fulfilment of the contractual obligations agreed in the pact between God and Jacob's grandfather. God had pledged Abraham that from his loins there would emerge seeds as multitudinous as the stars in the heavens:[23] "And I will make your seed like the dust of the earth—could a man count the dust, so, too, your seed might be counted." Abraham and his progeny were to be endowed with stupendous virility, with unsurpassed sexual prowess. Abraham himself would sire Isaac when he was 100 years old; no erectile dysfunctional problems were to afflict the children of Israel. No sickly saints anticipating prudish misogynist Paul would have the right to emerge to reprove and inhibit them.

But such satiated concupiscence could be forfeited; absolute fealty to the one and only invisible God was a pre-condition to the efficacy of the Great Covenant between God the Father and the Children of Israel. And to seal the bargain, to guarantee there would be no escape clause, every male at the age of eight days, as an act of symbolic castration, must be circumcised.[24] This was no mere pubertal rite or, as sometimes deployed in Biblical tales, an apotropaic device to ward off the hostility of a dangerous deity. The foreskin would ever bear witness to the agreed bargain that on earth God's children would be abundantly fruitful, kings would come from them, but there must be no hubris: they must know their place and acknowledge that they are subordinate to the Father who, in turn, would be their shield.

The sealed Covenant was not to be meddled with: rights and obligations were there nicely balanced; the ambivalence between all fathers and sons was acknowledged but constrained. When Jesus announced He was the Son of God, conceived without human coitus, and when His followers concurred, they were in total breach of the holy contract to which no amendment could be made. So they daringly unsealed the Covenant and, caring not that their virility depended upon its observance—for celibacy, not fertility was their ideal—drew up a new testament, far less onerous, far more imaginative, to which the uncircumcised could subscribe. And they did, by the millions. And when stubborn Jewry, faithful to the Covenant, disdained what it regarded as a soft option of doubtful efficacy, the angry Christian world thwarted the Covenant promise that the Hebrews would multiply as the stars in the heavens—by periodic culls, by pogroms, crusades and, ultimately, by holocaust. Now we have a Jewry that is but a remnant of a remnant.

To present in such a non-ecumenical mode an interpretation of the Jacob allegory and the Christ myth reveals, it will be said, my irredeemable bias. That will be a deserved reproach, for no greater act of serendipity has fallen upon me than, like Jesus, to have been born a Jew. But my father, full of minor faults, was no god. We wrestled too and, in the end, he, blessed be his name, loved me as I loved him.

Notes

1. *Genesis*, ch. 10, V. 8–9.
2. *Genesis*, ch. 22, V. 2.
3. *Genesis*, ch. 24, V. 2–3.
4. *Genesis*, ch. 47, V. 30.
5. *Matthew*, ch. 1, V. 18–21.
6. *Galatians*, ch. 1, V. 19.
7. Vermes, G. *The Nativity*, Penguin, 2006.
8. Gibbon, E. *The Decline and Fall of the Roman Empire*, ch. xxi, Penguin Classics, 1995.
9. *Gospel of Matthew*, ch. 1, V. 25.

10. Eisenmann, R. *James, the Brother of Jesus*, Faber and Faber, 1997.
11. Griffin, W. *The Nature of Fascism*, Routledge, 1993.
12. Ryecroft, C. *The Ablation of Parental Images. Psychoanalysis and Beyond*, Chatto & Windus, 1985.
13. See p. 71 above.
14. Gibbon, E. *The Decline and Fall of the Roman Empire, op. cit.*
15. Goodman, M. *Rome and Jerusalem: The Clash of Ancient Civilisations*, Allen Lane, 2007.
16. Simon, L. ed., *Ahad Ha-Am*, Oxford, 1966.
17. Goodman, M. *Rome and Jerusalem: The Clash of Ancient Civilisations, op. cit.*
18. *Galatians*, ch. 3.
19. *Book of the Jubilee.*
20. Brichto, Rabbi S., *Moses*, Sinclair-Stevenson, 2003.
21. Yoxall, J. *The Soul of a Cathedral*, in *Essays of Today*, Prichard, S.H. ed., Harrap, 1923.
22. Douglas, M. *Jacob's Tears*, OUP, 2004.
23. *Genesis*, ch. 13, V. 16.
24. *Exodus*, ch. 4, V. 25.

SOLOMON

CHAPTER THREE

The judgment of solomon

Then came there two women, that were harlots, unto the king, and stood before him.
And the one woman said, O my lord, I and this woman dwell in one house; and I was delivered of a child with her in the house.

And it came to pass the third day after that I was delivered, that this woman was delivered also; and we were together; there was no stranger with us in the house, save we two in the house.

And this woman's child died in the night; because she overlaid it.

And she arose at midnight, and took my son from beside me, while thine handmaid slept, and laid it in her bosom, and laid her dead child in my bosom.

And when I rose in the morning to give my child suck, behold, it was dead; but when I had considered it in the morning, behold, it was not my son, which I did bear.

And the other woman said, Nay; but the living is my son, and the dead is thy son. And this said, No; but the dead is thy son, and the living is my son. Thus they spake before the king.

Then said the king, The one saith, This is my son that liveth, and thy son is the dead; and the other saith, Nay; but thy son is the dead, and my son is the living.

And the king said, Bring me a sword. And they brought a sword before the king.

And the king said, Divide the living child in two, and give half to the one, and half to the other.

Then spake the woman whose the living child was unto the king, for her bowels yearned upon her son, and she said, O my lord, give her the living child, and in no wise slay it. But the other said, Let it be neither mine nor thine, but divide it.

Then the king answered and said, Give her the living child, and in no wise slay it; she is the mother thereof.[1]

The worth of a society is to be judged by the concern of one generation for the next. And fortunately I have, on occasions, been able to mobilize sufficient parental tenderness in the community to support my legislative efforts. But my hopes, and those of my liberal sociologist friends of the 1960s and 1970s,[2] that legislative changes encouraging the emergence of a democratic family system would benignly release the energy which for so long had been repressively engaged in the maintenance of a tyrannical authoritarian family system, have proved over-optimistic. The thraldom of the old order has, to the great advantage of women, very substantially ended but the nascent egalitarian system has proved too fragile to withstand the assaults made upon it by the narcissism politically promoted by contemporary capitalism. Our ambitious aspiration, that the legislative changes for which we fought, would help to create a warm, caring, sharing family unit finding its reflection in a more permissive society permeated by those values, is now, alas, seen as a vanity.

The rigidity of the traditional family unit, the container of misogyny, male domination, and strangulation of affect, is largely no longer in place. The modern family has become dangerously diversified: today we have second families; step-families; families where the children are not biologically related to one of the parents; adoptive families; families with lone, separated, unmarried, or same sex parents. Such emancipations from the menacing grasp of the "traditional" family have brought its miseries along with its freedoms. Too often they reflect, or add to, the disarray, selfishness and uncertainties so evident in our post-Thatcher/Blair Britain.

Those who laud the freedom attained from the maiming constraints of the traditional family should surely temper their enthusiasms. So often their insouciant treatment of marriage reveals how terrified they are of true commitment. Marriage is an institution that does not exist simply in and for itself but—although it may be quaint to affirm so today—it is an institution whose *raison d'être* is the foundation and maintenance of the family. The central consideration in the establishment of a mating relationship is the having and rearing of children whose needs will be satisfied during their years of complete and then partial dependence. The concluding emphases in the magisterial work of more than 70 years ago, *The History of Human Marriage*, by Edvard Westermarck, the famed Finnish anthropologist, remain apposite today:[3]

> ... it is originally for the benefit of the young that male and female continue to live together. We may therefore say that marriage is rooted in the family rather than the family in marriage. Indeed, among many peoples true married life does not begin for persons who are formally married or betrothed, or the marriage does not become definite, until a child is born or there are signs of pregnancy; while in other cases sexual relations which happen to lead to pregnancy or the birth of the child are, as a rule, followed by marriage or make marriage compulsory.

Those who flippantly treat the rites of the wedding as irrelevant and insignificant fail to acknowledge how entwined is marriage with family, and how its severance places at considerably extra risk the children we bring into the world. This consequence lamentably raises little alarm in England where I have learned, from my legislative efforts in the field of family law, that there is in place a seemingly endemic condition which finds its expression in a dislike by so many of their own children; it is a condition which has a chastening historical continuity.

In a cross-cultural study of child rearing 35 years ago, in six countries in the West and in Eastern Europe conducted by the American Urie Brofenbrenner and his team of social scientists concluded:[4]

> England is ... the only country in our sample which shows a level of parental involvement lower than our own with both

parents—and especially fathers—showing less affection, offering less companionship and intervening less frequently in the lives of their children.

Their conclusions corroborated the much earlier 1955 survey of the English character by the anthropologist Geoffrey Gorer. That survey illuminated how the controlled, stiff upper-lipped Englishman of his day gained his renowned poise by directing much of his aggression towards his own children.

Gorer's assumption that fundamentally the English character had changed little in the previous 50 years before he reported is probably unchallengeable. The curious pattern in England of the dislike of little children has a long and dishonourable history. That peculiarly English institution, The Royal Society for the Prevention of Cruelty to Animals, was founded in 1824; but it was not until 65 years later that the National Society for the Prevention of Cruelty to Children came into existence. When, in Liverpool, the first local society for protecting abused children took action to establish a Home for Children instead of a Home for Dogs, the president was compelled to explain, apologetically, to the unsympathetic citizens: "I am here for the prevention of cruelty and I cannot draw the line at children". The various Royal Commissions on the employment of children during the 19th century indeed reveal as much about the disturbed consciences of a section of the ruling class as about the exploitation of little children. It is hard not to suspect the prurient preoccupation of some of the Royal Commissions, like the societies for the prevention of cruelty, with the horrid thought of cruelty inflicted on the helpless: there is too eager a desire to harrow feelings, as a glance at the vivid literature describing the misdeeds wrought upon children show. These sick preoccupations continued into the 20th century; a survey in the early Fifties of the popular Sunday papers showed that almost half the published material was devoted to cruelty to children and animals, and to punishment inflicted upon the perpetrators. The trend and mood continues. The tabloids today delight in "outing" alleged paedophiles; reports of child abuse, with no detail spared, have never been more widely circulated and relished.

The internet now has afforded new opportunities for child abusers to advertise their misshapen, ugly needs, and for a prurient popular press to celebrate with excitement as it catalogues the fetishes and, glowing with its own virtue, condemns the wretched and dangerously immature practitioners. The UK's Internet Watch Foundation, in 2007, reported with dismay that the number of images of serious child abuse had quadrupled over the previous three years. Despite the changes in sentencing guidelines which now attach longer terms of imprisonment to internet sex offences, and enable those caught grooming children online to be gaoled for ten years, still the images, increasingly hard-core, pour out to meet consumer demand from an increasing number of sick and often dangerous voyeurs.

The seriousness of the phenomenon cannot be complacently minimized by pleading it is, unfortunately, one finding expression in all Western countries, that it is not specific to England or the United Kingdom. I doubt if anyone can now take such a relaxed view in the light of the damning 2007 report of the United Nations Children's Fund which tells of the widespread parental indifference in the UK to the emotional needs of their own children; such a neglect inevitably makes The UK's many unhappy children singularly receptive to the lures of the sick aberrations now canvassed on some 3,000 websites.

The report measures and compares overall child well-being across six dimensions; material well-being, health and safety, education, peer and family relationships, behaviours and risks, and young people's subjective sense of their own well-being. In total, 40 separate indicators of child well-being—from relative poverty and child safety, to educational achievement and drug abuse—are brought together in this overview to present a picture of the lives of children. The United Kingdom ranks in the bottom third of the countries' rankings for five of the six dimensions reviewed; it lags behind in terms of relative poverty and deprivation, quality of children's relationship with their parents and peers, child health and safety, behaviour and risk-taking, and subjective well-being. The UK's children are found to be the unhappiest of all those within the 21 industrialized countries studied in the report.

The UNICEF report does not attempt to explain the differences between the treatment of children in the countries studied; it simply records them. Such a survey, revealing that more than one-quarter of the UK's children feel uncared for and neglected, leaves us to ask why the nation's children are the unhappiest in the Western world. More than in the rest of Europe, parents either do not care enough about children to make time for them, or feel they cannot afford to make time for them. Working long hours to pay the mortgage becomes the priority, not the child. With high, and increasing, numbers of single parents, step-parents, full-time working mothers and irresponsible and absent fathers, children are pushed out of their rightful place within their parents' lives. Meantime, the fiscal policies of the Thatcher and Blair governments, responding to the imperatives of contemporary capitalism, have ensured that women have been denied the choice to be state-subsidized full-time mothers. Only 6 per cent of women want to work full-time, yet 53 per cent of working mothers are in full-time jobs. In the conduct of the feral children on the hellish estates of south London we are witnessing an extreme manifestation of the consequences of the widespread child neglect that prevails in the UK. Unhappily, striated in the British culture is an extraordinary parental hostility to children which, at worst, finds expression in child abuse and, less ingrained but little less tragic in its consequence, in a widespread indifference to the children's fate. Whatever the aetiology may be, in the collective unconscious of the British the interpretation of the birth of a child as a threat foreshadowing the extinguishment of the parent is singularly embedded. In all my legislative forays into the field of family law—whether I was seeking to amend the laws governing adoption and fostering, or when I was fighting to give a right to an unborn child to claim compensation if born damaged as a consequence of an injury sustained through negligence, or when I was insisting in my divorce law battles that it should be declared by statute that in matrimonial disputes the over-riding and paramount concern should be the interests of the child, or when I was trying to overhaul the laws relating to infanticide, or trying to modify the abortion law—always the issues were bedevilled in the public debates in and outside the Commons by an undercurrent of resentment that I should dare, in all circumstances, to put the child first and thus, by denying choice, derogate the proprietorial rights of the adult.

Only a society possessed by such ambivalences towards its children would, despite its unprecedented affluence, accept that in its midst hundreds of thousands of children are to continue living in poverty. An analysis by the Institute for Fiscal Studies of the numbers of children in poverty as revealed by the Office for National Statistics, has shown that child poverty was, in 2007, up by 100,000. Even the unambitious 1999 government target of cutting child poverty by 50 per cent by 2010 is not being achieved; nor will it be unless there is an acceptance of the need for higher taxes from the better-off.[5] We have had the spectacle of Gordon Brown, when chancellor of the exchequer, repeatedly saying that he wished he was under the same sort of pressure on child poverty at home as he faced over debt relief abroad; but there is no such pressure. A guilt-ridden one-off charitable donation for the children of Africa can be wrested from the public. But the timorous politicians know well that a sustained levy by way of tax-rises would be regarded by the City, and most of the electorate, as intolerable. So a million children continue to be deprived.

To disentangle the skein, to select and pick out the particular historical and sociological threads that have shaped this singular British propensity to withhold love and treat children as threats not blessings, may be an unachievable task; but, since the pathological is ever the caricature of the normative, this British response to the emotional demands and conflicts of parentage may be regarded as a maladaptation but certainly never totally alien to the general human condition. It is in the Greek myths and the Hebrew legends that we see exteriorized a recital of the rages accompanying the battles waged against biological imperatives within the interior life of every man and woman when unto them a child is born. To still our own turbulences, and for the sake of our defenceless children, we would do well to hearken to the lessons taught us by those ancient tales.

***

Mirrored in the Greek myth of Persephone, and the separate myth of Laius, we see acted out admonitory illustrations of the unacknowledged murderous and sexual violences against their own children ever harboured in the unconscious of the psyche of all parents. In the story of Persephone we witness the terrifying rage of a domineering aggressive mother losing absolute control of a daughter; in the tale of Laius we recoil as the threatened father attempts to pre-empt the parricidal assault he fears will eliminate him. If the truths contained within these tales are assimilated, the possibility exists for a benign tempering of the motivations informing the parent-child relationship; and the possibility arises too of a self-aware society, no longer frightened of itself, able to be governed by family laws that are maturing, not punitive. But such a happy resolution is unattainable unless first there is a recognition of the inherent conflict within the mother-child dyad. For those prepared to listen, the Persephone story tells us in chilling detail the nature of that conflict.

The maiden Persephone, Demeter's daughter by Zeus, always brightened her mother's days. While she was picking flowers in a field with her virginal friends an astonishing narcissus caught her youthful eye. As she went to pick the bloom, the earth opened at her feet. Hades, God of the Underworld, carried the maiden off. Disconsolate, in dark despair, the grieving mother wandered far and wide to seek her daughter and her joy. When the search was not successful, in mounting anger she threatened to put an end to every growing thing, as was within her power. Faced with this potential catastrophe, Zeus was compelled to intervene and sent his messenger to Hades to conclude a pact that Persephone divide her time between her husband and her mother. When mother and daughter were reunited, Demeter's happiness was dimmed by hearing that her child had eaten pomegranate seeds offered by her husband. Now her daughter would never belong to her as fully as before. In her fury, Demeter issued a curse: vegetation would only thrive when the two were together and would die back every year during their separation; winter would follow summer. This is not a happy-ever-after story. The reconciliation between mother and daughter is soured; the tale is one replete with ambivalences.

It was with the ambiguities within the Persephone myth well in mind that the formidable existentialist feminist, Simone de Beauvoir,[6] portrayed for us the conflictual situation between mother and child precipitated by every pregnancy:

> Pregnancy is above all a drama that is acted out within the woman herself. She feels it as at once an enrichment and as injury; the foetus is a part of her body, and it is a parasite that feeds on it; she possesses it, and she is possessed by it; it represents the future and, carrying it, she feels herself vast as the world; but this very opulence annihilates her, she feels that she herself is no longer anything. A new life is going to manifest itself and justify its own separate existence, she is proud of it; but she also feels herself tossed and driven, the plaything of obscure forces. ... Caught up in the great cycle of the species, she affirms life in the teeth of time and death ... this production of herself is,

for a woman, the foreshadowing of her own death. ... Even if the woman deeply desires to have a child her body vigorously revolts when obliged to undergo the reproductive process. ... The significance of pregnancy being thus ambiguous, it is natural that woman should assume an ambivalent attitude towards it.

Citing the clinical findings of the early psychoanalysts Wilhelm Stekel and Helen Deutsch, de Beauvoir emphasizes how the woman's hostility to the foetus finds psychosomatic expression in expulsive ailments, in vomiting, in diarrhoea, and in miscarriages: "Almost all spontaneous miscarriages are of psychic origin". She could have ominously added that such hostility does not cease on parturition; it can find its ultimate expression in a mother killing her newborn child, in infanticide.

***

More terrible anguish cannot be imagined than that suffered by a woman emerging from the trauma of childbirth to discover she has not a living child to suckle, but one she has strangled, suffocated, or decapitated. In her ghastly predicament she may sometimes go into complete denial and stubbornly repudiate all accusations that she is the killer; more usually she falls into a deep depression. At her time of greatest need for support and for understanding, our frightened society, recoiling with horror, unconsciously aware that the wretched woman has acted out a terrible destructive desire that possesses all, mercilessly responds by inflicting punishment on the hapless woman. By punishing her it expunges the guilt felt by all parents for having harboured in their unconscious death-wishes against their own child; to serve and alleviate their guilt, the woman, mentally disturbed though she may be, must be made a sacrificial victim: she must be hauled before the courts, her action advertised, and charged with infanticide.

Reflecting the ambivalences irrevocably laced into the mother-child relationship, infanticide is a curious offence to remain within our criminal code.[7] It is the only offence known to our law where the prosecution, in order to gain a conviction, has to establish the absurdity that the wrongdoing was done wilfully and at the same time the wrongdoer was not responsible for the deed. Upon the prosecution falls the task of showing not only that the mother killed her child under the age of 12 months, but that, at the time of the killing, the balance of the mother's mind was disturbed because she had not fully recovered from the effect of the birth or because of the effect of lactation. Having proved the tumult of mind of the unfortunate mother, in defiance of every canon of criminal responsibility and with a rare sadism masking the affected mercy, the law decrees that the punishment to be meted out shall not be that accorded to a murderer, but that the woman should be treated as if she had committed manslaughter. In theory this means that the sick woman could be sentenced to life imprisonment. Nineteenth century juries knew that, at or about the time of birth, dogs, cats, sows, white mice, rabbits—all of them—sometimes kill their own young. Those juries were not prepared to bring in a verdict of murder which attracted a death sentence. It was to prevent such acquittals that the present infanticide law was originally introduced.

In 1964, and again in 1969, I attempted in Parliament to undermine further the punitive elements within our infanticide laws. My attempts were made not only out of concern for the three or four mothers who each year were unnecessarily brought to trial in courts to face the charge that in theory could attract such a severe sentence. Rather, I was seeking to illuminate the dark forces that lay behind, and were responsible for, the distorted and bizarre legal elements that constituted the offence; and, by obtaining implicit acknowledgement of those forces from the community, summon it to have the courage to roll forward the frontiers of compassion within our criminal law. In my attempted reforms I was moving into deep and troubled waters. As every picture gallery reveals, not all the idyllic paintings of the Madonna and Child camouflage either the troubled demeanour of many a Virgin, or the murderous stance of many a violent Lamb. There are neurotic compulsions, social and psychological, to resist the unmasking of the over-determined, coy, and sweet image of the mother and child. In our fairy stories we may reveal ourselves in tales of killing and devouring parents; but expounding changes in the law of infanticide, I was to find, was different from re-telling the grim tale of Red Riding Hood.

When I introduced my first Infanticide Bill I did not attempt to spell out the subtleties of the existing law to Alice Bacon who unfortunately was Minister of State at the Home Office. She was a good woman, a spinster and former elementary schoolteacher who had,

I was aware, made unusual efforts and sacrifice for the elderly and in dealing with her own family, and her well-developed sense of service found expression in her politics. But she had been promoted well beyond her ability. She had secured the appointment because she held in Leeds the neighbouring constituency to that of Hugh Gaitskell. He wanted an untroubled base and he could depend on her absolute loyalty to protect his rear. I tried, therefore, in a very unsophisticated presentation, to spell out the issues to her but my approach brought about little understanding of the points at issue. Her initial response only revealed to me the inadequacies of her advising officials. The letters they were drafting for her signature showed a complete misunderstanding of the law of infanticide. The Home Office officials were totally confused between the law relating to diminished responsibility in homicide cases and the offence of infanticide. My modest aim was to end the rite of the existing long-drawn agony which compelled the woman to be brought before magistrates in preliminary proceedings two or three times for the taking of depositions, and then to endure the strain of many weeks' waiting before being brought for trial to face all the pomp and paraphernalia of the High Court. I wanted a magistrates' court to have the power to dispose of the whole matter speedily and finally, and for there to be restriction on press reporting of the essentially private tragedy. But the officials, resisting any change, began irrelevantly and desperately plumbing the depths of the Homicide Act, which dealt with the degree of impairment of mental responsibility that a defence must establish to gain a reduction in a charge of murder. As I insisted, in exasperation, to Alice Bacon, that this was a discreditable display of bad law, she arranged a confrontation between me and the officials in her room at Whitehall. It was easy enough to win the argument with the ill-informed officials. Alice Bacon did not grasp all the details of the dialogue but it was clear to her that the departmental view was ill-considered. Yet, under the department's surveillance, she could only look at me with despair and could not come a whit nearer to meeting my demands. Without her aid, and given the hostility of the department, I knew I had lost the battle, and my Bill fell.

In the five years that followed, however, I persisted whenever an opportunity arose to draw attention, in and out of the House, to the cruel consequences of the anomalies in infanticide law. In 1969, aware of my efforts, a generous Welsh colleague, successful in the annual private member Bills ballot, offered me the opportunity to re-introduce my Infanticide Bill. The publication of this second Bill, the widespread and sympathetic press notices it received, the encouraging responses coming from MPs and the public interest in social problems, led me to hope that some progress could now be made. But it was not to be. By this time Shirley Williams had become Minister of State at the Home Office. Now I was to be defeated by the Pope.

Shirley Williams was not only a pretty woman; she was, and is, a highly intelligent woman, one always governed by a severe Catholic conscience. She was too intellectually fastidious to use the blundering banal departmental arguments that had thwarted my 1964 Bill; she well understood the anomalies of the existing law. But, camouflaging her Catholic prejudice in favour of the redemptive power of punishment, and using the *faux-naïf* charm that endeared her to many of her susceptible male colleagues, she sought to persuade me that my Bill was legally defective. Her efforts would have received Rome's full approbation; they were well in tune with Pope Pius XII's classical discourses on punishment.

Nine years later I was to find myself again in conflict with her when she once again displayed her agility to conceal her doctrinal commitments; she sabotaged all my efforts to create a government-appointed committee to encourage and govern research into human fertilization in vitro. I wanted the desperately infertile couple to have an opportunity to have children of their own and I believed it necessary to prepare legislatively for the wondrous advent of in vitro fertilization[8] which I believed would not be long postponed. But Shirley Williams was determined to uphold the Vatican; she found shelter from my lambastings in the conservative pronouncements of the Medical Research Council which declared they would not "support research into these fields until there was satisfactory evidence from work with animals of the safety of the techniques". It was not until four years had passed, after the Medical Research Council had recanted and after I had pressurized Margaret Thatcher and forced a Commons debate on the issue, that the government acceded to my demand; the required committee was set up and opened the way for what was to become available under regulatory control, albeit, as it has proved, one inefficiently enforced, in and out of the National Health Service.

But I was to leave the Commons without having gained any such postponed victory in my attempts to reform the infanticide laws. The objections Shirley Williams had to my 1969 Bill were focused on the issue of punishment. Catholic penal reformers notoriously, like the late Lord Longford, cling to the doctrine of retribution; they will not accept that guilt can sometimes be an illusion. For them, it is an awful reality, even if not the final reality, and it is not in law but in grace, which dwarfs all calculations of individual merit and demerit, that the master concept governing responsibility must be found. They ever seek to persuade agnostic penal reformers that no rehabilitation can come to a delinquent until he has achieved redemption by recognition of his sin; and that this recognition comes when he sees his punishment as an act of love from the community. The sticking point, therefore, between Shirley Williams and me was reached when she supported the departmental defeatist view that the insuperable defect in my Bill was that it reduced the penalty of infanticide to less than the maximum two years' imprisonment attached to the offence of neglecting, assaulting or ill-treating a child. Her Catholic conscience came through in every gap in her argument; it was in vain that I sought to show the law acquitted the mother found guilty of infanticide of responsibility and that it was a false analogy to make comparisons with the "wilful" offence of assaulting a child. Her preoccupation with punishment I found a distasteful, popish trait. For me, the fundamental question to be faced when dealing with any offender is not whether he should be punished but whether he and society is likely to benefit from the imposed punishment. When, however, granted absolution by statute, the vicarious masochistic delights gained by enforcers as they identify with the agonies of their victims are, for those schooled in the theology of martyrdom, too exquisite to be relinquished. I realized I could not successfully take my Bill further with my Catholic colleague and I reluctantly accepted her offer that in return for my withdrawing the Bill she would have the whole offence referred for particular attention to the judges' Criminal Law Review Committee. Her propitiatory gesture doubtless lightened the load of the guilt she felt at rejecting my pleas and yet, nevertheless, simultaneously, enabled her to enjoy some of the subtle pleasures of guilt-feelings so often accompanying the Catholic conscience. For my part, I had little doubt that the judges would tardily sit on the issue and, in the end, take no action; and such proved to be the case. The law on infanticide has remained untouched to this day.

Every year, therefore, three or four women, most of whom having been initially charged with murder, continue to be brought to the courts to be convicted of infanticide. Except the hapless mother, all participating in the elaborate prolonged and public charade know full well that the sentencing court will, at the end of a very long day, dispose of the case by stigmatizing the defendant as a murderer and then release her, subject to a hospital order or probation order or a supervisory order with a condition of mental treatment. Our society demands, however, that before pronouncing what is, in effect, a pre-determined sentence, the wretched woman, to be purged of her offence, must first be pilloried and her shame blazoned abroad in ritualized trial in both the lower and higher courts of the land. Responding to this societal demand, the Law Commission, to its shame, specifically re-affirmed in 2006 that these sadistic rituals must remain in place; the sick woman must continue to be brought before the courts of England and Wales.

The setting up of the Law Commission was the one significant reforming achievement of the lack-lustre first Wilson government of 1964. Its main progenitor was the great lawyer Gerald Gardiner who had made his acceptance of the lord chancellorship conditional upon the Commission being set up. He, in turn, appointed as its first chairman Sir Leslie Scarman, later Lord Justice Scarman, a politically skilled and committed liberal lawyer of rare distinction. The commissioners who served under him in its early years were of similar ilk, and included Stephen Cretney,[9] the academic lawyer uniquely qualified in the field of family law. My friendship with Gardiner, Scarman, and Cretney arose out of my indebtedness to them for the encouragement, advice, and research material they proffered to me as I pursued my reforming private member Bills in the Commons. Those were the glory days of the Law Commission when it made its humane and radical recommendations for law reform to a receptive legislature. But over the years, conservative lord chancellors and timid commissioners have done their worst. The Commission has long since lost its dynamism and spirited independence of governments more concerned that no law changes should offend the prejudices, however ill-founded, of the electorate or of the privileges of vested interests. By the 1980s, zealous young solicitors and barristers who had enrolled as servants of the Commission to be in the vanguard of law reform were disenchanted, and peeled off, sometimes fluently articulating their dismay.[10] Judging by the Law Commission's 2006 report on infanticide, their early forebodings were well-founded.

This report is a review of the general law of homicide; the law relating to infanticide was only an incidental part of their considerations. This infanticide section is distinguished by its provincialism and its prurience; no comparisons whatsoever are drawn with the response in other countries to the tragedies arising from post-natal depression that can afflict mothers in every land. What is, however, provided in excruciating detail, is a tabulation of the methods used by the severely disturbed mothers who, after suffering their labour pains, ended the lives of the babes they had newly created. We are informed how many babes had, in the preceding 12 years, been suffocated, how many strangled, how many drowned, how many battered, how many poisoned, how many thrown from a bridge, how many knifed by a sharp instrument. Such gory recitals would qualify for a place on a pornographic website where, doubtless, they could excite voyeurs nostalgic for the days when a visit to Bedlam was an entertainment; their deployment here in the Commission's report is suspect. Here, they are not deployed to illustrate the terrible madness that must have possessed the hapless mothers. If used for that purpose it would have led to the obvious conclusion that the Commission should not, in a laboured procrustean exercise, attempt, as it has, to yet again squeeze infanticide into the existing criminal law of homicide. Rather, the recital of the frenzied women's irrational conduct could have led to a declaration that there was a need for a canvass of possible humane societal responses—medically, sociologically, and psychiatrically informed—that would find expression in determinations made in a forum distanced from, and not integrated into, courts designed to dispose of criminals.

The report's emphases on the horrors of infanticide should not be dismissed as marginal irrelevancies or as asides in which draughtsmen or statistically-minded research workers indulge in some vicarious sadistic fantasizing; they are of greater significance. The crimes to which we are most attracted are the ones which we most condemn: thus we resist temptation, protecting ourselves from acting out our own deviances by punishing those who dared to do what we have secretly desired to do. It is the zealous puritan who will seek out and condemn the slightest flick of lust. By gratuitously and unnecessarily adumbrating the specific tortures inflicted upon babes by demented mothers the Law Commission ensures that all the notorious child-hating propensities endemic to the English culture are activated. Then, horrified by the image depicted of the mother, we recoil and refuse to acknowledge that it is our reflection: it must belong to another. To preserve his own identity he exonerates himself and projects all the guilts of his own unconscious homicidal impulses upon the crazed mother; her guilt purges his, he is innocent, she is guilty. A report that triggers the operation of such a psychological mechanism is certain in England to receive public approbation of its conclusion: that infanticide must remain a crime, for we are presently living, by odd circumstance, in a society which particularly facilitates the operation of such a psychological mechanism.

With the legacy of Margaret Thatcher, daughter of Beatrice Roberts, carefully preserved by Blair and New Labour, we continue, unemancipated, to be governed by the ethos and values Thatcher brought to Britain. Her disciples and apologists are justified in making large claims on her behalf; the impress her personal predicaments had upon public policy should not be underestimated. The political consequences precipitated by the antagonism between Margaret and her mother provide a modern illustration of the myth of Demeter and Persephone, of the destructiveness that can be unleashed when mother and daughter struggle unforgivingly with each other, when the resentments and hostility within the dyadic relationship are never assuaged, and when there is never a reconciliation between the two. In my psychobiography of Thatcher[11] I have told of the extraordinary efforts made by her to ablate her mother, to erase her name from her *Who's Who* entry, to cease, when a teenager, to communicate with her and to refer to her only reluctantly and in deprecatory terms. Thatcher took that battle with her mother into the public arena; traditional "Old" Labour was a party identifying with the mother, a party whose self-perception and ideals were essentially mother-orientated, even as yesterday's Conservative Party was father-orientated; the Labour Party was the "Welfare Party", maternally concerned, the provider, the bountiful caring one, the party that created the tendering National Health Service and gave the protection to the stumbling in our society of the National Insurance Act, the creator of the 1945 welfare state. With great effect, Thatcher displaced all her rage against her mother in an onslaught on what she described as "the nanny state", stigmatizing it as a cultivator of dependency and a subverter of individual effort and aspiration. Margaret Thatcher was engaged in matricide not politics, and the uncaring Thatcherite society we now have in place proclaims her victory. A probe into such a society's motivations is indeed a most unwelcome intervention; deploying Greek myths and psychoanalytic insights when faced with mothers slaying their babes is too dangerous an exercise: it would tell us too much about ourselves which we do not wish to know. It is easier to follow the Law Commission's ignoble example and respond with punishment.

***

The Persephone myth raises the alarm: terrible consequences follow if the biologically determined hostility of mother to daughter is not curbed. The Laius myth is similarly no less admonitory: mayhem results if the unrestrained father unleashes his vengeance upon his infant son. In our contemporary UK society, stigmatized by international assessors as notorious for its deficient responses to our children's emotional needs, the Laius myth has especial relevances and resonances.

Laius, significantly, for he is a dangerous man to encounter, is given little acknowledgement in our culture; we know him only as a victim of his son, Oedipus. Freud's remarkable selectivity in his rendering of Sophocles' *Oedipus Rex* told us nothing of Laius' crimes.[12] Freud was otherwise concerned: he was seeking to establish that the continuing force of Sophocles' tragedy was due to its evocations of forgotten infantile impulses common to all mankind. It is the inner forces luring us to kill our fathers and sleep with our mothers which Freud brings to our attention; Freud's eye is turned towards inwardness, towards inner drives and fantasies. In his presentation, therefore, Laius has no real presence other than as the victim of Oedipal rivalry.

Yet in the full legend Laius himself becomes an orphan child at the age of one and his throne is usurped by his uncle. Expelled from his home, he becomes a wanderer, a pederast whose homosexual crimes lead to his being cursed by the father of the boy whom he has sodomized. The curse that follows his buggery is that he will long remain childless and then be murdered by his son. Laius, fearful of the prophecy, abjures sexual intercourse with Jocasta until, finally, she intoxicates and seduces him. It is the child of that seduction, Oedipus, whom Laius sadistically and fearfully exposes to bring about the child's death. He acts cruelly and evilly towards his infant son, even pinioning his foot to stigmatize him; and thus the child is orphaned and driven out to become a wanderer. In Freud's synoptic version we are given an interpretation with all the emphases being placed upon the child's sexual desire, upon his hatred and envy of the parents. In the full tale, as in real life, what is to be remarked upon is the desire, hatred, and envy of the parent.[13] Child murder is a far more frequent offence than parricide.

If a 20th century man, responding to the didactic warnings spelled out in the Greek legend, gazes into a mirror, he finds no difficulty in recognizing the image of Laius confronting him. In the 19th century it was perhaps possible that mythological figures and besporting gods could be distanced as inhabitants of an alien land conducting themselves in ways unknown to man; today we can no longer be deaf to the resonances in place. Now that no permanence in the parental couple is to be assumed, when marriage is no longer necessarily the parental norm, when there is a dramatic rise in serial families and when divorce has ceased to be unusual, we cannot regard the behaviour of the protagonists in the Greek tragedy as bizarre.[14] In the light of present-day Western experience of the undoing or mutation of family norms, the stories of Ancient Greece can seem strangely contemporary; everywhere in those stories we find step-parents, single parents, step-siblings, half-siblings, second families and adoptions—the last three in *Oedipus the King* alone. Modern man, living in a society so afflicted with familial disorders, is especially susceptible to act out, albeit usually more subtly, the violences Laius directed against his own son.

And, if we are not to be misled by Freud's abbreviated version of the tale, we should recall that Laius' actions, unlike those of Oedipus, were wilful, not accidental. When Oedipus, hoping to avoid the fulfilment of Delphi's oracle that he would slay his father, quit his foster-parents and then met the murderous Laius at the crossroads, he raised his arm against the furious unknown stranger who attempted to strike him down; Oedipus acted in self-defence and ignorance. It is surely Oedipus who is the victim not Laius in this fateful encounter; and it is the Laius lurking within every father that needs to be contained, and never more so than in a society where traditional constraints are fraught or have been abandoned.

The full legend, happily, gives us some encouragement that those constraints can be exercised and, indeed, can be beneficially morphed. In his old age Oedipus was honoured and shepherded by his daughter and by a good princess. More, according to the interpretation developed by the psychoanalyst Malcolm Pines,[15] Oedipus, who had wandered the earth repenting his unwitting parricide, was, at the end of his days, "redeemed" by King Theseus, who was himself "the good son of a good loving father who was the civilised opposite of Laius, the fatherless and primitive autocrat".

There are, therefore, intimations within the story teaching that all is not bleak, that the father-son relationship need not be irrevocably disastrous; that tenderness, care, and concern can triumph over hostility and indifference; that one generation can transcend its self-regard and bequeath the legacy of love to the next.

But such instruction is unwelcome to a society like ours now wallowing in its own narcissism. It was no less unwelcome in the 1960s, the era so often fallaciously represented as "swinging", as one sprinkled with stardust where, repudiating aggression, singing songs of peace and love, we danced together and, liberated, in perfect harmony, we responded to a beat proclaiming the brotherhood and sisterhood of the human race. The reality was quite otherwise; that idyll never existed. The dominant *zeitgeist* remained in place initially little affected by the frolicking on its periphery. And at no time did it more show its ugly face to me than when I began my long, arduous, and ultimately successful campaign to totally overhaul our adoption and fostering laws; the extraordinary resistances I encountered once again revealed how widespread was parental indifference to the ultimate fate of their children. My interventions were resented; they were correctly perceived as assaults upon the proposition that children are parental property with no fundamental rights of their own.

***

The older I become, the less stable is that crutch, the chronology of memory, but it was, I think, some time in 1964 that a zealous children's officer in Camden whose name, to my shame, I have forgotten, in despair with the Home Office's traditional negative responses, approached me, asked my aid, and invited me to speak to a children's officers' conference. I agreed. In the event, it was the children's officers who spoke to me, not I to them. The Camden children's officer had precipitated the passage of the Children's Act which I eventually engineered on to the statute book 11 years later, in 1975. It was a reforming Act that, almost 25 years later, in 1999 attracted this verdict from Stephen Cretney, the former law commissioner and legal historian: "The Act is a landmark in 20th century child law ... The Act has stood the test of time".[16] Now, the very late autumn of my life, when I muse upon the legislative changes for which I must take a large measure of personal responsibility, this Act was the most outrageous, one that intervened into the very heart of family life, and was the one that I can most confidently assert added to the capacity of hundreds of thousands to enjoy a happier life. It remains the Act that, in retrospect, makes me feel all the hard slog and drudgery of my parliamentary life was well worthwhile.

Attending that children's officers' conference had made me aware that the need for sweeping legal changes in our children's laws was overwhelming. Because of the lack of any comprehensive adoption service giving support and guidance to the unmarried mother as well as would-be adopters, and available to all those needing it throughout the country, the choosing by society of parents for thousands of children each year was little more than a sinister game of roulette. Scores of voluntary adoption societies existed, unevenly distributed throughout the country, some purporting to serve a locality and others claiming to operate nationally. Many of them had standards of service which were abysmal; they lacked any professional skills or staff, dealing only on the basis of often bizarre criteria. The dilettante nature of the characteristics of too many of the adoption societies was encouraged by the perfunctory surveillance to which, by law, their operations were subject. Indeed, approval of their registration had become reduced to little more than a formality and was done by local authorities, more than half of whom shirked exercising their own existing powers to make their social services departments act as adoption agencies.

Outside the purview of these adoption societies of such varying quality, many adoptions were arranged privately by matrons, gynaecologists, health visitors and busybodies. Choosing parents for someone else's child was certainly too awful a responsibility to be left to any one person, but the muddlers and meddlers who for morbid or mercenary motives intervened to play God were given a dangerously free hand under our laws. One of the most hazardous direct adoptions were those arranged by a mother with colluding grandparents, aunts or elder sisters who wished to create legal relationships which differed from and distorted the natural relationship between not only child and adopters, but also of the child to his own mother. Too often in such adoptions the real circumstances of the illegitimacy of the child were hidden and the child's later discovery that his "parents" were really his grandparents and that his older "sister" was really his mother was a final damaging blow to a child who had already been brought up in an inevitably guilty and anxiety-ridden home.

Led by that children's officers' conference, I needed no further prompting. Perhaps even more than the children's officers I appreciated the full extent of the damage being inflicted upon the affected children since, from the time of my adolescence, I had steeped myself in the fascinating writings of that most daring and elastic of Freud's first collaborators, the Hungarian Jew, Sandor Ferenczi: no one had more brought home to me the travails of an unwanted child. More than 75 years ago he told how the chances of adult happiness for the child who feels an unwelcome guest in the family could be blighted:[17]

> [a] child has to be induced, by means of an immense expenditure of love, tenderness and care, to forgive his parents for having brought him into the world without any intention of his part; otherwise destructive drives begin to stir immediately. And this is not really surprising, since the infant is still much closer to individual non-being. and not divided from it by so much bitter experience as the adult. Slipping back into this non-being might therefore come much more easily to children. The "life-force" which wears itself against the difficulties of life has not therefore any great innate strength and it becomes established only when tactful treatment and upbringing gradually gives rise to progressive immunisation against physical and psychical injuries.

An adopted child, already rejected or by external circumstances compulsorily abandoned by the parents, has greater needs than most if he is not to be afflicted by a diminished desire for life. Moral and philosophic pessimism, scepticism, and mistrust can become character traits which can especially burden the mismatched adopted child. According to Ferenczi, and to Georg Groddeck, the German physician who was the father of psychosomatic medicine, such "unwelcome guests" in adulthood have a vulnerability to illness and to suicide that substantially exceeds the norm.

Initially, increasingly aware of the damage that can result from the casual adoption laws in place, and knowing the issues I was raising impinged upon a statistically significant section of the electorate—the natural parents giving up their children, the would-be adoptives, the foster-parents and adults who had been adopted—I was innocent and arrogant enough to believe that my propagandist talents would ensure a speedy response to my proposals. My optimism was misplaced. I was making incorrect assumptions about England that were based upon the warmer and more affectionate family units of the Welsh valleys when I was a lad, and upon the passionate Jewish family life with which I was so familiar.

When I entered the Commons, in my constituency, then still a coal mining seat, women who worked outside the home were suspect and acquiescent men who encouraged or accepted the notion of a working wife were despised by the mining community. But the influence of those "Mams" of south Wales valleys was nevertheless all-pervasive; they were free of the self-doubts which afflict so many women today and who define their self-worth in quite different terms.

Without washing -machines, driers or dishwashers, without bathrooms or running hot water, they received into their spotless homes their menfolk from the deep pits. With pit-head baths only exceptionally in existence then, the miners were covered with coal-dust and wives readily filled the tin baths and tenderly washed away the grime of toil. On Mondays, the wash-days, the miner's wife spent her time at her scrubbing board and cheerfully hung out the clothes on the lines in the cramped backyard. But she certainly did not feel exploited or oppressed, for the division of the duties and responsibilities between husband and wife were unambiguously defined. She was the queen of the household and the treasurer. She had no need to engage in a battle for "equality". When pay-day came, the miner came home from the pits and pushed his unopened wage packet into the apron pocket of his waiting wife, sitting outside the terraced home, and accepted without demur what she would then give back to him as pocket money; she managed the finances of the household.

In turn, the husband was totally kept out of the kitchen. Cooking and washing-up were not within his province, but parenthood was most certainly shared. The macho miner, in-between shifts while his wife was engaged in her considerable chores, would take the baby wrapped comfortingly around him in a shawl, Welsh fashion, and join his mates similarly encumbered at the street corners where, amidst their talk of whippets, rugby, and local Lodge politics, the babies slumbered on. The carping within so many marriages today as to who should do what, as overworked women return home to face fatigued husbands and domestic chores, was unknown. There were, of course, drunken husbands and domestic violence marring the ideal of the family life prevailing in the coalfields. But community pressures and disapproval operated severely upon miscreants who did not conform.

As I pursued my campaign to alter Britain's children's laws, I was to discover how in England most children were reared within a home environment far different from that enjoyed by the children of the extended families of the south Wales valleys who so often suffered economic deprivations but rarely endured the emotional starvation which the recent (2007) UNICEF report tells us continues to be the lot of so many: we have to assume therefore that in this regard the report related to their English counterparts. The family life of the valleys which was the background of my parents, as of my earliest years, corroborated the values maintained within the traditional Jewish family unit in which I was reared. There the danger was an excess, not a lack, of emotional involvement between parents and children. The resistances to my propagandizing initially perplexed me until I appreciated how alien to my Welsh-Jewish childhood was the early upbringing of so many of those who constituted the wider electorate to which I was appealing. Those who invested so little in the emotional development of their own children were unresponsive to a call to consider the emotional needs of other children abandoned by their parents.

The difficulties I met in my attempts to overhaul our adoption laws were not, however, due only to obstructive historical forces.

I found it unusually difficult to present the defects in our then existing adoption practices in sufficiently simple, dramatic, yet conciliatory terms, to ensure an understanding and a response from the wider public. Adoption is an ambitious technical method of resolving sterility, illegitimacy, and the nurture of the rejected or unattached child. It is also an imaginative and sensitive human enterprise where biology jostles passion, and where irresponsibility, inadequacy, or wickedness is met by pity, concern, and love. To presume to intervene by laws in this subtle and complex process is to invite condemnation as an intruder: an insistence that the adopted child, to gain a confident identity, has the right to know his biological parents, can be interpreted as an impudent intrusion. Emphasizing the sperm of a father, not as a mere fertilizer but as the carrier of DNA, the book in which much of the recipe for a new human being is written, can be regarded as a provocative insult to the infertile adoptive father; reason and insight embedded within such laws, however mildly coercive, can be speedily resented. I only erased a perception of me as an interfering busybody when I sensed the interest that the "property"—the child—was an issue: when a conflict arose between the desire of a foster-parent to adopt a child whom she had tended for years and the natural mother who belatedly wished to reclaim her child. Because of such conflict situations, by the posing of provocative questions in the frame of a maieutic dialogue, it was possible to act the pedagogue to a now attentive and disturbed public who could be taught that the complex decisions such disputes provoked were paradigms of the judgments that belonged to every adoption situation. The indignation felt when the battles over the future of a child were brought to public attention could be fanned into a blaze of protest as women empathized with the foster mother, the natural mother or, indeed, the child. I consciously, by speeches, questions in the House, and through the media, publicized the dilemmas and put into circulation phrases designed to catch the headlines; my description of "tug-of-war" children or "tug-of-love" children soon became the currency of sub-editors looking for an arresting paragraph.

Apart from the involvement of mothers at surface level in a dispute over parental and proprietorial rights, there were aroused at a more profound level the deep-seated emotions that have kept prising for thousands of years the legend of the most famous adjudication in history: Solomon's renowned judgment. By tapping the self same springs which have perennially sustained the vigour of that biblical tale, I was to release forces which were to compel a government enquiry into the whole of our adoption law and practices.

The ancient Hebrew story of contending mothers,[18] which in my battle for reform was to play such a significant part, is usually romantically recalled as the triumph, because of Solomon's insight, of the selfless mother over a cruel woman who was ready to have the babe killed. The adult memory tends to suppress the recorded facts of the story which is founded on harlotry and infanticide. Both the women concerned were prostitutes living alone in a brothel. Each had a child in the same house at about the same time with, strangely, no one else present. The one mother smothered her own babe by "accident", and then at night put her dead child by the side of the good sleeping mother, taking from her unsuspecting sleeping colleague the live child. On the morrow the good mother awoke to find only a dead child to suckle. Immediately asserting the dead child was not hers, she appealed to the king. The killing mother, who so desperately wanted to replace her lost child, then improbably agreed to Solomon's suggestion that the live child be hacked to pieces. This is indeed a strange story replete with odd embroidery and most unlikely responses. Yet its fascination remains in our secular world.

Is not the clue to its continued acceptance that secretly we know that this is not the story of two mothers and two children but of one mother and one babe? It bears psychological witness to the ambivalence of every woman to her own child, of her love for him and of her hate, of her feelings of fulfilment and of her feelings of destructiveness. The schizoid splitting in the tale, of the one woman into two, into good and bad, is imperfectly completed: the good mother still has her badness symbolized by her prostitute status so that subliminally we may learn without fear that evil and antagonism must live in every mother side by side with tenderness and maternalism. In the first part of the story the mother kills the child, but in the second part hate is defeated by love and the babe lives again in unison with the true mother. Solomon, the wisest of kings, confirms that although woman must have conflict between her rôle as individual and her rôle as mother, a healthy society enables the woman to resolve the struggle and attain happiness and self-esteem in a symbiotic relationship with her wondrous creation.

In every tug-of-war situation there is enacted before every woman the selfsame drama of the loving mother and the rejecting mother. And since both such mothers are encapsulated within every woman, it is not surprising that such incidents arouse a tumult of emotions. Most of the battles between foster-parents who had children in long-term care and the natural parents arose in fact out of poor case work by overburdened social workers who failed to maintain an adequate contact between foster-parent and natural mother. But although laws in themselves cannot remedy the failures which precipitate such conflicts, their very existence enabled me to use them for fuller discussion of all adoption malpractices. Members of Parliament who had such instances occurring in their constituencies came to discuss them with me, and with such Members I was able to form an all-party group committed to pressurizing the Home Office to review our adoption and fostering laws. The Home Office still stalled; its Children's Department was already overstretched with preparations for other legislation and did not wish to take on further burdens. As our pressure mounted they pleaded, predictably, that more research was needed before any moves could be made. Then, after unrewarding years of attempting to coax and to alarm public opinion, there came a serendipitous intervention.

In 1967 Jim Callaghan became home secretary. He came to his new office shell-shocked. Devaluation and his subsequent resignation from the chancellorship of the exchequer had left him stunned and depleted. He had been poor in his boyhood and it led him to be over-fascinated by money. Mixing with bankers and economists had shored him up, leaving him with a profound sense of security that he had rarely been able to enjoy. The total collapse of his assumptions and of the pound was felt as more than a policy failure; he was a shaken man. Bewildered, he invited me—as doubtless he invited other backbenchers who had in the past fully involved themselves in political programmes that were part of the responsibility of the Home Office—to come and talk to him privately; he wanted instruction. I seized the moment and told him he could be remembered as the man who had revolutionized Britain's child laws. The notion of being "the Children's Protector" immediately appealed to him: as a very young boy, Callaghan lost his seaman father and the widow was left to fight a bitter struggle to maintain the family. The impress of those early years was irrevocably stamped upon the adult man; in this case, it acted to my advantage.

Callaghan agreed to my suggestions that an advisory committee be immediately set up to review the laws and make proposals for legislative changes; that it should be composed of those with expertise in the field of childcare and those familiar with the operations of the existing laws; and that I should sit upon it. The Home Office civil servants, as ever, stalled, claiming their Children's Department was already over-stretched. Then, in a rearguard action, they sought to limit the terms of reference of the proposed committee. But my incitement of Callaghan to resist proved successful and for three of my most arduous parliamentary years I sat with the committee taking evidence; finally we produced an exhaustive and unanimous report whose recommendations could be legislatively implemented.

Soon after the report's presentation, my colleague David Owen drew a high place in the annual Private Members' ballot which entitled him to the time to bring in a Bill. He readily agreed to sponsor one implementing the committee's proposals. Together we steered the Bill through the Commons and then, before it reached the statute book, an election was called and the Bill fell. On Parliament's return, however, the Labour government took it over and, although it was still to be some years before it was fully implemented, it did become the Children's Act in 1975.

Now the workings of that Act clearly need reviewing, not least because of the arrival of in vitro fertilization. And, with 60,000 children in England today being looked after by the state, there is certainly a need to ensure that we have laws and practices in place that will encourage, not deter, those with the courage and nobility to take traumatized children out of care and undertake the adoption of disturbed little ones who have often endured neglect, instability, and terrible violence. But whatever changes may come, the basic principles enshrined in that Act will be a permanent feature of Britain's children's laws.

It is a quirk of mine that I am much happier when I am warding off brickbats than when receiving encomiums. In this instance, however, I was pleased when, shortly before the legislative implementation of the advisory committee's recommendations, Jim Callaghan wrote to me spontaneously, and over-generously:[19]

> This is another reform that your own activity and zeal has been largely responsible for. You will have a wonderful collection of worthwhile scalps under your belt before you finish. And

you do much more good in terms of human happiness than 90 per cent of the work done in Parliament on what are called "political issues".

That verdict upon the Children's Act which I engineered, by the man who was soon to be prime minister of the UK, is not recorded here out of conceit; rather, it is a recitation of a clear intimation that it is possible for the politician to engage in successful counter-cultural assaults in our country and, although within the culture of, in particular, England, there are few more undesirable motifs than an indifference or antagonism to children, it is nevertheless challengeable.

Events since, that 1975 Act precipitated another challenge. Outrageous cruelties inflicted upon an African child sent to a member of her extended family in England fuelled a campaign for changes in social services' involvement with young children and, eventually, led to the 2004 Children's Act, devised to join up the dots and ensure that education and social services worked together in providing services for children. It has been criticized as legislation offering responsibility to everyone but giving it to nobody, but it has led to the creation of a supervizing children's commissioner, a post currently held by the renowned paediatrician Professor Sir Al Aynsley-Green. Evidently appalled at the continuing lack of focus on children's issues, he declared this to be a reflection of "a cultural attitude that children are relatively unimportant". When he had reviewed the statutory Children's Plans that local authorities in England are required to have in place, he spelled out his chastening response:[20]

> We have to recognise that 30 years of disinvestment and lack of focus on children's issues cannot be solved overnight. I feel ashamed to have been a paediatrician for 30 years and failed to shout from the rooftops about the problems in children's services.

Since then, he has had no need to shout from the rooftops; he can speak to Ed Balls, Secretary of State for the newly-created Department for Children, Schools and Families. The creation of this superdepartment, an empire with huge spending powers, may become bureaucratically choked but, more optimistically, it could be a happy augury; charged with the tasks of initiating and invigilating all legislation and ministerial action that may either benignly or adversely impinge upon children's welfare, its creation could result in the governance of England being permeated with a "children first not last" ethos. Much depends upon the support he will now gain from his friend, the prime minister, to whom he was an aide when both were at the Treasury. Balls rightly said, on accepting—and, indeed, choosing—his appointment, that his task was "quite daunting".

In his interventions Balls will meet what Professor Sir Aynsley-Green—indicating he was making a well-informed worldwide comparison—declared as a "very peculiar" English reluctance to cherish children on the margins of our society. It is a reluctance that has its source, in my view, in the incapacity or selfishness of so many English parents to bestow sufficient love upon their children. Inevitably those children when adults, deficient of love, cannot give what they have never received. In an article he wrote in August 2005 for the civil service network web page, the professor has appeared to have encountered the same syndrome as I found in place in the resistance to my reforming children's laws in the 1970s, which has again been identified in the UNICEF report of February 2007.

But Balls will be contending too with other inimical trends within our narcissistic society. He has one particularly difficult task: to design, for the sake of our children, legislative, administrative, and fiscal changes aimed at emphasizing and encouraging awareness and recognition of the overwhelming significance of fatherhood. This will not be approved by the outdated 20th century gender feminists whose voices in the political arena are not, unfortunately, stilled. The judgment of Solomon will, regrettably, provide Balls with no precedent enabling him to plead a case for the father because no fathers make an appearance in King Solomon's court; the disputed children, born in a brothel, were the children of prostitutes, the true fathers unknown to each of the mothers and fated irrevocably to be unknown to the surviving child. Solomon, in the absence of any father, did his best for the unmarried mother and child, applauded her readiness to sacrifice all, even the right to her babe, for the sake of that child; by his adjudication, he exhorted the mothers of Ancient Israel to follow that mother's example, to overcome their destructiveness, and so to be rewarded with royal approval and a loving child. Yet not even the wisdom of Solomon, or the boundless love of the mother for her child, could find a way of removing the initial handicap inescapably falling upon that babe, as upon every child, boy or girl, born into a fatherless household.

A little girl needs a relationship with her father in order to open up wider horizons of difference so that she can later manage her intimate relationships with men. As family therapists Pincus and Dare have written:[21]

> A little girl needs to know that her father is a bit in love with her (just as the adolescent girl whose father has absolutely no erotic interest in her cannot believe that anyone else can love her); a little girl needs also to believe that her mother takes her seriously as a rival to her father's affections; only so can she take herself and her own life seriously too.

And, for the son, the father can provide a rôle model not only in how to manage male aggression and power within and outside the family, but also how to bestow concern, support and love on another. The essential rôle of a father is to provide his sons with a separate model of confident and caring masculinity, and to ensure that the little ones have a clear window to an outside world. Every child needs the other parent to mediate, to avoid the suffocating and potentially manipulative closeness of the dyadic relationship with one parent.

The need to have welfare and fiscal policies explicitly encouraging the establishment and stability of the two-parent family has never been greater as we witness the children of the black community and of the white "underclass", lacking male models in the home, daily wreaking their vengeance against a society which ignores their fatherless plight.

If Balls is bold enough to insist upon such policy emphases, he is likely to have little encouragement from the present minister for women, Harriet Harman, who, in the mercifully little contact I had with her in the Commons, I found to possess a conceit matching her obtuseness. In a declaratory pamphlet she once opined that "it is essential for men to change their rôle in the household and do more of the unpaid work"[22] so that there may be an end to the "separate spheres and models of family life". Confidently she asserts that "it cannot be ... assumed that men are bound to be an asset to family life, or that the presence of fathers in families is necessarily a means to social harmony and cohesion". Such an approach reveals a compulsive need for total autonomy. For her, evidently, inter-dependence means, as she explicitly declares, "equivalent skills, status and power'—and how meanly is the distribution measured to ensure that not one iota more is given than is received. It is an approach to male-female relationships worthy of cheating hucksters in the market-place and what is being sold, as has been challengingly asserted, is indeed "a programme for equality on female terms alone".[23] And thus wrapped up in such an ideology, such women seek to hide their fears for they lack the courage to let go lest that should lead to dependence upon another. Trusting neither themselves nor the other, they are perforce illiterate in the land of love. They provoke havoc in their marginalization of the man within the family, in their minimizing of the especial rôle of the man as father and their insistence that he must be a surrogate mother to ensure his wife, untrammelled, can enter the workplace. This agenda of the 20th century gender-feminist continues to leave its impress on the UK's welfare and fiscal policies: by incitement and coercion they ensure the augmentation of our cheap part-time labour force and the delivery of women out of the home into the willing maws of devouring employers. Much of the criticism by Melanie Phillips[24] of the thrust of Gordon Brown's 1998 budget policies when Balls was his aide at the Treasury remains valid:

> It collapses men's rôle as family breadwinner, which is to be imposed upon women instead, while mothers looking after their own children are to be devalued and discouraged. ... It will keep women dependent upon the State which now merely changes its rôle from surrogate male breadwinner to a new surrogate function as a female carer, looking after children while mothers are pushed out to work. ... The intention is precisely to undermine the male breadwinner and trash hands-on motherhood. Full-time mothering is now to be viewed with contempt. ... Women are to be manoeuvred into work even when they are nursing their babies. ... The State will pay strangers to look after children. This reflects the myth that children are generally better off in substitute care than with their families.

If Balls is to succeed in a quest to establish a framework within which a stable two-parent family life flourishes, not wilts, he will need to slough off the departmental prejudices in place during his short span in 2006 as economic secretary to the Treasury; and if by fiscal advantage he seeks to encourage the ideal—the creation of two-parent families—he will need political courage to withstand the onslaughts of those who will, falsely, immediately accuse him of a puritanical attempt to discriminate against the unmarried and the one-parent family unit. Balls has indeed a "daunting" assignment.

Repeatedly during the 20th century major legislative and administrative changes proposing the prioritization of children's needs have been thwarted. Children, unlike adults, have no votes and a sulky self-regarding electorate have been vexed when their parental rights are questioned or challenged. I am ever mindful of the fate of the report of a Royal Commission chaired by Judge Sir Morris Finer, a man whose friendship I was much privileged to enjoy. During the 1960s, in and out of the Commons, I had given all the support I could to the valiant efforts of the National Council of the Unmarried Mother and her Child, the lobby led by the redoubtable Margaret Bramall,[25] to draw attention to the disabilities and plight of so many children born out of wedlock. Our agitations ultimately resulted in the appointment by the Labour government in 1969 of a Royal Commission under the chairmanship of Morris Finer. When, after years of scrupulous enquiry, the completed report was submitted in 1974 it contained 230 recommendations. *The Observer* accurately hailed it as one of the major social documents of the 20th century. Morris Finer's premature death, the timorousness of politicians fearful of handling hot potatoes, and the indifference of the public ensured the report's burial; it has remained shelved.

In December 2007 we found Ed Balls laudably produced a detailed 10-year Children's Plan,[26] a plan to "make England the best place in the world for children to grow up". It is impressive in its interventionist ambition but leaves serious doubts about whether that ambition will ever be fulfilled. Today, anyone embarking upon a radical reappraisal of the inadequate support, institutionally, legislatively, and fiscally, given to children, will find entrenched similar resistances to those which saw off the implementation of the recommendations of the Finer Report. To overcome them, Balls, in his adjudications, will need not only some of the wisdom of Solomon but also, if his newly-created empire is to triumph, to emulate the ruthlessness of the young king of Israel. As the days of King David "drew nigh that he should die" he charged his son Solomon: "I go the way of all the earth; be thou strong therefore, and show thyself a man." In one of the most bloody chapters in the Bible we see Solomon fulfilling the paternal command; all who would subvert his authority, including his elder brother and meddlesome priests, were slain: "And the kingdom was established in the hand of Solomon." In the exercise of his remit Balls will need to display a similar lack of squeamishness. Only thus will some relief come to the many unhappy and anxiety-ridden children[27] of the United Kingdom.

Notes

1. *1 Kings iii,* 16–27.
2. Fletcher, R. *The Making of the Modern Family*, essay, Ciba Foundation Blueprint *The Family and its Future*, Churchill, J. & A. 1970; and Fletcher, R. *The Shaking of the Foundations: Family and Society*, Routledge, 1988.
3. Westermarck, E.A. *The History of Human Marriage*, Macmillan, 1921; and Westermarck, E.A. *The Future of Marriage in Western Civilisation*, Macmillan, 1936.
4. Brofenbrenner, U. *Two Worlds of Childhood*, Simon & Schuster, 1972.
5. Elliott, L. *Only the rich can end child poverty*, in *The Guardian*, 2nd April 2007.
6. de Beauvoir, S. *The Second Sex*, Jonathan Cape, 1953.
7. Abse, L. *Private Member*, MacDonald & Co, 1973, pp. 96–103.
8. Abse, L. *Politics of in Vitro Fertilisation*, in *In Vitro Fertilisation*, eds. Fishel, S. & Symonds, E.S., IRL Kraus, 1986.
9. Cretney, S. *Family Law in the Twentieth Century: A History*, Oxford University Press, 2005.
10. Oerton, A. *A Lament for the Law Commission*, Countrywise Press, 1987.
11. Abse, L. *Margaret, Daughter of Beatrice*, Jonathan Cape, 1989.
12. Ross, K.M. *Oedipus Revisited: Laius and the Laius Complex*, in *Psychoanalytical Studies of the Child*, 37, Newhaven, CT, Yale University Press.
13. Pines, M. *Circular Reflections*, Jessica Kingsley, 1998, p. 125.
14. Bowlby, R. *Freudian Mythologies: Greek Tragedy and Modern Identities*, Oxford University Press, 2007.
15. Pines, M. *Circular Reflections, op. cit.*
16. Cretney, S.M. *Looking Back—Looking Forward: 150 Years of Family Law*, Oxford University Press, 2008.

17. Ferenczi, S. *The Unwelcome Child and his Death Drive*, in *Collected Writings*, Penguin, 1999.
18. See p. 91.
19. Callaghan, J. private letter.
20. Aynsley-Green, A. quoted in *The Sunday Times Magazine*, 5th August 2007.
21. Pincus, L. & Dare, C. *Secrets in the Family*, Faber & Faber, 1978.
22. Abse, L. *Fellatio, Masochism, Politics and Love*, Robson Books, 2000, pp. 142–143.
23. Phillips, M. *The Sex-Change Society: Feminised Britain and the Neutered Male*, Social Market Foundation, November 1999.
24. Phillips, M. *Times Literary Supplement*, 20th March 1998; Phillips, M. *Man's Job is to Win the Bread, a Woman's Job is to Spend it*, in *The Observer*, 22nd March 1998.
25. Obituary, Margaret Bramall, *The Guardian*, 17th August 2007.
26. Balls, E. quoted in *The Guardian*, 12th December 2007.
27. *Community Soundings*, Cambridge University Report quoted in *The Guardian*, 12th October 2007.

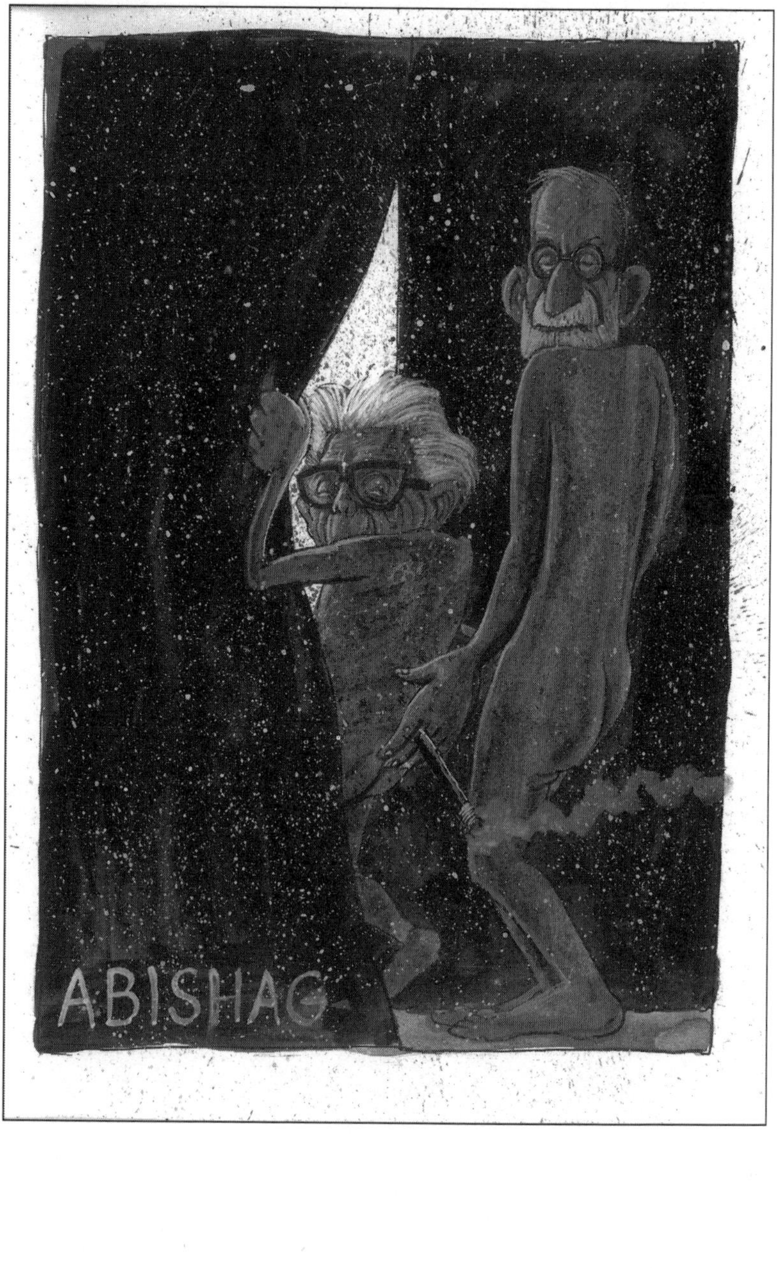
ABISHAG

CHAPTER FOUR

Abishag: The lure of incest

Nearly 90 years ago, as a very little boy sitting on the kitchen floor watching my mother cooking, I was first introduced to Jewry's dietary laws. At about my eye-level when I stood up there were two dresser drawers, one with a red knob, another green; I liked to play with them. After a little accident I was careful, to avoid further admonishment, never to pull them out lest the cutlery they contained should overspill. My mother, I noticed, treated both drawers with similar circumspection. They were not to be opened at the same time; the knives, forks, and spoons of the one were never ever to be mixed with the other. Soon I was to learn that the drawer with the green knob was named *Milchadika* drawer, the other the *Fleischik*, the cutlery from one to be used for milk and vegetarian meals and the other only for meat dishes.

In the 20th century my mother was scrupulously observing the injunction imposed upon her ancestors some 2,000–3,000 years earlier: "Thou shalt not seethe the kid in his mother's milk."[1] So imperious is the command, it is repeated three times in the Pentateuch and, acknowledging the hazards of unwittingly breaking so intimidating a law, in my Orthodox mother's Jewish household there was not to be any mixture of meat and milk dishes.

At my first questioning of this strict rule against mixtures, my mother explained it was part of a diet laid down by God which, if followed, would ensure we ate only what was good for our health. It gave us immunity from epidemics that raged among Gentiles who ate *trefe*—unclean—food and did not confine themselves to the kosher food sanctified by God which, of course, she always gave to me; and so I should eat it all up and be a good boy and then I would grow up strong and healthy.

Perhaps it was an awareness that his precocious grandchild was gradually becoming sceptical of his mother's explanations of the elaborate food rituals practised in his home, that prompted my Talmudic grandfather's early intervention. In the rough and tumble playground of the Welsh working-class primary school where my brother and I were the only Jews, ever wrestling and fighting, I would have found no corroboration of my playmates being particularly handicapped by their *trefe* eating habits; and, when playing in the street, I would have observed that my mates, after breaking off and popping into their homes for a piece of bread and dripping and a strong milky cup of tea, returned replenished, not stricken, to the fray. My grandfather, seeing the need, was soon providing me with a rationale more likely to ensure my allegiance to the ancient dietary rules. Before I reached my *bar mitzvah* I was aware of the 12th century Maimonides' high-minded explanation of their purpose:[2]

> The dietary laws train us in the mastery over our appetites; they accustom us to restrain the growth of desire, the indulgence in seeking that which is present, and the disposition to consider the pleasure of eating and drinking the end of man's existence.

Maimonides was giving his laudatory justification for the rules categorized in Leviticus. There the original prohibition of Exodus of seething the kid in his mother's milk has been much elaborated, providing an extraordinary list of what food can not only not be mixed, but what can and cannot be eaten, and what combinations, even of seeds and textiles, are to be regarded as abominable miscegenations attracting the wrath of the Lord. But notwithstanding Maimonides' exegesis, the only explicit object of these laws that is distinctly mentioned in the Pentateuch is the promotion of Holiness.[3] At the end of one of the sections, the dietary laws conclude thus:[4] "For I am the Lord that brought you out of the land of Egypt, to be your God; ye shall therefore be holy, for I am holy."

Repetitively, insistently, we are enjoined that the attainment of purity, the prerequisite to becoming holy even as God Himself, is the maintenance of the divisions between the animals that can be eaten and those that cannot:[5]

> I am the Lord your God who set you apart from all the peoples. And you shall set apart the clean from the unclean beast, and the unclean diet from the clean, and you shall not make yourselves despicable through beast and bird and all that crawls on the ground, which I set apart for you as unclean. And you shall be holy to me, for I the Lord am holy.

Here we see at work the single imperative verb that focuses the major theme of Leviticus: it is *hivdil*—the Hebrew word for "divide." Elegantly the Hebraic scholar Robert Alter[6] has elevated the significance in that Leviticus *hivdil*; that verb, he reminds us, stands at the beginning of the story told in Genesis of the creation: "And God saw the light, that it was good, and God divided the light from the darkness ... And God made the vault and divided the water between the vault from the water above the vault, and so it was." In this vision of cosmogony, the condition before the world was called into being was a chaotic interfusion of disparate elements. Alter proposes that what provides a framework for the development of human nature, conceived in God's image, and of human civilization, is a process of division and installation: light from darkness, day from night, the upper waters from the lower waters, and dry land from those lower waters. That same process is, Alter claims, repeatedly manifested in the dietary laws of Leviticus.

Such a commendation of Jewry's menu, unchanged for thousands of years, would have been fully endorsed by my Talmudic maternal grandfather; it would, with no less zeal, have been mocked by my atheist paternal grandmother. My two sets of grandparents dwelt but a few hundred yards apart in the same road in Cardiff, but they lived in entirely different worlds; since they competed for their grandchildren, I, as a child, had the good fortune to live in both. Both these grandparents, such significant figures within my family constellation, had come in their youth to Wales, the one from Russian

Poland, the other from the Baltic, from East Prussian Kônigsberg to which, from a small village in what is now Lithuania, my paternal grandmother had moved with her parents as a child. In German-speaking Kônigsberg the Haskalah, the Jewish movement claiming to bring the benefits of the Enlightenment to Jewry, had scorched her. When she came as a young woman to Cardiff she looked with scorn on the small Jewish community living there within their self-created ghetto and still clinging to what she regarded as the archaic values of the *shtetls*, the settlements within the Russian Pale which they had so recently quit. Alone, of all the Jewish women in the community, she advertised her atheism by her flagrant disobedience of the dietary laws; ostentatiously she bought her meat in non-kosher butcher-shops and in Cardiff's fish market; while other Jewish wives were carefully selecting their fish for the gefilte fish Sabbath supper, she would outrage them by openly buying her shrimps, oysters, and lobsters—all the shellfish so severely prohibited by Leviticus.

By so doing she was far more fundamentally and effectively attacking God and the Bible than our contemporary militant atheists of Richard Dawkins' ilk. Their puerile assaults tell us of their unresolved Oedipal problems as, in adolescent defiance, they rage against God the Father and reveal their fundamentalist creed as little more than cowardly over-compensatory doubt. Their failure to understand that much of the content of religious faith is metaphorical, poetic, and symbolic, reveals a failure of sensibility. The vulgarity of their prosaic formulations estranges even agnostics repelled by the coarseness of their literal argument. Like Nietzsche who in his anti-Christianity diatribes declared not that God did not exist but that He was now dead, my grandmother's credo was more subtle and far more subversive. By taking away from God the right to determine her diet, to insist that her kitchen was her own domain, that she would be her own chef, mixing her own ingredients and deciding the order of courses according not to any formula but to her own caprice, she was not engaged in childish tantrums. She was deliberately sweeping aside all Maimonides' ascetic rationale counselling the benefits of constraint, and, more, she was defying the basic principle of division which, the rabbis taught, accorded with God's own template. She would unhesitatingly, if the mood so took her, prepare a meal of kid seethed in its mother's milk.

Unlike today's evangelical atheists who, lacking the guts to really take on God, tell us there is no "evidence" that He is here, my grandmother was too Jewish—for God had been too long in the family—to so deny His presence. And she had intuited that by breaking the dietary laws of Leviticus she was also breaching the walls that protected that inner sanctum, the Holy of Holies in the Temple, from which emanated the laws regulating the divisions, not merely between animals, fish and fowl, but those that prevail between all members of the human race and between all generations.

The dietary laws are in effect but a corroborative addendum, albeit a significant one, to the Almighty's commandment specifying in detail the boundaries that must be maintained in human relationships:[7]

> Ye shall therefore keep my statutes, and my judgements; which if a man do, he shall live in them; I am the Lord.
>
> None of you shall approach to any that is near of kin to him, to uncover their nakedness; I am the Lord.
>
> The nakedness of thy father, or the nakedness of thy mother, shalt thou not uncover; she is thy mother; thou shalt not uncover her nakedness.
>
> The nakedness of thy father's wife shalt thou not uncover; it is thy father's nakedness.
>
> The nakedness of thy sister, the daughter of thy father, or daughter of thy mother, whether she be born at home, or born abroad, even their nakedness thou shalt not uncover.
>
> The nakedness of thy son's daughter, or of thy daughter's daughter, even their nakedness thou shalt not uncover; for theirs is thine own nakedness.
>
> The nakedness of thy father's wife's daughter, begotten of thy father, she is thy sister, thou shalt not uncover her nakedness.
>
> Thou shalt not uncover the nakedness of thy father's sister; she is thy father's near kinswoman.
>
> Thou shalt not uncover the nakedness of thy mother's sister; for she is thy mother's near kinswoman.
>
> Thou shalt not uncover the nakedness of thy father's brother, thou shall not approach to his wife; she is thine aunt.
>
> Thou shalt not uncover the nakedness of thy daughter in law; she is thy son's wife; thou shalt not uncover her nakedness.
>
> Thou shalt not uncover the nakedness of thy brother's wife; it is thy brother's nakedness.

> Thou shalt not uncover the nakedness of a woman and her daughter, neither shalt thou take her son's daughter, or her daughter's daughter, to uncover her nakedness; for they are her near kinswomen; it is wickedness.
>
> Neither shalt thou take a wife to her sister, to vex her, to uncover her nakedness, beside the other in her life time.
>
> Also thou shalt not approach unto a woman to uncover her nakedness, as long as she is put apart for her uncleanness.
>
> Moreover thou shalt not lie carnally with thy neighbour's wife, to defile thyself with her.
>
> And thou shalt not let any of thy seed pass through the fire to Molech, neither shalt thou profane the name of thy God; I am the Lord.
>
> Thou shalt not lie with mankind as with womankind; it is abomination.
>
> Neither shalt thou lie with any beast to defile thyself therewith; neither shall any woman stand before a beast to lie down thereto; it is confusion.
>
> Defile not ye yourselves in any of these things; for in all these the nations are defiled which I cast out before you.

The consequence of disobedience of these ordinances was awful: no longer would Israel enjoy the privilege of being divided, or set apart, from all other peoples, of being a holy people living *imitato Dei*. Israel would, if it dared to trespass, be "spewed out", reduced to "vomit" and shit, a repellent mixture. There is a terrible anxiety pervading all the coercive regulations, a fear that unless severely and punitively controlled, lust would implode and society disintegrate. Only a God aware of the almost compulsive attractions of the transgression would have listed in such detail the deviations to which mankind is prone—incest, buggery, adultery, bestiality, pederasty. The severity of the sentences imposed upon culprits who in the slightest fashion deviated from the normative betrays a lack of confidence by the God of Leviticus; His savage penalties and sentencing policy have an air of panic.

Our present-day pusillanimous militant atheists, into denial, avoiding confrontation by pretending that there is no God to attack, are poor stuff; but the true atheist knows God and His weakness and possesses the strategy to allay Him and assault Him at His most vulnerable point. No-one illustrates this stance more than the Marquis de Sade who proclaimed in his *120 Days of Sodom* the precepts of his "Code of Laws". Even as Division is the leitmotif of the laws of Leviticus, so Mixture is the defining heading of Sade's alternative canon.[8] By his command, the individual merges into the group and their sexual intercourse is practised uninhibitedly, without any boundaries. All men and women, children and old people, virgins and whores, nuns and bawds, mothers and sons, fathers and daughters, brothers and sisters, uncles and nephews, noblemen and rabble[9] "higgledy-piggledy will wallow on the flagstones, on the earth, and, like animals, will interchange, will mix, will commit incest, adultery and sodomy."

Under Sade's code, children and parents as a category are abolished. "Ceremonies" are to be in place marrying children to adults; there are to be no generation gaps, no barriers separating man from woman, child from adult, mother from son, daughter from father, brother from sister. Nor must the erotic zones be separated for they are now declared to be interchangeable. In Sade's fantasy, God's measured and ordered universe is dethroned. Sade's kingdom is where undifferentiation, confusion, prevails. The aberrant offers exquisite pleasures, all inhibitions mocked: "God is shallow and ridiculous ... We have nothing but contempt for the god you are foolish enough to believe in ... He is a creature of the imagination." Sade is no hesitant non-believer like those who in contemporary mode diffidently express their reservations. Sade is the true atheist. His conviction is founded not on mere intellectual argument; it is founded on perversion. And that is why the God of Leviticus fears him.

For in each and all of us there is a latent perverse core capable of being activated. If we have not learned this from our own dreams or from the foreplay we have enjoyed in our intimacies, then there is abundant clinical evidence from both French and British analysts, often from different perspectives, instructing us that perversion is not to be considered only as a sexual disorder affecting a relatively small number; it is endemic to the human condition:[10] "Perversions" an eminent French analyst has taught us, "are a dimension of the human psyche in general, a temptation in the mind common to all of us."

Sade, alluringly, presents to us all those temptations and the Leviticus God, panic-stricken that we shall yield to them, is no less aware, as His sanguinary laws reveal, of the selfsame temptations. The philosopher Kierkegaard's insight—that what a man most dreads, he yearns for, and that what one fears, one desires is nowhere more apposite than in the thunderous prohibitions of Leviticus. Fear of death itself, the unbearable tension of expectation, can become a motive for suicide; fear of pregnancy can become a motive for conception. The fierce over-determined denunciation in Leviticus shows the writers of this book are afflicted with the same malady; they are possessed with a terrible fear of the lure of incest between the generations. The Exodus prohibition, the Ur-command of which the laws of Leviticus are an extraordinary elaboration, is that a kid must not be seethed in its mother's milk. This is the forbidden mixture, a coming together of mother and child with no boundaries, no division between them: this poisonous brew must, at all costs, be avoided. To drink one spoonful is analogous to the commission of the terrible crime of incest with your mother.

For the monotheist Jews, breaking the kosher rule had particular heinous and sinister implications, for their monotheism had precariously emerged in a region where polytheism prevailed. The quality of isolation, of separation, that characterized Jewish eating habits insulated them from the practices of the surrounding pagans. Indeed, among some of the neighbouring peoples, seething the kid in his mother's milk formed part of the worship of their goddesses. The Biblical command is therefore no rant against a peccadillo; it is a warning against the dangers of regression and a return to the archaic matriarchal law that governed early primitive societies. There, God the Father was excluded in favour of the union between mother and child. The man who does not respect *Kashrut* is thus perceived as challenging the very existence of the one and only God. Only by following the Leviticus laws would the Jews remain, as the Bible proclaims, a Holy people. *Kashrut* is therefore no culinary or aesthetic preference: for the Jews to eat kosher was to define themselves as a separate people, chosen by a God with whom, because they too were "holy", they ceaselessly identified.

For thousands of years in all the lands into which Jews have been dispersed, at each and every meal the observance of *Kashrut* has reminded them that they are "a peculiar people", and this has comforted them. Repetitively, through their diet, they did not permit any flirtation with an incestuous relationship to enter their minds; they pledged themselves in between each mouthful of food never to flirt with any fantasy of incestuous union with their mothers.

ABISHAG: THE LURE OF INCEST   135

By their abstinence, they demonstrated their allegiance to the one and only God the Father and proclaimed their observance of the Covenant, thus they were assured that He would ensure that they would be redeemed and come again unto Zion.

Our unimaginative contemporary militant atheist scientists, and the raggle-taggle crew of journalists and academics who champion them, would have us treat such expectations as illusory and the Biblical rituals that guarantee their fulfilment as mumbo-jumbo. But these critics are severely handicapped; they are deaf. Feeling that there had to be some harmonizing principle behind the patterns of the cosmos, Einstein, the great Jew scientist, long ago diagnosed their ailment: "The fanatical atheists are creatures who cannot hear the music of the spheres."[11]

In Leviticus, the shortest of the five books of Moses, that music is played out thunderously; it is meant to be heard and understood even by the simplest so that there is no obfuscation, no rhetoric, no equivocation, no recourse to the grand stately cadence we find displayed in the other books of the Torah. Its message is clear, certain and brief. Its language is not that of a refined priestly caste; it is the blunt language of the security guards' room. Commentators, repelled by its coarseness, have sometimes striven to prettify its contents, and interpreted its brutal and peremptory commands as part of a system of "correspondences". The Catholic anthropologist Mary Douglas has proposed that the detail in the regimens of rituals depicted manifest, analogically, a correspondence with a concept like Sinai or the Tabernacle.[12] Such a reading is over-sophisticated, seeking to disguise the essentially functional purpose of Leviticus. It is the book that, above all others in the Bible, engages in the protection of monotheism and the Mosaic creed from any polytheistic encroachments.

The impatient, corrupted by their liberal permissiveness, dismiss Leviticus as a catalogue of oppressive and archaic practices of a cult of the Ancient World; their enthusiasm to label all rituals as superstitions unbecoming to modern man totally misleads them. For, although like all security operations it has its excesses, its obsessiveness has one over-riding purpose: to insist that man throws away his toys, the gods he can fantasize and manipulate to provide him with answers, however mendacious, that he wishes to receive. Now he must grow up, quit the nursery inventions and face reality: there is only one God and He alone makes the rules. It is a tough world, but that is how it is; obeying the rules of Leviticus is a necessary rite of passage to attain the maturity to live, not with silly idols, but with an invisible God, never to be depicted in any form, never to be glimpsed in human form on earth.

Only the incurious cannot but wonder how such a demanding and austere monotheistic doctrine enforced by such terrifying penalties could have emerged in a little, thinly-populated land, no larger than Wales, surrounded by two mighty empires, the Assyrian and Egyptian, both of which were wholly dedicated to pagan worship of scores of well-established gods and goddesses. The Book of Leviticus was assembled by priestly writers in the sixth century BCE but its contents were not new; they were precipitated by events that had taken place 1,000 years earlier and it is only if we turn to those events, when the astounding Akhenaton reigned as Pharaoh over Egypt, can we begin to understand how Leviticus came into being and why many of its tenets still challenge us in the 21st century.

***

No historical figure has captured my imagination more than the Pharaoh who, 14 centuries before Christ was born, founded and imposed upon his subjects during his 17-year turbulent reign the first anti-polytheistic creed. The revolution of Akhenaton was not only the first but also the most radical and violent eruption of counter-religion in the history of mankind.[13] Temples were closed and images of old Egyptian gods were destroyed, their names erased and their cults discontinued. No derogation from the worship of Akhenaton's one god was permitted. The revered Egyptologist James Breasted wound up his classic study of Akhenaton's reign in these words:[14]

> There died with him such a spirit as the world had never seen before—a brave soul, undauntedly facing the momentum of immemorial tradition, and thereby stepping out from the long line of conventional and colourless pharaohs, that he might disseminate ideas far and beyond the capacity of his age to understand. Among the Hebrews, seven or eight hundred years later, we look for such men; but the modern world has yet adequately to value or even acquaint itself with this man who in an age so remote and under conditions so adverse, became not only the

ABISHAG: THE LURE OF INCEST   137

world's first idealist and the world's first *individual*, but also the earliest monotheist, and the first prophet of internationalism— the most remarkable figure of the Ancient World before the Hebrews.

That Akhenaton should be so awesomely eulogized is unsurprising but care must be taken not to be so dazzled by his charisma that idealization leads us to an over-valuation of his achievements and an under-valuation of the vigour of his opponents. He had dared to challenge gods still possessed of considerable vitality. As recently as in the reign of his grandfather, Thutmosis IV, the gods of old Egypt had been at the zenith of their power.[15] They were the gods of a nation which can be said to have existed for more than 2,000 years, during which a plethora of polytheistic beliefs had developed. The tribal gods which had first abounded had evolved to become specific to individual cities and some had then subsumed such local gods and had been elevated into national gods. Of these, the presiding deity, Amun, originally the god of Thebes, was the most powerful and in an endeavour to contain his rival national god of the city of Heliopolis, the sun-god Ra, the Theban priests had striven to annex him, to identify the two deities under the one name of Amun-Ra, king of the gods. The manoeuvre was only a partial success; the priests of Heliopolis were ever resentful and the rivalries and tensions between the two groups were continuously reflected in the court of the Pharaoh. It was at a time of such acute religious controversy that Akhenaton, little more than a boy, came to the throne.

As the boy grew into manhood his resentment, prompted by the increasing attempts by the Theban priesthood to usurp the state, grew. The Theban gods became ever more distasteful to him and as part of the political élite's intrigues of the time he strengthened his allegiance to the sun-god of Heliopolis now rejoicing under the name of Aton. How eventually he rid Aton of the old associations and yet another god, how he dared to proclaim that the sun itself was but a symbol and that it was its heat, its life-giving intangible essence, that made the sun the foremost deity, is the wondrous story of one god-intoxicated man's attempt to emancipate humanity from thousands of years of superstition. This remarkable advance towards monotheism was however in a form, as the committed Christian archaeologist and excavator Arthur Weigall stressed, that made it a forerunner anticipatory of Christianity rather than Mosaic doctrine.

Akhenaton had the same confidence as Christ in challenging the establishment for he, like Christ, believed he was the Son of the God that he worshipped. More, the notion that he was the Son of God on earth—a concept of the physical presence of God that was to be abhorrent to the later Mosaic believers—brought him to express the wish that his Father would ever be gentle to him, thus creating a god that was loving, tender, and compassionate. The destructiveness of the sun was never referred to in Akhenaton's exposition of Aton; the pitiless orb under which Egypt sweats and groans each summer had nothing in common with the gentle Father conceived of by Akhenaton. This is not a judgmental god. There is no wrath in him. He is not a stranger speaking through the roar of thunder. Thirteen hundred years before the birth of Christ, Akhenaton was preaching "God is Love", a forgiving merciful god.

Akhenaton's god is the progenitor of the New Testament God, not the God of Justice of the Old Testament. Aton is a deity to whose tender heart human bloodshed made no appeal. Unlike his belligerent predecessors who had built the Egyptian Empire, Akhenaton was so opposed to war that he persistently refused to offer armed resistance to the subsequent revolts which occurred in his Asiatic dominions. His pacifism, so akin to contemporary Christian pacifism, was to be a contributory cause of his eventual downfall. Akhenaton's god was indeed no macho god laying down the law like Israel's God at Sinai; instead, what was attributed to him were all the feminine virtues.

And as he was, so Akhenaton, son of Aton, was depicted. In all the various images exhumed by the archaeologists, Akhenaton is depicted as effeminate, lacking a phallus or, more usually, with an explicit hermaphrodite anatomy. The manner in which he directed he should be depicted, with all physical characteristics heavily emphasized—sometimes to the point of caricature, sometimes grotesquely—clearly mean he was determined that his self-perception, and his people's perception of him, should be that of a leader possessed of the powers of the hermaphrodite. And those powers, he intimated, were a reflection of those possessed by Aton who was in effect both god and goddess. Later on such notions were emphatically not to be found in place in the uncompromising Mosaic Code, but the Mariolatry embedded within Christianity—with the Virgin Mary playing the same succouring rôle as that attributed to the feminine dimensions of Aton—resonate with the doctrine expounded with the two men believing in their own divinity, Akhenaton and Jesus.

There are other significant congruences between the tenets of Akhenaton's religion and those that were later to emerge in Christianity; both creeds affirm a belief in the individual after-life, and both do so in terms that are quite alien to Jewish doctrine. Akhenaton believed that when a man died his soul continued to exist as a kind of astral, immaterial ghost, sometimes resting in the dreamy halls of heaven and sometimes visiting, in shadowy form, the haunts of the earthly life:[16]

> By some of the inscriptions one is led to suppose, as in the Fourth Article of the Christian faith, so in the teachings of Akhenaton, the body was thought to take again after death its "flesh, bones, and all things appertaining to the perfection of man's nature".

Akhenaton was too tender-hearted to postulate a hell in which, as the Christian was later to believe, an evil man would, after Judgment, be cast into an inferno. He expurgated from his doctrine the old Egyptian threat that man on death would be brought before the throne of Osiris and his soul weighed and, if found wanting, would be devoured by a monster; if the scales turned in his favour he would be accepted into a blissful heaven. In place of such a deterrent Akhenaton, as discovered inscriptions reveal, warned the wicked that there would be no future life for them—that they would be annihilated.

All these emphases upon the nature of the immortality that would be the reward for each Aton-believer are not dissimilar in kind to those to be found within the Christian credo proffering life ever after to those who come to Jesus. But such individual salvation and reward was not on offer in the monotheistic credo which the Hebrews, under Moses, brought out of Egypt. Theirs was a religion whose aim was not the salvation of the individual but the well-being and perfection of a group, of the Jews, and ultimately of the whole human race; the aim is always defined in terms of the collective. Indeed, we see in its most fruitful period, that of the divine revelation and the Prophets, Judaism eschewed any unambiguous ideal of individual immortality and of reward and punishment after death. These preoccupations, so obsessive in Akhenaton's code and Christian theology, are absent:[17]

> The religious and moral inspiration of the Prophets was derived not from any belief of that kind but from the conviction of their belonging to the chosen people which had, according to their belief, a divine call to make national life the embodiment of the highest form of religion and morality.

Often this Jewish insistence to eschew speculation about individual immortality has been deliberately obscured by the subtle mistranslation of the Hebrew Bible. The Christian renditions to be found in the King James Bible have imaginatively provided us with superb poetry but sometimes accuracy has been relegated to aesthetics—as in the notorious example of Psalm 23, that most comforting psalm known to all of us beginning "The Lord is my shepherd; I shall not want". That wondrous poem has, by its ending, skewed the psalmist's intention. It concludes with intimations of immortality: "I will dwell in the house of the Lord for ever." A Christian notion of the after-life is here grafted upon a Hebrew text where no such promise is held out; "and I shall dwell in the house of the Lord for many long days" is a direct and more accurate translation for, as Robert Alter has put it:[18] "The viewpoint of the poem is in and of the here and now and it is in no way eschatological." And that anti-Akhenaton and anti-Christian perspective of the limited span of life awarded to the individual was to remain in place. Even in later times, after the Babylonian exile had put an end to the free national life of the Jews, the response to a desire for an individual salvation was tempered; always it was subordinated to a religious consciousness which had as its highest aim a collective goal. The tradition has been maintained and today in the synagogue, in the daily and festival prayer-books, we find only a minority of the prayers turn on the personal needs of the individual worshipper while the overwhelming majority deal with the concerns of the nation and of the whole human race.

The distinctions that were in Akhenaton's religion and those which were soon to emerge in the Mosaic doctrines are, however, certainly not confined to issues relating to immortality. They are

ABISHAG: THE LURE OF INCEST   141

differences that Freud in the most audacious of his works, *Moses and Monotheism*, where he wishes to demonstrate the monotheistic congruences between the two religions, has tended to smudge. What essentially distinguishes Mosaic doctrine from Akhenaton's worship of Aton, and indeed from Christianity, is its absolute determination to make religious and moral consciousness independent of any definite human form, and to attach it without any mediating term to an abstract incorporeal ideal. Even as we cannot conceive of Christianity without Jesus, so Aton-worship cannot be imagined without Akhenaton; both religions link religious and moral consciousness with the figure of a particular man who is to be regarded as the ideal, as absolute perfection, the worship of whom is an essential part of the religion which is inconceivable without him.

In the Aton religion the rôle of Akhenaton was flaunted; indeed the German Egyptologist Jan Assmann, evidently finding the religion so saturated with Akhenaton's egotism and noting that its tenets and hymns are all related to the king as the ultimate god of creation, denies it any theistic claim whatsoever and describes it as a "pharaoh-centric" religion.[19] Akhenaton instituted not only a religion of love but also of self-adoration. Sculpture, as an art form, was evidently his great delight but for the most part it was he, and members of his family, who are portrayed. His exhibitionism was unlimited: in scanty attire, in thin tunics, he had himself portrayed thousands of times. Despite the wanton destruction of so many of his depictions during the counter-revolution that ultimately deposed him, it is said that this only son of his god has left us possessing more original portrayals in sculpture, bas-relief, and paintings of himself and his family "than of all the kings and queens together, from William the Conqueror to the present Queen".[20]

All this is in striking contrast to posterity having at its disposal no graven image of the man Moses who, lacking Akhenaton's astonishing delusions of grandeur, permitted his narcissism to be assuaged by making the immodest but limited claim that although he was not the equal, or son, of God he was nevertheless the messenger of his invisible God. To thus, by contrast, emphasize the conceits of Akhenaton is not necessarily to join in the derogation of his designation by those modern historians who have dismissed his monotheism as at most mere henotheism—the belief in a supreme god without any assertion of his unique nature; but nevertheless the exercise, yet again, alerts us to the distinctiveness of Mosaic doctrine from that of Akhenaton's.[21]

And above all others there is one issue revealing that there is between the two religions a chasm, not mere nice theological differences: it is the gap which Leviticus, in terrifying terms, warns us can never be bridged; any attempt to bridge that gap brings disaster; at all costs one must avoid walking near its edge. Fearful that any close human relationship could be dangerously evocative of incestuous desires between father and daughter, and mother and son, Leviticus wisely extends the taboo against coupling between any who could be deemed to be members of an extended family. But, as the text makes clear, the Mosaic prohibition is primarily directed against any sex between father and daughter or mother and son; that is the ultimate taboo.[22] It was that ultimate taboo that Akhenaton is believed to have publicly and persistently broken. There is considerable evidence, although challenged by some, that the young Akhenaton married his own mother, Queen Tiy.

It was the psychoanalyst Karl Abrahams, one of the earliest followers of Freud who, in 1912, long before Freud had written of Akhenaton in his *Moses and Monotheism*, drew attention to the singular attachment of Akhenaton to his mother and postulated that it was the hidden source of Akhenaton's religious innovations.[23] Abrahams suggested it was Akhenaton's rivalry with his father Amenhotep for the possession of his mother that had led him to erase the name of the god Amun and turn to the worship of Aton; that Akhenaton, in mutilating the name of his father in all available inscriptions, and by assuming the new name of Akhenaton, was attempting to wipe out the memory of his sire; by destroying his name, his *ka*, his soul in the after-life would be delivered to destruction.

Abrahams' 1912 thesis, a half-century later, was daringly developed by the provocative Russian historian Emmanuel Verlikovsky who marshalled much persuasive evidence that Akhenaton's warm relationship with Queen Tiy was consummated, and that she bore him a son who Akhenaton acknowledged he had sired. Although incest between brother and sister was a regular and accepted traditional feature of the Egyptian royal household, incest between mother and son was generally regarded as an abomination—but it was not so regarded by the people from whose family Tiy had sprung, the Mitanni people who dwelt in a region of Northern Iran and whose kings prayed to Indo-Iranian gods:[24]

> The Iranians (Persians) had an approach to the problem of incest very different to that of other peoples of antiquity. They had an ethical religious concept and practice of xvaetvadadha which means, according to ancient authors and modern scholars alike, the marriage of parents with their children ... The ancient Iranian texts commend and in certain religious ceremonies even command that xvaetvadadha ...

Akhenaton did not seek to conceal the nature of his relationship with Tiy and it does indeed seem most probable that the affront this occasioned played a considerable part in the inevitable and successful counter-revolution by those who swept him from Egypt's history, stigmatized him as a criminal and reinstated the old gods. Anyone who had been much influenced by Akhenaton's expositions or had been, as a prince, part of Akhenaton's entourage which, Freud has canvassed, was the lot of Moses, could only remain in Egypt as a renegade or as an outlaw. Freud put forward in his hypothesis that one of the consequences for Moses after Akhenaton's downfall was:[25]

> *The death of Akhenaton and the abolition of his religion meant the end of all his expectations. He could remain in Egypt only as an outlaw or as a renegade. Perhaps as a governor of a frontier province he had come in contact with a Semitic tribe which had immigrated into it a few generations earlier. Under the necessity of his disappointment and loneliness he turned to these foreigners and with them sought compensation for his losses. He chose them as his people and tried to realise his ideals in them.*

Acting according to his ideals, Moses, finding the polytheism of the counter-revolution intolerable, set out to found a new kingdom with a new people "to whom he would present the worship, the religion, which Egypt had disdained". But the precepts embodied in the religion that Moses brought to the Hebrews were far harsher than those enunciated by his mentor Akhenaton; they gave no absolution for failing, as incestuous and narcissistic

Akhenaton did, to achieve the necessary instinctual renunciations. Not for Moses any dependence on the sun-god of Aton to which Akhenaton continued to adhere. There was to be no image, however masked or attenuated, of God; one must worship a God one could not see, one without name or countenance. This meant, as Freud stressed, that:

> A sensory perception was given second place to what may be called an abstract idea—a triumph of intellectuality over sensuality or, strictly speaking, an instinctual renunciation ...

It was a huge demand for any leader to make upon his followers; and it was to be a demand that repeatedly they and their descendants could not always meet. When Egyptologists today complain that "the Hebrew Moses of the Bible has kept an image of Egypt alive in Western tradition that was thoroughly antithetic to Western ideals, the image of Egypt as the land of despotism, hubris, sorcery, brute-worship, and idolatry",[26] they do not fully appreciate how what they deem to be Egyptophobia was a defensive action. The condemnations against all the attractions luring the Hebrews back to the fleshpots of Egypt, the prohibitions acting as deterrents to those who would lapse, had one over-riding aim: to sustain what Freud called "the great advance in intellectuality".

If that advance was to be held, if there was to be no retreat to the comfort zone of Egyptian polytheism and the more permissive religion of Akhenaton, then, no matter what distortions had to be made, the text of the Biblical canon had in every possible way to disavow influences upon Mosaic doctrine. Nowhere do we see this more dramatically or obscurely illustrated than in the recitation in the text that the son of Moses, or perhaps Moses himself—the text is so obscure that scholars have failed definitively to unravel its contents—was not initially circumcised. Angered by the tale that the Moses family was one of the uncircumcised, that the man who was to lead out of Egypt God's holy people (holy because of the Covenant made between Abraham and God and endorsed by the rite of circumcision) had not followed the ancient commandment, the scribes adopted a fearful and ambivalent oral legend—that God was about to kill Moses for being uncircumcised but he was saved at the last minute by his wife performing the operation herself, apparently upon the son. Rather than giving any acknowledgement that Moses was an Egyptian and would therefore have followed the traditional practice which Herodotus[27] has told us prevailed in Egypt, and which is something confirmed by discovered mummies and pictures in tombs, this weird tale is in indeed a tortuous attempt to establish that Moses was a Hebrew, and that his message came from God and not from some polytheistic Egyptian lore.

But often the scribes collating the oral and written legends that were to become the canonical contents of the Hebrew Bible did not so densely obfuscate the dangerous nostalgia for Egypt and its temptations that needed to be expurgated if the Mosaic laws were to be upheld. Sometimes they could not forbear to tell of the delights that Egyptian transgressions could bring and, vicariously, in the telling, they would share those thrills before reluctantly submitting to the command of Leviticus; and then firmly, but with obvious regret, they would end their flirtation with Egypt's and Akhenaton's condonation of deviances, not least of incestuous indulgences.

All these ambivalences are revealed to us if we delve into the Biblical legends telling of the miscreants who dared to defy Leviticus' prohibitions against incest. In the little enchanting tale of Abishag, the beauty queen of Ancient Israel, we shall see all these ambivalences explicitly and daringly revealed.

***

Dazzled as we must be by the great poetry of the Hebrew Bible that can only have been the work of inspired individual poets, we tend to forget how much of the canon is in fact the end- product of hard-working consensus-seeking committees. There are notable occasions when we see the process at work, when the Temple scribes gathered together the many oral and written accounts, fabled or accurate, of Israel's history that were in circulation, and then edited and selected those they deemed to be appropriate to be placed in what was in effect the reference library of the Temple; it was by drawing upon such material that the Bible was eventually created.[28,29]

Sometimes such collations were precipitated by outside events. The Persians sought, in their dealings with conquered nations, to provide their rule with a solid base by sanctifying a codified law of the land as the law of the Persian king. It was in pursuit of such a policy that around 450 BCE Ezra was mandated by the governing Persian authorities to provide the province of Judah with a national constitution.[30] To fuse the many and various extant documents to produce the required national law would have been a huge task. Ezra could only have achieved it with the aid of the priestly scribes who, working probably in groups, would have submitted their consensus material to him. It was their work, under Ezra's supervision and with his approval, that constitutes what was, much later, to be canonized as the Five Books of Moses.

Another significant sifting of available oral and written material came about two centuries later. It was a period when there was a growing class of literate laymen and when widespread Messianic expectations were abroad, and apparently it was in response to this *zeitgeist* that the scribes of the Jerusalem Temple prepared, in what seems a flurry of committee work, definitive editions of the works which we now have in the Bible as the Psalms, the Book of Proverbs and the Books of various Prophets.

To be fluent in committee-speak is, perforce, a considerable advantage in interpreting and assessing Bible texts; it is an advantage which, albeit with a sense of shame, I can immodestly claim. I have spent, perhaps squandered, literally many years of my life as chairman of far too many committees not to have learned the language. From my teens, when I was chairman in Cardiff of the young socialists, to my adult years as chairman of the Cardiff Labour Party, then as chairman of city council committees and, later, in the Commons, I was at various times presiding over the Welsh Parliamentary Party and acting as the chairman in invigilating select committees, I have lived my working life entangled in dreary but necessary committee work. I have sat on Home Office advisory committees on abortion, on adoption, on penal affairs; I have spent years as chairman of a charitable trust, as a member of a university council, and served upon the governing bodies of an opera company and an art college—even this lamentably and chasteningly does not exhaust the list. I proffer it merely as a plea that I may be regarded as sufficiently qualified not to be judged presumptuous in insisting Holy Writ must be read irreverently.

Almost invariably the committees upon which I sat had one overriding objective: the achievement, if at all possible, by its members of unanimity. Committee reports or recommendations undermined by dissent or minority reports lack authority; and that is the quality that the Temple scribes had to seek when they worked together on a presentation that would be deemed to be Holy Writ. Such consensus required compromises, and it is surely not anachronistic to assert that the same psycho-dynamics that operate in the notoriously quarrelsome academic committees in today's universities were at work when the opinionated priestly scribes made their determinations; compromises then, as now, would not have been easily reached.

Inevitably compromises tend to lack clear and unequivocal definition because ambiguity is often necessary to bridge the differences between contending protagonists. Awkward findings may be omitted and facts suppressed, potential mine-fields carefully left unexploded, and sometimes the gaps in the final summation are of greater significance than the proffered rendition. In Biblical texts repeatedly we find oddities and inconsequentialities but, once the gaps are given as much attention as the substantive material, there is revealed a perfectly coherent statement full of important information.[31] We need to be very wary when we find Biblical texts that appear nonsensical; much may be hidden by committee-speech babble.

But whatever internecine disputations may have taken place between the scribes and which we find reflected in the often subtle circumlocutions and ambiguities of the final text, there was never within that text any erosion or qualification of the dogma that God is one and invisible and that there was to be no yielding to the temptations of Egypt's polyandry or Akhenaton's monolatry. Egypt's offer of life after death seems to have left the priestly scribes strangely unmoved; perhaps they regarded it as a confidence trick. Certainly they in no way sought to disguise the chilling message that "We must all die; we are like water that is poured out on the ground and cannot be gathered up".[32] But the same indifference could not be shown to the sensual permissiveness proffered by Egypt. The physical pleasures available on this earth, not in some conjured-up afterworld, above all in the incestuous couplings condoned by Egypt, could not be easily resisted. Repeatedly we find we are regaled by near-pornographic tales when the scribes are fluttering like moths around the flame as they tell us of incestuous liaisons and of the punishments wreaked upon the miscreants engaged in incestuous practices. One such illustrative story is that of the rape of Tamar.[33]

The tale is to be found within the wondrous Books of Samuel. All the leading characters in the books—Samuel, Saul, David, Joab, Jonathan, Amnon, Absalom, and others—are full of human contradictions, wavering between the polarities of love and hate, duty and the pleasure principle, compassion and brutality, humility and over-arching arrogance and ambition. The whole work is a great historical romance. The hold of these two books on the reader, it has been pertinently said, is that of a novelist or playwright rather than that of a historian. Sidney Brichto, in his illuminative interpretative translation[34] of a work that is essentially a great literary classic, has proffered an explanation as to how such an unlikely work has entered the canon. Brichto convincingly suggests that this story in Samuel of the emergence of kings in Israel is a compromise; that it was precipitated by the demand for human monarchs by the undisciplined tribes of Israel who lacked sufficient faith in the source of their deliverance from Egypt and their conquest of the Promised Land. They, reassuringly, were granted earthly kings by God and in return they reaffirmed allegiance to the invisible Him.

But the Him to whom they gave obeisance, although they pretended otherwise, as was often the mode in the gods of all nations, was created in their own image. There is no more striking illustration of the operation of the psychological mechanism of projection than is to be found in the *Genesis* fallacy that man was created in the image of God; on the contrary, He is created by man in his image. And nowhere in the Bible is this imaginative fallacy more exposed than in the conduct of the interventionist God of Samuel[35] who

> is given the leading rôle of hero. It is He who moves the plot along, determining the success and failure of the human protagonist with inexplicable changes of attitude, more consistent with the vagaries of the human heart than that of a perfect deity.

All the vagaries of the human heart are indeed to be found in this imperfect deity. When the flawed deity unloads his anguishes upon his worshippers, sometimes they masochistically submit to his severe admonitions and sometimes they rebel. Always between God and Man tensions and ambivalences abound, tumult envelopes the narrative. Samuel is not a book to be commended to those who turn to religion for consolation, to escape from painful reality. In Samuel one certainly has corroboration of the view of the renowned theologian Gabriel Josipovici[36] who affirms that the Bible shows that:

> In the end the only thing that can truly heal and console us is not the voice of consolation but the voice of reality. That is the way the world is—neither fair nor equitable. What are you going to do about it? How are you going to live so as to be contented and fulfilled? And it contains no answers, only shows us various forms of response to these questions.

And because in Samuel reality is not shirked, the erotic compulsions that universally challenge every man and woman are starkly depicted, never sentimentalized. In the tale of the rape of Tamar, lust, deceit, betrayal, shame, and self-disgust are mercilessly anatomized. Israel's struggle to resist the ever-present Egyptian temptation of incest is epitomized in Amnon's transgressive desire for his own sister.

The basic story is simple. Amnon, son of King David, lusts for his beautiful half-sister; Tamar, prompted by a corrupting cousin on the pretence that Amnon is ill and needs to have food brought to him, unsuspectingly is lured by Amnon to his supposed sick-bed and there, failing to seduce her, he violently rapes her. But the priestly scribes do not recite the story abruptly; they linger lasciviously in their telling of the self-inflicted lacerations suffered byAmnon as he struggles with his incestuous desires; and when his lust is spent, we are told of an epiphany of self-disgust and shame, of the emptiness and loneliness afflicting both Amnon and his victim. As so often within the Books of Samuel, we are here given a coruscating display of word-craft in brilliant and varied deployment of dialogue, in several shifts of narrative perspective, and in literary allusion.

The story is far more than a recounting of the agonies and ecstasies of one man and his sister; it is therefore inspirationally told with an artistry worthy of its essentially allegorical content. Once again the warning is being given of the consequences of disobeying Leviticus and looking back to polytheistic Egypt where, as in the Eighteenth Dynasty, the throne was often inherited not by a son but by a daughter, and the son, by marrying the heiress, his sister or half-sister, acquired title to the throne. For a member of Israel's royal family to relapse into not dissimilar behaviour was a capital offence, and accordingly the God of Samuel saw that Amnon was, as punishment, killed by his elder brother. The tale is told confidently. A sister in the scale of relationships is a second degree relative and incest between siblings the scribes seemed able to handle without excessive panic; but it is otherwise when they are required to tell, or hint, of incest between first degree relations, between mother and son or father and daughter. Throughout the Bible and the Apocrypha we are repeatedly made aware how fraught with anxiety are the renderings of legends of incest between a parent and child; there we find that distortions, feints, and suppression abound. Fear of the attraction being condemned is ever present as with circumlocution and omission we learn of the perverted desires of the protagonists. The priestly élite had intuited what Freud made explicit in his seminal *Totem and Taboo*:[37] that civilization began with that primal taboo. The scribes often recoiled in horror even as they dutifully recorded the terrible transgression which could bring about a regression to barbarism and, as in the cities and plains of Sodom and Gomorrah, the obliteration of mankind.

In Sodom there were no boundaries; it is depicted in the Bible as the ultimate Sin City where differentiation between generations and sexes was unacknowledged, where virginity was scorned and where an overtly homosexual culture operated. When God sent His comely male messengers to visit Lot, who had taken up residence there, it was only His intervention that saved them from gang rape by the baying lustful citizens. There was no limit to their wickedness; nor to the attractiveness that their perversions excited. When God ordered Lot and his family to leave Sodom, which He would then destroy, Lot's sons-in-law, reluctant to leave the swinging city, were deaf to the warnings; they remained, and were destroyed; and Lot's wife, although told to run for her life, was torn by her desire to stay, reluctant to obey the command to renounce city life for the desolate desert. Hesitating in her flight, she stood still and turned around to gaze lingeringly at the city of exquisite transgressive desires. Her nostalgia betrayed her; for her sinful thoughts, she was punished: she was turned into a pillar of salt.

Here is to be found a tale foretold. Never return. The wandering Hebrews, looking back to the fleshpots of Egypt were to be condemned to 40 years of wandering and were never to enter the

Promised Land. The crime of nostalgia for an imagined world without inhibitions and prohibitions is irredeemable.

But despite the recrimination that follows the committal of the crime, despite the terrifying metamorphosis of Lot's wife, still the Genesis story-tellers could not desist in their desire to vicariously enjoy guilt-free incest. It so often fell to me as a young lawyer to seek to mitigate the offences of my criminal clients by pleading they committed it while drunk. That same stale and unconvincing defence is used to acquit Lot of responsibility for his incestuous gambols with his two daughters. We are told that after he left Sodom with his now attenuated family his elder daughter plied him with wine and, while he was in his soporific state, she lay with him: "He was not aware of her lying down nor her rising up". Nevertheless it evidently was a very active night and, finding it most fulfilling, Lot's daughter heartily recommended the performance to her younger sister who then enthusiastically followed her example. Once again, Lot is plied with drink and, once again, after the younger daughter has had her fill, he is totally exonerated. The verse is repeated: "And he perceived not when she lay down, nor when she arose."[38] For the behaviour of the daughters the text affords a shade more plausible excuse. The daughters claimed they had slept with their father not out of desire but because they, mistakenly believing that the retribution God had wrought on Sodom had wiped out all men, wished to ensure that Lot should have the blessing of descendants. At this point the textual editors must have gulped hard. They make no comment on the audacious excuse but they knew that the kicks they got out of telling of the incestuous romping of Lot's family, and the absolutions they were granting, could lead their readers into temptations. The whitewashing must cease and, somewhere, punishment meted out. And so they, disgracefully, found hapless scapegoats. It was decreed that the two innocent sons, Moab and Ammon, born of the incestuous unions, were destined to carry the guilt of their forebears: their descendants were to be treated as bastards, as pariahs, never to enter the community of Israel,[39] always to be excluded from the Promised Land.

Although usually presented less overtly than in the tale of Lot, the powerful desire for trans-generational sex and the punishment it attracts is a staple *leitmotiv* of many an anecdote in the Bible and the Apocrypha. Not daring to unequivocally depict copulation between father and daughter, a proximate tale is woven so that lustful old men can delight in, or seek to delight in, the possession of beautiful young women. Such a story is that of Susanna and the Elders.[40]

The story tells of two community elders who lust after the virtuous young wife, Susanna. They hide in the garden where she bathes in the nude and they emerge to threaten her that unless she sleeps with them, they will publicly declare that they found her *in flagrante delicto* with a young lover. She rejects them and refuses to yield to their blackmail. They carry out their threat but when she is put on trial for adultery, the Prophet Daniel appears and by a deft piece of cross-examination proves the elders are lying. The lascivious elders are consequently put to death for their mendacious slander.

The story is known to most of us not from a reading of the Apocrypha but from its notorious deployment as a celebration of the exquisite pleasures of voyeurism; the great European artists Titian, Tintoretto, Rubens, Gentileschi, Lely and many others have, in their glorious renderings, all joined the lurking prurient elders who from their hiding-place were aroused as they gazed upon the bathing naked and curvaceous Susanna.

The elders were in their gaze and importunings acting out the prohibited, breaking an ultimate taboo; and for that there could be only one consequence: they were sentenced to death. Whenever a hint of trans-generational incest enters a Biblical story the sentence the participants attract is mandatory; throughout the Bible and Apocrypha a terrible curse or death sentence always follows the actual or yearned-for consummation. Throughout the Bible and Apocrypha the tales are told as warnings to resist the temptations of trans-generational sex. Perhaps the most vivid, explicit and exotic of these admonitory stories is that told of young Absalom, the son of David who, rebelling against his father, defiantly proclaimed himself king and, to validate his claim, publicly fornicated with David's wives on the roof of the royal palace.[41] Such transgenerational incestuous misconduct was unforgivable: punishment must be inflicted upon Absalom to match his crime. His nemesis was, predictably, fated to be terrible and gruesome. While riding his mule, his hair became entangled with the lower branches of an overhanging tree and as the mule moved on, he was left dangling helplessly in the air only to be discovered by David's supporters.

His was to be a lingering death: three arrows were successively thrust into his body and only then was he cut down and killed. Yet in all these Bible stories, where retributive punishment is declared to be the price to be paid for yielding to the temptation of acting out in inter-generational sex actual or fantasized incest, there is a notable exception: no punishment looms over the enchanting tale of Abishag, Israel's young and virginal beauty queen who slept in the bed of the aged King David.

***

In the First Book of Kings the story of Abishag is simply told:

> Now King David was old and stricken in years; and they covered him with clothes, but he gat no heat.
> Wherefore his servants said unto him, Let there be sought for my lord the king a young virgin; and let her stand before the king, and let her cherish him, and let her lie in thy bosom, that my lord the king may get heat.
> So they sought for a fair damsel throughout all the coasts of Israel, and found Abishag a Shunammite, and brought her to the king.
> And the damsel was very fair, and cherished the king, and ministered to him; but the king knew her not.[42]

We should not be disarmed by this arch and elegant recounting of the tale; its affectation of transparency should not be allowed to deceive us; its *faux-naïveté* makes us wary. This is a story to be read with the repeated warnings from the time of the prophet Jeremiah down to Freud ringing in our ears: beware when an enchanting traditional story perpetuated by its oral telling is morphed into a written text. The "lying pens of the scribes" Jeremiah warned,[43] could subvert tradition by a mere sleight of the pen and a written text could encourage a superficial mode of thought that concentrated on information, sometimes spurious, rather than wisdom. The transition from an oral tradition to written text cannot only lead to religious stridency,[44] by giving the reader an unrealistic certainty about essentially ineffable matters,[45] but, more, by its editing, as Freud emphasized, it can so mutilate the story's content that its meaning can be "changed into its reverse".[46] Much of what Freud wrote in his scrutiny of the Biblical text of Exodus is applicable to the Abishag story to be found in Kings:

> On the one hand it has been subjected to revisions which have falsified it in the sense of their secret aims, have mutilated and amplified it and have even changed it into its reverse; on the other hand a solicitous piety has presided over it and has sought to preserve everything as it was, no matter whether it was consistent or contradicted itself. Thus almost everywhere noticeable gaps, disturbing repetitions and obvious contradictions have come about—indications which reveal things to us which it was not intended to communicate. In its implications the distortion of a text resembles a murder: the difficulty is not in perpetrating the deed, but in getting rid of its traces. We may well lend the word *Entstellung* [distortion] the double meaning to which it has a claim but of which today it makes no use. It should mean not only '*to change the appearance of something*' but also to '*put something in another place, to displace*'. Accordingly, in many instances of textual distortion, we may nevertheless count upon finding what has been suppressed and disallowed hidden away somewhere else, though changed and torn from its context.

Thus alerted by Freud, we anticipate the scribes, wrestling with a tale dangerously evocative of an incestuous father and daughter relationship, would strive to sanitize the story; our expectation is fully met. But before we patronize or mock the droll efforts of the redactors to de-sexualize, as they have, the Abishag tale, let us remind ourselves how tortuously and far more clumsily efforts were made, more than 2,500 years later in Protestant England, to come to terms with the Leviticus injunctions against incest when, thanks to Henry VIII, the convoluted dispensations, hitherto made available by accommodating popes to validate royal marriages that would otherwise breach the consanguinity laws, were no longer in place. Nowhere are the resulting dilemmas epitomized more clearly than in the extraordinary emotions aroused in the 19th and early 20th centuries when repeated attempts were made to emancipate the law from the restrictions against marriage imposed by the canonical table of the Book of Common Prayer. For the Church, marriage between husband and wife made husband and wife one flesh so, it was affirmed, just as it was forbidden to marry one's sister, it was no less incestuous for a widower to subsequently marry his sister-in-law. On at least 17 occasions a Deceased Wife's Sisters' Marriage Bill was presented in Parliament but on each occasion failed to reach the statute book. Gladstone thundered that "the purity of sisterly love itself" was "threatened to be tainted by the invasion of possible jealousies". In his view, although the family was fundamental to society and natural affection was the cement of the family, sexual attraction was different. To permit sexual attractions within the intimate family circle was to "confuse the two relationships and unsettle the whole basis of society". In the light of such opposition, it was not until 1907 that the Bill, albeit with many lacunae, was finally enacted and permitted a widower to marry his sister-in-law.[47]

Unlike the English legislators, when faced with the task of dealing with a situation enveloped in incestuous innuendoes, the apprehensive scribes refused to become entangled with its dangerous implications. They brazenly evaded any acknowledgement that any such existed; they went into denial. Abishag goes into the king's bedroom; there she "cherished" him; she "ministered" to him; but there was no sex. And lest it be thought that euphemisms had been used to conceal what happened between the sheets, defiantly and improbably the scribes add that "the king knew her not". They had no need, therefore, to mete out punishment to this couple; their relationship, they claimed, was pure and sexless.

Apart from the inherent improbability of the tale's denouement, there are many reasons to suspect that we are being presented with a heavily censored version of an original oral story that had, throughout the ages, so vigorously gripped the imagination that its claim to be included in the canon could not be resisted by the frightened redactors. So they censored the story and freed it from its temptations: Abishag remains a virgin; David is rendered impotent. Since the story is almost irrelevant to the narrative of the chapter in which it appears, it has indeed every appearance of being a belated compromise reluctantly interpolated.

But the killjoy scribes in so "murdering" the texts left—as Freud has remarked, is so often the legacy of text mutilators—too many traces of their crime for it to remain undiscovered. Following

Abishag's coming to David, he evidently rallied. Far from being a depressed and impotent wretch, unresponsive to his despairing attendant servants, we now see a hyper-active king determined that on his death his kingdom should remain intact and be governed wisely by the successor he had chosen. To that end we see David receiving and negotiating with his erstwhile lover Bathsheba, and with the prophet Nathan, taking the initiative and acting, successfully, to thwart the coup d'etat of the would-be usurper Adonijah, and then consolidating the state by abdicating and placing his son Solomon formally on the throne, provided with the benefit of his detailed advice and patronage. No man could have more courageously faced his death and ensured that his affairs, and those of the nation, were in order before he told his son: "Í go the way of all the earth." David achieved what is the hope of all: he died alive.

The mean snivelling scribes, rather than acknowledge the success of his relationship with Abishag that is displayed so vividly in the dynamism of his last years, depicted David as senile, whimpering, and impotent. But they failed in their attempt to protect their orthodoxies. Inter-generational sex reminiscent of incest should have ended in disaster and punishment but here, to their consternation, it was bounteously rewarded. The idiosyncratic, the creative eccentric, is happily ever a threat to the innate conservatism of rule-bound Establishments.

The redactors' obfuscations came no less to grief in their clumsy effort to pronounce Abishag an inadequate woman unable to arouse the sexual desire of the aged David. When David died, we do not find her languishing: she is too beautiful and desirable to be depicted as a retreating young woman withering in her virginity. On the contrary, the scribes, losing their thread, releasing their own repressed lusts, leave us with the distinct impression that she was a most seductive object of desire, a successful courtesan whom men would risk their lives to acquire.

This indeed was done by Adonijah, the elder brother of Solomon, who, despite the incestuous overtones of his lusting for his father's favoured paramour, conspired, on David's death, to possess Abishag and thus, as a pretender, become endowed with the aura of authority she would bring to him. The enraged Solomon, learning of the plot, condemned Adonijah to death. And so it has come about that, despite themselves, the ambivalent scribes have left us, in Abishag, not a dumb provincial beauty queen but, rather, a woman fit to be enshrined beside Eve and other alluring *femmes fatales* within the pantheon of our knowing Bible.

***

There will be those who will demur, who will pretend that such a contrary presentation of the Abishag story is a provocative tease. But, declaring an interest, I insist my interpretation is no theoretical speculation; it is arrogantly founded on proven experience—my own. When I passed my 80th birthday I was indeed, like David, old, stricken in years, and gat no heat. In the bleak years of my widowerhood, bereft of the sensuous Celtic imagination of my artist wife, I lived mechanically, alone in a very empty house. She had been a precariously poised woman to whom I had given anchorage and who, in return, had given me her startling vision. I had married her no doubt because for me she had that extra dimension. I could have married a much simpler woman and lived more prosaically, certainly less turbulently and passionately. On her death, all passion spent, I hated the silence of my home, and cursed the cancer that had killed her.

When, some years later, my psychoanalyst brother who held a chair in psychiatry in Virginia visited me, he was not deceived; the depression concealed beneath my controlled demeanour was soon apparent to his clinical eye. He deservedly had gained by his writings and lectures a national reputation in the USA in the field of marriage counselling in medical practice[48] and immediately applied his expertise to my condition, and with all the authority of an older brother peremptorily ordered me to speedily re-marry.

It was a disconcerting command, understandably ill-received by my adult children: it was not respectable; in your eighties you are supposed to gently fade away, not engage embarrassingly in new undignified matrimonial pranks. But it was the firm condition my brother attached to the proposed re-marriage that caused the ultimate outrage: the woman I was to marry must be, he insisted, much younger than me. When, after a short visit, he returned to the States, he left me years younger than when he arrived. I had been given the same advice the ageing David had received from his wise servants. Now with a fresh eye, I re-read my favourite mediaeval

Hebrew poet, Samuel Hanagid, the warrior who in the year 1050 AD exhorted:[49]

> In times of sorrow, take heart, even
> though you stand at death's door; the
> candle flares up before it dies, and
> wounded lions roar.

Now I would hearken to him and no longer would I yield to those poets from Sophocles to T.S. Eliot mourning and rationalizing their loss of youth and proclaiming the aridity of old age. The ageing Sophocles, when asked how sex was going, unconvincingly affected to have attained an anaphrodisical calm:[50,51] "I am very glad to have escaped all that, like a slave who has escaped from a savage and tyrannical master." Only one who has never been at ease with his sexuality could so eulogize old age as a liberator bringing freedom from desire. And similarly the embittered Eliot at the age of 54, projecting his own tortures and failures on to his, and everyone else's, old age, pours out his spleen:[52]

> Let me disclose the gifts reserved for age
> To set a crown upon your lifetime's effort.
> First, the cold friction of expiring sex
> Without enchantment, offering no promise
> But bitter tastelessness of shadow fruit
> As body and soul begin to fly asunder.

But I mocked Eliot's defeatist prognoses and, incited by Hanagid, moved on, scorning all the gloomy poets. For my boldness, I was rewarded. Serendipity intervened to meet my new expectation. When I met the Polish girl, a one-time qualified electrician during the Communist era in the Gdansk dockyards, she had worked her way in menial tasks, probably illegally, whilst a student at a college of art. From there she had obtained a bursary to the prestigious Royal College of Art where she was about to obtain her master's degree as a textile designer. She was comely, vital, possessed of all the sensibility of an authentic artist, but, above all, she fully met the qualification upon which my brother had insisted: she was half a century younger than me.

ABISHAG: THE LURE OF INCEST   159

With guile, patience and persistence I successfully wooed her. With cunning and stealth I forestalled the gutter press; I had already left the registry office for abroad before the scavengers were alerted to the marriage ceremony. My newly-wedded wife was bewildered by my precautions and chided me for my conceit in assuming my private life was of public interest. I knew otherwise. While, anonymously, I was quietly spending my honeymoon in a Portuguese hideout, the slobbering tabloids excitedly prepared salacious accounts of my scandalous breach of the norm. Reporting inter-generational sex lit them up: covert incest had to be exposed, mocked, and condemned; the outrage had to be advertised, and enviously they searched for embellishments which would titillate their readers even as, simultaneously, in the telling, they could enjoy their own masturbatory thrills. The embarrassed holy scribes of yore had coyly sought to conceal the erotic when recording the Abishag tale. Here the sex-obsessed reporters, familiar only with rutting not love, wished to emblazon it abroad. These illiterates would not even have heard of the early 17th-century Robert Burton who, in his profound nuanced *Anatomy of Melancholy*, spoke truly when he told us how various true love can be, and reflected: "love's limits are ample and great, and a spacious walk it hath".[53]

Looming behind every sight by an observer of an elderly commanding authoritarian figure is a perception of his own father; the responses to an old man and his conduct are pre-figured by those shaped in the early Oedipal years of the viewer. The scribes, like all little boys, fundamentally hated to believe that their fathers had ever romped with their mothers; one response to the painful reality is to fantasize that they were born of an immaculate conception, that there was no sex; this fantasy colours the scribes' judgment that David "knew not" Abishag.

The press hirelings who pursued me were no less entangled in their Oedipal conflicts. Although the precipitate was identical, their response was somewhat different: their mothers, they wished to believe, had not chosen their fathers over them but had been forced to the bed by the tyrannical father; now they would punish the rapist, besmirch him with scandal, and mock his folly. With that in mind, accompanied by photographers, they descended upon the village in Tuscany where I had long had my holiday home, and to which they wrongly assumed that I had fled; they left empty-handed. And, meantime, while I was in idyllic Portugal enjoying my renewed status as a husband, another tabloid sent a team of scavengers to Poland to scour the gutters of Gdansk. In vain did they seek for dirt. My wife's relatives whom they harassed had survived under communist rule and had a particular contempt for all informants; the interrogators were given short shrift.

Thus frustrated, awaiting our return, the pack took up positions to besiege my London home; paparazzi trespassed into my garden, selecting positions from which, clandestinely, they hoped to take derisive pictures of the honeymoon couple. But I outmanoeuvred the sniggering wretches. I pressed the buttons of friendship with responsible journalists which my parliamentary years had made available to me. I gave two "exclusive" interviews, one to an upmarket daily, one to a popular weekly and, accompanied by sedate photographs, sympathetic and understanding articles immediately appeared. Thus pre-empted, the lurid screeds that had been prepared by the hacks telling of a predatory immigrant who had seduced a dirty old man in his dotage became stale: they were spiked. The disappointed reporters returned to their sewers and the television producers clamouring for interviews were given dusty answers. The storm blew over.

Now almost a decade has passed. During all this time, even as Abishag cherished and ministered to David, so I too have been blessed by the cherishing and ministering I have received. And, even as King David responded to his awakening with Abishag by a bout of hyper-activity, so I too, as a nonagenarian, have responded to my awakening and been able, over our years together, to dedicate to my muse three books which I hope are worthy of her.

And all this is because, *pace* the lying scribes, even as David knew Abishag, I too have known the woman I love.

Notes

1. *Exodus*, ch. 23, V. 19.
2. Maimonides, M. *The Guide*, 111, ch. xxv, p. 167.
3. Friedlander, M. *The Jewish Religion*, Shapiro, Vallentyne & Co., 1931.
4. *Leviticus*, ch. 11, V. 45.
5. *Leviticus*, ch. 20, V. 24–26.

6. Alter, R. *The Five Books of Moses*, Norton, W.W., 2004.
7. *Leviticus*, ch. 18, V. 5–24.
8. Chasseguet-Smirgel, J. *Creativity and Perversion*, Free Association Books, 1992.
9. Sade, D.A.F. Marquis de, *The 120 Days of Sodom, and Other Writings*, Random House, NY, 1966.
10. Chasseguet-Smirgel, J. *Creativity and Perversion, op. cit.*; Glover, E., *Aggression and Sado-Masochism in the Pathology and Treatment of Sexual Deviations*, ed. Rosen, E., Oxford University Press, 1964; Glasser, M., *Some Aspects of the Rôle of Aggression in the Perversions*, essay in *Sexual Deviations*, ed. Rosen, E., Oxford University Press, 1979; Abse, L., *The Man Behind the Smile: Tony Blair and the Politics of Perversion*, p. 169, Robson Books, 1996.
11. Isaacson, W. *Einstein, his Life and Universe*, Simon & Schuster, 2007.
12. Douglas, M. *Jacob's Tears: The Priestly Work of Reconciliation*, Oxford University Press, 2004.
13. Assmann, J. *Moses the Egyptian, op. cit.*
14. Breasted, J.H. *Ikhnaton, the Religious Revolutionary*, in *Cambridge Ancient History*, 1st edn, Vol. II, ch. 6, Cambridge, 1924.
15. Weigall, A. *The Life and Times of Akhenaton, Pharaoh of Egypt*, G.P. Putnam's Sons, New York, 1923.
16. Weigall, A., *The Life and Times of Akhenaton, Pharaoh of Egypt, op. cit.*
17. Ha-Am, H. *Philosophia Judaica*, East & West Library, Oxford, 1946.
18. Alter, R. *The Book of Psalms: A Translation with Commentary*, Norton, 2007.
19. Assmann, J. *Moses the Egyptian*, Harvard University Press, 1997.
20. Velikovski, I. *Oedipus and Akhenaton*, Abacus, 1960.
21. Aldred, C. *Akhenaton, Pharaoh of Egypt*, Thames & Hudson, 1968.
22. *Leviticus*, ch. 18, V. 6–8, *op. cit.*
23. Abrahams, K. in *Imago*, No. 1, 1912. (A translation of Abrahams' paper was published in *The Psycho-analytical Quarterly* for 1935).
24. Verlikovsky, E. *Oedipus and Akhenaton*, Sidgewick & Jackson, 1960.
25. Freud, S. *Moses and Monotheism*, SE, Vol. xxiii, Hogarth Press.
26. Assmann, J. *Moses the Egyptian, op. cit.*
27. Herodotus, *Histories*, Book Two, ch. 104.
28. Van der Toorn, K. *Scribal Culture and the Making of the Hebrew Bible*, Harvard University Press, 2007.
29. Alter, R. *Committee Speak*, in *The London Review of Books*, 9th July 2007.
30. *Ezra*, ch. 7, V. 14.
31. Kugel, J.K. *The Ladder of Jacob: Ancient Interpretations of the Biblical Story of Jacob and his Children*, Princeton University Press, 2006.

32. *The Book of Samuel II*, ch. 14, V. 14.
33. *The Book of Samuel II*, ch. 13.
34. Brichto, S. *The People's Bible: Book of Samuel*, Sinclair-Stevenson, 2000.
35. Brichto, S. *The People's Bible: Book of Samuel, op. cit.*
36. Josipovici, G. Lecture given at University of Boston, in *Times Literary Supplement*, 24th February 2006.
37. Freud, S. *Totem and Taboo*, SE, Vol. xiii, Hogarth Press.
38. *Genesis*, ch. 19, V. 33 & 35.
39. Brichto, S., *The People's Bible: Book of Genesis, op. cit.*
40. *Apocrypha* in *The New English Bible*, Oxford and Cambridge University Presses, 1970.
41. *The Second Book of Samuel*, ch. 18.
42. *The First Book of Kings*, ch. 1, V. 1–4.
43. *The Book of the Prophet Jeremiah*, ch. 8–9.
44. Soloveitchik, H. *Rupture and Reconstruction*, in *Tradition*, 28, 1994.
45. Armstrong, K. *The Bible: The Biography*, Atlantic Books, 2007.
46. Freud, S. *Moses and Monotheism, op. cit.*
47. Cretney, S. *Family Law in the Twentieth Century*, Oxford University Press, 2003.
48. Abse, D.W. *Marriage Counselling in Medical Practice: A Symposium*, University of North Carolina Press, 1964.
49. Hanagid, S. in *The Penguin Book of Hebrew Verse*, Penguin Books, 1981.
50. Plato, *Republic*. Kermode, F. in *London Review of Books* article, 13th December 2007.
51. Small, H. *The Long Life*, Oxford University Press, 2007.
52. Eliot, T.S. *Little Giddings*.
53. Burton, R. *The Anatomy of Melancholy*, Dent, 1968.

NOAH

CHAPTER FIVE

The nakedness of Noah

Wine is a mocker, strong drink is raging; and whosoever is deceived thereby is not wise.[1]

The Old Testament's admonition was first spelled out to me by my caring Nonconformist teachers at my Welsh working-class primary school. To be certain that its full significance was well understood my class of nine-year-olds would be shepherded into a nearby Methodist hall and there shown a terrifying slide-show of brains: the misshapen, ugly brains of alcohol-sodden drunkards, and wonderful beautiful brains of abstainers. The slides would be dramatically interpreted to us by proud officials of the Band of Hope, wearers of the blue ribbon, a status symbol in south Wales of the widely respected men who had signed the pledge and renounced the demon drink. And after the most diverting show, which I would so much enjoy, I would go home to my Friday evening Sabbath supper where, before being served my mother's chicken soup, kreplach and gefilte fish, I loudly declaimed in Hebrew the enjoined ancient benediction, the *Kiddush*, as a blessing on the excruciating kosher wine which, as a boy, I then drank as if it were nectar:

> Blessed art Thou O Lord our God, King of the Universe, who createst the fruit of the vine.

As a boy, as now, I was untroubled by the seeming inconsistencies within the doctrinal teachings telling me of the potency of wine to which I was exposed; except for those imprisoned by an obsessional neurotic temperament which demands that truth give way to consistency, there is indeed no paradox in the Biblical emphases upon the sacramental dialectical relationship between wine as a blessing and wine as a curse; only if God's fruit of the vine is wondrously intoxicating could its spoliation bring about the enormity of the curses raining down upon errant abusers of God's gift. Repeatedly in legend and allegory the Biblical narrative invokes wine as the catalyst precipitating God's love or wrath.

More, so thaumatological are its properties that it becomes the symbol of divinity itself: "I am the true vine" saith the Lord; and with such omnipotence being attributed to the grape, the psalmist in an exquisite allegorical reading, turns to the vine to rejoice in God's peculiar care for His chosen people:[2]

> Thou has brought a vine out of Egypt; thou hast cast out the heathen, and planted it.
> Thou preparedst room before it, and didst cause it to take deep root, and it filled the land.
> The hills were covered with the shadow of it, and the boughs thereof were like the goodly cedars.
> She sent out her boughs unto the sea, and her branches unto the river.

The psalmist, in his founding of the allegory upon the blessedness of the vine, was anticipatory, for wine was later to receive the endorsement that pulsates throughout Christian doctrine; indeed, there are enthusiastic Christian wine critics who claim the hidden story of the Gospels is the story of wine itself.[3] Their claim is not pretentious for the story of Jesus' first miracle gives it credence. It was at a wedding-feast in Cana[4] that Mary nudged her Son, when it was found that there was a dearth of wine for the guests, to turn water into wine and so, prematurely, begin the mission which was to shape Western civilization.

Jesus was evidently no mean oenologist; we are told that host and guests alike at Cana found the wine unsurpassable, and I cannot doubt that the wine Jesus, as a connoisseur, offered as a gift to His disciples at the Last Supper was of similar quality. At this moment of time I cannot but particularly envy them for I am now drinking my last bottle of superb 1975 Barbaresco from my depleted wine cellar. At the age of 74, 16 years ago, I selfishly decided to buy no more wine but to begin drinking up my carefully acquired horde of Italian wines; but, to my chagrin, I have outlived my cellar. But the wine babble that I have enjoyed with my friends at my table was of a different order to the solemn conversation at the Last Supper. There Jesus describes the wine He offers as the "blood of the new testament"[5] and asks them to drink it then and for all time "in remembrance of Me"; the wine had been transformed into the symbol of the Passion.

Roger Scruton, philosopher and wine critic, has told us that viniculture aspires, with partial success, towards the Divine Idea of wine and that at Cana it found a perfect instance. Today:

> The miracle is re-enacted when the liquid in the glass is suddenly revealed as the presence, here and now, of the Platonic Form of wine ... a revelation which can no more be captured in words than can the meaning of a Beethoven quartet.

The discriminating don's enthusiasm is commendable but it should come with a health warning. Such "divine" potions must be carefully measured: an overdose can have catastrophic consequences. The Biblical legends associate wine not only with the blessing of the Redemption; it can also be a harbinger of doom and dissension among mankind. There has never been recorded a more terrible incitement to mayhem than that contained in the tale of the drunken Noah: his binge has contributed to the suffering and death of millions.

***

Noah, survivor of God's curse of the Flood and destined to be the sole progenitor of all mankind, pronounced his sinister malediction after a drunken bout that had left him senseless. But it cannot be dismissed or excused as the bad-tempered outburst of a man suffering a hangover. It is unclouded, precise, measured, and unequivocal, a blunt apologia able without distortion to be used as justification, as it has been, by racialists for millennia; it preaches an evil doctrine of hierarchy, an ordained superiority of one race over another. Noah's vineyard was indeed to yield bitter fruit.[6]

> And Noah began to be an husbandman, and he planted a vineyard;
> And he drank of the wine, and was drunken; and he was uncovered within his tent.
> And Ham, the father of Canaan, saw the nakedness of his father, and told his two brethren without.
> And Shem and Japheth took a garment, and laid it upon both their shoulders, and went backward, and covered the nakedness of their father; and their faces were backward, and they saw not their father's nakedness.
> And Noah awoke from his wine, and knew what his younger son had done unto him.
> And he said, Cursed be Canaan; a servant of servants shall he be unto his brethren.
> And he said, Blessed be the Lord God of Shem; and Canaan shall be his servant.
> God shall enlarge Japheth, and he shall dwell in the tents of Shem; and Canaan shall be his servant.

The odd displacement in the curse which we find falling on Canaan, the son of Ham, rather than upon Ham the perpetrator of the violation, has been unconvincingly used to suggest the curse of enslavement was only of local significance, that it did not fall on all mankind, and thus the whole story is made "to justify the—much hoped-for—subject status of the Canaanites in relation to the descendants of Shem, the Israelites".[7] While, given the terrible racial discords that over the years its citing has fuelled, it is pardonable that attempts should be made to restrict the scope of the curse, the brutal truth is that all the oppressors of the blacks, the apartheid doctrinarians of South Africa, the fundamentalists of the southern States of America, the Christian slave-traders of Europe, have the Biblical text on their side. It diminishes the book of Genesis to treat it as a depository within which may be found the history of conflicts between squabbling Middle Eastern tribes. The unfolding of the history of the Noah family, like the Creation legend itself, is the crucial focus of a larger universal history. And since the Bible was conceived and written by men, it reflects all their contradictions and prejudices as well as their idealism; and as we chasteningly learn from the Noah story, of all prejudices, racial prejudice has the longest of histories.

Later scribes in later times sought to mitigate the consequences of Noah's curse, as when they told of God afflicting Miriam, Moses' sister, with a type of leprosy[8]—and thus temporarily isolated her as a pariah in punishment for her racialist criticism of the marriage of Moses to the dark-skinned Kushite woman. More usually, however, any modification of the curse is, at best, ambivalent. In the Song of Songs the "belovèd" is comely despite, not because of, her blackness:[9]

> I am black, but comely, O ye daughters of Jerusalem, as the tents of Kedar, as the curtains of Solomon.
> Look not upon me, because I am black, because the sun hath looked upon me; my mother's children were angry with me; they made me the keeper of the vineyards; but mine own vineyard have I not kept.

But her eloquent plea for more than tolerance has a dusty answer. We find the curse untempered and reaffirmed as irremovable by the Prophets: "Can the Ethiopian change his skin, or the leopard his spots?" declaims Jeremiah.[10]

Ironically, today, many of the black Ethiopian Jews, fancifully claiming that they are the descendants of Menelik, the son of King Solomon and the visiting Queen of Sheba (and who, to Israel's credit, have been received into the modern state) are bitterly complaining that they have not escaped Jeremiah's stigma and are suffering racial discrimination in the very land from which they claim to have sprung. Noah's curse, it seems, cannot be erased. The damage it has done is irreparable. Even the Holocaust has not exhausted the racialist curse's potency and now, in the 21st century, it hovers about Barack Obama's campaign for the presidency of the United States, reverberates in the responses to the black rioting in the suburbs of Paris and is shamelessly, with some success, exploited by the fascist British National Party in London's Barking and Dagenham districts.

The awesome consequences of the curse compel us to look anew at the precipitate which Old Testament scribes have claimed as its cause. Apologists may seek to persuade us a gaze can be lethal, that looks can kill, and that the text implies that Ham is being punished for harbouring in his "peep" parricidal wishes, for which he and his descendants deserve retribution. But even if any weight is given to such a limp defence of the curse, still there remain huge and significant gaps in the chronicler's tale; either the original story has been heavily censored or, even from the beginning, the events in Noah's tent were too awful to be told. We do not expect our legends to follow strict rules of causality but that an inadvertent glimpse by a son of his father's nakedness should have such dire consequences for one part of the human race is indeed a singularly unconvincing recounting. The myth as told conceals more than it reveals. One of the most lively of modern-day rabbis, recognizing the lacunae in the story, has suggested that Ham laughed at the drunken Noah's nakedness and that this was the cause of Noah's anger.[11] Such an anodyne explanation, that a son's innocent tease of a father should cause such a disproportionate response, is not persuasive; there are far more likely and far more explosive interpretations to be found in the interstices of the abrupt verses. Something more than a concupiscent gaze had taken place in the encounter. The accusation can be made and justified that within the tent Ham had found the temptation of homosexual incest too alluring to be resisted.

When any sacred taboo is broken, a curse must fall upon the miscreant. That is the iron rule to be found in all the Greek and Hebrew myths. And when so terrible a curse so replete with injustice is in place, then we know a taboo has been violated. It is the full horror of such a transgression that envelopes the Biblical fable. The chronicler seeks to acquit the father of guilt, pleading his drunken stupor as extenuation. But a scapegoat has to be found. For so heinous an offence as this was, the punishment must be forever a permanent deterrent to those who otherwise may yield to the temptation of acting out the primal fantasy of becoming the exclusive lover of the father that Freud has taught us envelopes all male infants.

The rabbis of yore were not deceived by the existing bland texts: they speedily rumbled that more than a gaze had taken place, that the tale was one of a sexual encounter.[12] That they came to such a

THE NAKEDNESS OF NOAH   171

conclusion is unsurprising: the clue would have been available to them since, as so often in the Hebrew Bible, "to see the nakedness" means "to copulate with.[13] In the Babylonian Talmud we find that all the debating rabbis considering the Noah story agreed that a sexual encounter had taken place; where they differed with each other was the nature of the encounter. Some insisted that Ham had raped his father; others argued that Ham had castrated him and, since no textual proof of any emasculation was available, they postulated that Ham feared that Noah would procreate again, siring, at the very least, a fourth son—thereby diminishing Ham's share of the world. It was an interpretation not confined to Jewish circles: Bishop Theophilus of Antioch, the early Greek Church father, was canvassing such a possibility in AD 181.

From a Freudian perspective, as we shall see, the two themes are not mutually exclusive, particularly as there appears to be general agreement among Biblical scholars that the belief that anal intercourse had taken place was the original interpretation of the tale and the castration hypothesis was a later speculation. In a commanding survey of past and present assessments of the nature of the fateful encounter, the historian Benjamin Braude, at the 2003 Yale Conference on "Collective degradation: Slavery and the construction of race", opted for the buggery interpretation, arguing that:[14]

> Based on a range of sources—Mesopotamian tablets, intra-Biblical exegesis, obliquely the earliest expansions of Biblical stories, as well as Rabbinic and Patristic comments—that what was done to Noah was some kind of sexual violence, most likely anal intercourse.

Braude is no Freudian but his conclusion, that buggery had taken place, is congruent with a psychoanalytic reading of the Noah story, for it is indeed a tale richly illustrative of what Freud has named as the "negative Oedipus complex".

The sinister insightful fable tells us that after the Great Flood that drowned the sinful world, even although mankind was given a second chance through the survival of Noah and his family, still the wondrous and sanguine covenantal rainbow would not act as a shield if a particular temptation was not resisted. There was one transgression that was irredeemable: that of incestuous homosexuality. It was abominable and its practice would, and did, bring disaster upon a large accursed section of the human race. In the 20th century Freud, drawing on his clinical investigations, explicated to an unbelieving world the psycho-dynamics operating within legends like that of Noah. He was corroborating what thousands of years earlier the creators of the myths had divined. He chose to name the syndrome after a legendary Greek and called it the Oedipus complex; he could equally well have identified it with the fraught relationships within the Noah family, the family from whom, the Bible tells us, we are all descended.

Although now, in the 21st century, a notion of the Oedipus complex is glibly bandied about in our general culture, its full implications—those which illuminate the Noah legend—are, in and out of psychoanalytical circles, cowardly evaded. Too often it is presented almost as a fairy tale, a childish rite of passage, a phase we all pass through between the ages of three and five when unconsciously we are possessed with a wish to possess the parent of the opposite sex and to eliminate that of the same sex. Thus presented, our culture is able to accommodate comfortably what can be interpreted as a reassuringly normative story. We begin by desiring and wanting to kill off our parents. Registering the horror, not to mention the impossibility, of this project, we more or less relinquish it. We renounce our first infantile desires and wait; then, in a diaphasic interlude, we, as adolescents, recapitulate, in disguised form, our early rebellions and eventually, if all goes well, we work through the consequent turbulence, and as adults find people who are sufficiently reminiscent of our parents to be exciting, but sufficiently different so that we can consummate our desire. We want some things but, repentant, we realize the errors of our ways and we find the substitutes that can satisfy us. The story thus portrayed is one of human development, one that is both possible and potentially satisfying. Within this anodyne developmental version of the Oedipus complex, doubtless we can end the story by saying that as adults we can live happily after. Repeatedly, however, Freud insisted that the telling of this gentle simplification of the phenomenon may be attractive for "schematisation" purposes but that it was a wholly inadequate explication of its content. He warned:[15]

> ... the simple Oedipus complex is by no means its commonest form, but rather represents the simplification or schematisation which ... is often justified for practical purposes. Closer study

usually discloses the more complete Oedipus complex, which is two-fold, positive and negative, and is due to the bi-sexuality originally present in children; that is to say, a boy has not merely an ambivalent attitude towards his father and an affectionate object-choice towards his mother, but at the same time he also behaves like a girl and displays an affectionate feminine attitude to his father and a corresponding jealousy and hostility towards his mother ... it may even be that the ambivalence displayed in the relations to the parents should be attributed entirely to bi-sexuality and that it is not ... developed out of identification in consequence of rivalry.

From within the primal fantasy that Freud has described of the boy becoming the exclusive lover of the father, there emerges a terrible threat: the consummation requires, perforce, emasculation. Feminine submissiveness, a readiness to receive physically the father, means a price has to be paid: the penis has to be forfeited. The Babylonian rabbis who argued whether buggery or castration had taken place in Noah's tent were reflecting the contradictions inherent in the fantasy. To merge totally as one with the father demands vaginal intercourse and total phallic loss: that was unendurable. A second-best, a hazardous compromise, was the unsatisfactory but partial assuaging of the desire to possess or to be possessed by the father. Anal intercourse was the vain hope of resolving the dilemma. And that was the dangerous, and spurious, solution enacted and cursed in the foetid tent of Noah.

But by attempting to take such an escape route, the route named by Freud as the "negative Oedipus complex", the fundamental teleological function of the primal attachment to the father is thwarted. The developmental purpose of this desire to be as one with the father is to have a penis like the father, to participate in the father's penis.[16] The negative Oedipus complex is a rite of passage, an apprenticeship, a preparation for the complete Oedipus complex, when, having learned the ways of man, the son can enter into masculine competition with the father to gain the mother and then, when he finally realizes that that impossible wish must be renounced, to find as he grows up compensation in other women in his mother's image. Such a son has found his way to genitality; but the boy who has never graduated from his apprenticeship cannot so advance: he remains arrested, condemned to sterile anality.

The Bible never tells winsome fairy stories. Ever its recital of the Hebrew fables are didactic, weighty, and multi-layered, and the story of the conflicts and tensions within the prototypical Noah family is no exception. Here we are told of the sexual constraints that are imperative if the ascent of the once nearly wiped-out mankind is to continue, if in civilized fashion, distanced from primitive prehistoric man who knew neither endogamy nor exogamy, mankind is to proliferate and cover the whole earth. Either we advance into the world of genitality or we regress and, yielding to the attractions of coprophilia,[17] retreat to the safety of the anal zone where our eroticism can be played out unencumbered by women and where procreation is excluded. In the Noah story, God has inflicted a terrible reprimand on those who are, impertinently, defying His command: "Be fruitful and multiply and replenish the earth".[18]

Only if we acknowledge that the curse was a response to an attempted subversion of that life-affirming doctrine will we understand why it fell upon a son deemed to be black; then we are less perplexed that of the three siblings born to the same parents only Ham was not white. His visage was ever to be associated with barren anal intercourse. His pleasures were found in the passage from which the dark faeces emerge; he revelled in shit when the evolutionary imperative demanded he should have responded with disgust. The good sons, politically correct, were repelled by their father's nakedness and would not look upon their father's buttocks; Ham found them inviting and yielded to temptation. He became black as sin, the pure brothers remained white as snow. In the normative development of the babe in its pre-Oedipal stages, the infant, initially fascinated by the dark brown excreta he has proudly produced, if he is to move on, has to be emancipated from his coprophilia; an estoppel is needed to overcome his wish to smell his perfumed product and his desire to play with it, to smear his white skin with the colourful cosmetic cream. The perception that the dense dark material that oozed from his anus is beautiful must be erased. The mechanism that psychoanalysts have named as "reaction-formation" comes to evolution's aid and the socially unacceptable impulses are mastered by exaggeration, by hypertrophy of the opposing tendency: the exquisite perfume becomes a stink; the lush excrement is morphed into the untouchable; what was alluring becomes repulsive.

But when Ham fucked his father, he heralded the demolition of all those inhibiting barriers which curb desires to return to the fantasized world of the cloaca. There, naked, wallowing in undifferentiated faecal mixtures, all interchanging indiscriminately, no bodily orifice banned, incest, adultery and sodomy prevailing, every possible permutation of erotic zones and their functions practised, gender erased and categories of parent and child abolished, the destruction of reality is effected and the pervert's goal is reached in an anal universe where all differences, generational differences above all, are abolished.

Ham's penetration of Noah was more than a violation of his father: he was taunting God. The deservedly renowned French psychoanalyst Janine Chasseguet-Smirgel has instructed us: "The man who does not respect the law of differentiation challenges God"[19]—and that is precisely what Ham did, for the God of *Genesis* who brought order to chaos was the creative God of division:[20]

> And the earth was without form, and void; and darkness was upon the face of the deep. And the Spirit of God moved upon the face of the waters.
> And God said, Let there be light; and there was light.
> And God saw the light, that it was good; and God divided the light from the darkness.
> And God called the light Day, and the darkness he called Night. And the evening and the morning were the first day.
> And God said, Let there be a firmament in the midst of the waters, and let it divide the waters from the waters.
> And God made the firmament, and divided the waters which were under the firmament from the waters which were above the firmament; and it was so.

And differentiation, an insistence upon an absence of hybridization with no intermingling of the species, continues in the following verses:[21]

> And God said, Let the earth bring forth grass, the herb yielding seed, and the fruit tree yielding fruit after his kind, whose seed is in itself, upon the earth; and it was so.

And the earth brought forth grass, and herb yielding seed after his kind, and the tree yielding fruit, whose seed was in itself, after his kind; and God saw that it was good.

The adverbial phrase "after his kind" is repeated like a leitmotif; separation, not mixture, is the prerequisite for God to declare it was "good". Ham, in his homosexual incestuous act, was denying boundaries; it was more than an impertinence, it was a takeover bid. The ordered world would be overwhelmed and another world, that of mush and disorder would come into existence. This was an attempted dethronement of God. It merited not a mild rebuke but a punishment proportionate to the enormity of the offence. Even as God was to brand Cain with a mark advertising his sin, so Ham and his descendants were to be distinguished forever from their fellows. In a terrible act of retribution, Ham's nose—indeed his whole body—was to be rubbed into shit. He was never to be free from the ordure and colouration of the excreta whose properties had so excited him; he was indelibly stained.

***

There are some who cannot tolerate such a vengeful presentation of their God and have therefore striven to exonerate Him. One Jewish historian insisted, to a sceptical academia, that the "stigma" of colour attached to Ham is based on a misreading of Hebrew and other Semitic languages, and that this has led to a mistaken belief that the word "Ham" means "dark black" or "heat".[22] Be that as it may, what is chasteningly clear is that for centuries wherever the Noah story is read and absorbed into the general culture, it incites colour prejudice. It is in Protestant regions, where the Old Testament played so significant a part in determining the dominant ethos, that we find miscegenation was declared to be a criminal offence. Repeatedly when, in my younger days, I travelled to pre-independence Portuguese Mozambique, to the Belgian Congo and British colonies like Kenya, I was struck by the contrast between the attitudes where the colonial power was Catholic and where it was Protestant; miscegenation was taboo wherever, in one form or other, apartheid prevailed, but it was deliberately, without inhibition, used in Catholic dependencies as an imperialist tool to enlist a half-black elite as collaborators in the governance of a colony. The Catholic Church has never encouraged the laity to read the Bible; it is too dangerous a book to be let out of the hands of the priesthood. But in Protestant countries, where collective Bible-readings were so often at the centre of family life, the Bible stories were told and re-told—and the tale of Noah has certainly seeped with toxic consequences into fundamentalist Protestant thought.

Fundamentalist Protestantism gave us the Boers of South Africa and the slave-owners of the Southern States of America. Unconsciously and often consciously they ever equated black with filth and associated sex with dirt; unemancipated from their anal fantasies, still yearning for the pleasures found in their imaginings of irresponsible promiscuous revelling, they sought to rid themselves of their own scatological pruriences by casting them upon black men and women. In the darkness of the enslaved their tainted perverse lusts would be hidden; the blacks would be ghettoized and in the enclave there would be sited the sewage farm into which the detritus of the white man's filthy regressive desires would fall.

But there were serious technical defects in the engineering of this project. The expelled waste was not lifeless; it was not filtered. It was an admixture, a compost, a generative fertilizer, a breeding-ground, a depository in which all the libidinous desires directed by man to woman could flourish. Now the fantasy becomes a nightmare. Unwittingly the white man has bequeathed to his victim his potency, and multiplied ten-fold his procreative capacity. Ham and his descendants would outnumber those of Shem and Japheth. They would, as Margaret Thatcher once memorably warned Britain, "be swamped". To the white man uncertain of his own vitality, the black man has now become a symbol of uncontrolled animal lust, a rapist who menaces the white man's woman and who well deserves a Ku Klux Klan lynching.

And even when lynching ceased and slavery was abolished in Protestant America, still the stereotyping image of the sexually aggressive black persisted. He could not be treated as a human being equal to the white man. Ironically, the abolitionist imagery itself assisted in perpetuating the stereotype. The well-intentioned abolitionist medallion that inscribed the famous quotation, "Am I not a man and a brother?" enshrined and crystallized the idea of a docile subservient black inferiority; the medallion's image of a pathetic supplicant slave on bended knees was an attempt to reassure the white man that the black was tamed. The most famous monument to Abraham Lincoln is itself a representation of the respectful abased figure to be found in the abolitionist emblem. Lincoln stands erect, one arm stretched out over the head of a nearly naked ideal docile slave. The iconography tells us how the emancipators have failed to emancipate themselves from their own fears. No wonder black art historians have described the monument as the visual equivalent of a cringing "Uncle Tom" paying his obeisances to a patronizing philanthropic white man who has granted him his manumission and absolution. The monument reveals, not conceals, the fears of the apprehensive white man that his expurgating stratagem, of denying his own waywardness and projecting all his inordinate lustfulness and transgressive desires upon the black, may fail.

Despite all the anti-discrimination and anti-segregation legislation that has come about in the USA, the image of the black man as the container of the illicit trespasses of the white man remains in place; neither America's Congress nor Supreme Court has succeeded in eradicating Noah's curse. America may be integrated by law but by practice and perception it is segregated; to this day even the most acclaimed black icons are suspect. When, in 2008, for the first time, American *Vogue*, arbiters of contemporary fashion, placed a black man on its cover, it advertised all the continuing ambivalences which America has towards the vigour and sexuality of its black citizens. The picture was of a muscular 6 ft. 9 in. LeBron James, the famed hero of US basketball. But it was no compliment to his physique and sporting talents: he is depicted striking a pose reminiscent of King Kong. Even as, in 1887, the sculptor Fremiet carved his notorious bronze statue of a gorilla carrying off a white woman, and even as Hollywood gave us the now legendary movie still of King Kong clambering up the Empire State Building clutching a young and beautiful white woman in his huge paw, so *Vogue* exteriorizes the white American's repressed fears by depicting LeBron James holding on to a delectable white supermodel. In vain did black spokesmen protest at this debasement. *Vogue* had twitched the curtain but a little to reveal what since Noah's day is dangerously harboured in the white man's psyche.

In Europe the syndrome is often similarly but more cunningly portrayed. We find sculptors' representations of slavery are essentially placatory: the black or dark victims are empathetically portrayed; they smoulder with sensuality but are submissive and unthreatening. And paintings abound in similar mode. It is in Europe's empire-building phase, particularly in the 18th and 19th centuries, when the white man was brought closer to his dark-skinned subjects, that we find, despite his conquests, he is most lacking confidence in his own erectile capacity and is most envious of the huge penis which his febrile imagination attributes to the black man; to protect himself from his dangerous ambivalences towards his victim, he enlists the artist to provide yet more safeguards. This is the era when, overtly or implicitly, the feared black man is castrated; the artist, responding to societal apprehensions, unmans the black and in innumerable harem scenes depicts him as the huge eunuch, the sexually impotent guardian of the beautiful nude odalisques, all unattainable to him.

But it is not only the black man who must suffer humiliation; so must the concubine in the harem. Her destiny has been determined; her brown colouration identifies her as a descendant of Ham. The lighter pigment of her skin, a shade less than black, bestows upon her an especially alluring temptation evoking, as it does, reminiscences of hazardous buried coprophilic delights. She is dangerous and must be disarmed; she must therefore be depicted as passive and under total control. It is in the works of Delacroix and Jean-Léon Gérôme and the French "Oriental School" that we find the apogee of European paintings of this genre. In exotic creations overt statements abound that this woman is a property, a possession with no rights, wholly under the domination of man. The artist invites us, as titillated observers, to gaze as voyeurs disapprovingly upon deliciously unconstrained barbaric practices of a very dark man attending a slave market and there for his pleasure, choosing one of the numb naked and terrified not quite white but fair-skinned girls on parade. By such subtle transportations and evasions Europe's exploitative imperialists, through their hireling artists, ensure that Noah's curse is perpetuated. Vicariously and guilt free, the white European can participate in the erotic indulgences of the dark "oriental" slave purchaser and simultaneously condemn him. Meanwhile, excitedly, he can view the seductive black skin of the native slave, confident that all the temptations that he has transposed from himself onto her are safely entrapped by her status: she, and his regressive temptations, are safely locked up in a well-guarded harem.

Yet, so great is his apprehension, still the white man fears that somehow she could escape from the fantasized high security harem in which she, as the container of his perverse lusts, has been imprisoned; still he is frightened that the curse will lose its efficacy, that the separation that the curse guarantees will expire. To allay these societal anxieties we find the pliant resourceful artist ingeniously devises alternative stratagems.

In Manet's notorious "Olympia" we find one such stratagem ostentatiously advertised. A pretty black girl, out of the harem but still in servitude, is shown as servant to a reclining inviting languorous naked white woman; the blackness of the servant girl is presented as a stimulant, as an aphrodisiac, encouraging the European voyeur, thus aroused, to dare to turn his devouring lustful gaze upon the awaiting white diva. And in many other deviations a black servant-girl is given a no less humiliating rôle; the painter robs her of her own sexual attractiveness and puts it at the service of her white mistress. Repeatedly in bath scenes by Gérôme, Depat-Ponson and Bouchard we find a lovely demure white woman being bathed and massaged by a vigorous ugly black woman who is preparing her for service in her lover's bed. In all such portrayals the subordination of the black figures, their dehumanization, their equation with deviant sex, proclaims the ancient curse was, to the profit of the upholders, fully in place as Europe placed its yoke upon the dark-skinned peoples of its colonies.

With the end of Empire, however, with de-colonization and the domestic need of the metropolitan countries for a reserve of cheap and plentiful labour, such labour by the millions was brought into Europe. At first they submitted to their fate. In Britain the curse upon them was substantially unchallenged until the 1980s. Then came the "slave" revolts. Race riots from Toxteth to Brixton shook the confidence and complacency of the white "masters" who, out of self-interest rather than from nobler motivation, tightened anti-discriminatory racial legislation and, by targeting funding and services, and by imposing minimum wage rates, attempted to dilute the malediction instituted by Noah. Thus, under the proclaimed rubric of multi-culturism, the reality that ghettoization, not integration prevails, has been evaded. And now, with globalization, and in particular with the free movement of labour within the European Community bringing millions of white immigrants, awakened xenophobia afflicts a significant section of the indigenous populations deaf to the pleas of politicians and employers that these immigrants bring economic benefits for all. The apologists for persisting in open door or half-open door immigration policies would wish the political arguments to shift decisively away from race to economics. This may be a rational step but it is one out of kilter with the prejudices of the majority and, lamentably, colour cannot be thus laundered out of the debate.

Since diagnosis must precede cure, if we are to have any hope of overcoming the still prevailing and deep-seated colour prejudice, we surely need to explore in depth why black and dark hues in themselves can so persistently, from and before Noah down to the present day, create such ambivalent antagonism. How does it come about that a dab of black or dark brown evokes such dangerous emotions totally absent at the sight of blue or grey? How can this prejudice's ubiquity be explained, and by what means has its predisposition been transmitted from generation to generation? We can, I believe, find answers to our questions within the work of one of the earliest followers of Freud, the Hungarian Jew Sandor Ferenczi, the irreverent psychoanalyst whose speculations enraged so many of his professional colleagues but who, to the end, Freud, recognizing his genius, and tolerant of his aberrations, admired and defended. His densely-written book, *Thalassa, A Theory of Genitality*,[23] a mere 100 pages long, more cited than read, too explosive to be treated as part of the canon by timid psychoanalysts, provides us with a profound and disconcerting explanation. In this book, drawing on knowledge gained by his treatment of those men who found themselves impotent, or those afflicted with *ejaculatio precox*, or those capable of erection and intromission but incapable of ejaculation, Ferenczi vividly reminds us that when normative libidinal development takes us to the stage where all our component instincts, oral and anal, come under the primacy of the genital organs, within genital activity there still remains striated abounding unrenounced coprophilic pleasures. The clinical picture he presents of his impotent patients reveals their malfunctioning is related to the deleterious invasion of anality during their attempted or actual copulations; evocation of coprophilic delights may enhance the thrills of the fuck but in the case of his patients such recall overwhelmed their genitality and left them stricken. The spotlight Ferenczi places on the rôle of anality in coitus, alerting us to the mixture of eroticisms that accompany our copulations, has a most significant relevance when we seek to de-mystify a myth such as that of Noah which sets out and warns against the usurpation of our anality over our prolific heterosexual intercourse. His theory of genitality leads us to the uncomfortable truth that in colour prejudice, in our attraction and repellence to black/brown faeces, we are dealing with an intractable biological factor, an irrevocable determination that accompanies every ejaculation of every man. These days, when increasingly behavioural-genetic studies are leading to greater emphases being given to the heritability of personality traits,[24] Ferenczi's theory is perhaps less startling than when he first proposed it in 1915. Inescapably it brings us to a sombre and disquieting conclusion, welcome only to avowed racialists. But the instruction it gives us means that we must not be content to treat colour prejudice as a cultural creation. Its aetiology tells us otherwise: we are dealing with a phenomenon lacking pliant malleability. Only if we are blinkered we can optimistically believe that liberal anti-discriminatory measures, well-meaning exhortations to practise tolerance, and special fiscal and housing strategies to assist disadvantaged areas where poor black and minority ethnic people live cheek by jowl with poverty-stricken whites, will in themselves erase the curse of Noah, end Shem's swagger and Ham's inferiority. Denying the very existence of the territory from which the curse has sprung is a self-defeating ploy, in that its roots remain untouched, firmly embedded and, even worse, enable the vociferous racialist, unmasked, under the cover of his oft-times sophisticated justifying rationalizations, to propagate his obscene doctrines without acknowledging or revealing the sick psycho-dynamics prompting his displays of rage and indignation. Such a man was Enoch Powell who, apart from Benjamin Disraeli whose extravagant unconcealed racialism stemmed from a different source, can be categorized as the most articulate racist in British political history. No assessment of the working of Noah's curse in contemporary Britain would be complete without some scrutiny of this brilliant tortured Biblical scholar. It was my privilege to be hated and feared by him.

***

For some 20 years, Enoch Powell's office at Westminster was a few yards away from mine—on the first floor of an annexe to the House of Commons. Almost every day of the parliamentary calendar we would pass and re-pass each other and, when the division bell rang in our rooms, we would emerge simultaneously and walk across the ancient courtyard side by side, all of two feet behind each other, to register our votes in the Chamber. Never in all those years did one word pass between us. His hostility towards me was unremitting. If, inadvertently, his gaze caught mine, his staring phallic eyes smouldered with hate. I had once pierced his carapace, and the wound I had inflicted never healed.

The great debater, master of rhetoric, was not troubled by those who, outraged by his incitements, albeit less articulate than him, challenged his presumptions and logic; indeed, when they attempted to tongue-lash him he would dramatically enjoy his flagellations, and in his martyrdom would, and did, engage the sympathies of millions of his empathizing fellow citizens. Resonances of his notorious "rivers of blood" speech have in no way faded. On the 40th anniversary of that address, present immigration problems and the association of terrorism with dark-skinned Muslim perpetrators, have given full opportunity for him to be recalled as a wronged inspired prophet. And always, his apologists, like himself, deny they are racialists; they claim their concern is that the indigenous culture will be overwhelmed, that, as Powell put it, "numbers are of the essence", that blacks and browns would become the majority in our cities if immigration is not severely curtailed.

But Powell's eloquent formulation, ever insisting his alarums arose solely out of a concern of the consequences of the burgeoning birth-rate of non-white immigrants, was a half-truth, one that paradoxically acted as a camouflage and yet advertised the true source of his apocalyptic warnings. His persistent fascination with birth-rates of those with darker skins than his was not simply, as he claimed, a matter of numbers. It was essentially prurient; discomfited and uncertain of his own sexuality, the man who once during a television appearance, shared with his wife and daughter, displayed breathtaking insensitivity when, in the presence of his family, told of his wish to be a monk, was in his campaigning engaged in an inquisition into the love-making of those he felt were menacingly vigorous in bed. He feared the blacks' sexual and progenitive capabilities; his preoccupation was not with birth but with copulation. And, impatient of Powell's pretence that he was not a racialist but concerned only with "numbers", I told a packed Commons in May 1970 that "The speeches of the Rt Hon Member for Wolverhampton South-West are really about how many times a week a black man copulates, not about the birth-rate ... The language of the Birmingham racialists reveals their fear of the potency of the black man—the sexual rivalry felt by those uncertain of their own Wolverhampton virility ... Let there be no doubt—if we had fewer eunuchs we would have less Enochs."[25] The House, perhaps intemperately, roared with approving laughter. Powell could withstand, even enjoy, criticism but my quip, piercing his carapace, he found intolerable. Incandescent, he completely lost his cool. He speedily made representations to the Leader of the House, Fred Peart—who earlier, in another context, had reminded a Labour back-bencher of the "decencies" to be observed between MPs—demanding to know what action he would take against me in view of my misbehaviour. Peart, ever charming and ineffectual and the least likely of men ever to take a confrontational stance, tried to pour oil on troubled waters and replied tactfully but evasively that he could "understand" Powell's feelings, but the issue was a matter for the Speaker, not him. This reply provoked rather than soothed Powell who retorted that "... it is not a question of my feelings. It is a question of the credit and good repute of the House as a whole, which is damaged when its Members cast obscene aspersions on one another on the floor of the Chamber."[26] For nearly two weeks Powell continued to brood, nursing his hurt, but then, no longer able to contain his rage, belatedly he called upon the Speaker, Horace King, to rebuke me. But the Speaker punctiliously replied to him that he "did not think at the time any unparliamentary language had been used" and added: "I cannot think I would have been on firm ground if I had attempted to intervene." Enraged by the Speaker's dusty answer, Powell, now out of control, proceeded to attack the Speaker himself. He wrote to King saying he wished to place upon record his belief "that Mr Speaker's responsibility is not limited to requiring the withdrawal of words which are technically 'unparliamentary', or to maintaining observance of the rules of order. ... most of us, I believe, feel that the standard of decency in the House has deteriorated in the Parliament just ending. I do not think that in retrospect the Chair can hope to be clear of responsibility."[27] Unsurprisingly, Horace King had by now had enough and rebuked Powell saying that his letter was "the most distressing one that I have received since I took office";

he also pointed out that if Powell felt so badly about his conduct it was his duty to oppose his re-election as Speaker. That so experienced and masterly a parliamentarian as Powell should have gone to pieces and responded so ineptly and wildly to my Enoch quip was because he had particular reasons to doubt the strength of his own heterosexuality. I have little doubt that as a young man he had a German lover, and that episodic homosexual experience bore down upon him all his life, leaving him with a stammering guilt-ridden sexuality, one envious and fearful of the fantasized sexual prowess that he projected upon the black man. In 1988, when the former Dean of Westminster interviewed him in connection with a book, Powell "confessed" to his early homosexuality and read to the clergyman passages from his collection *First Poems* explaining the homosexual love behind the writing. Powell was not talking of some adolescent fumbling but of a more searing experience, and how traumatic that was can be observed when we learn how he responded to the loss of what he called his "beloved country"—Germany—and thus his lover.

Powell was five years older than me. But as a provincial lad in my very early teens I was profoundly conscious, despite the attraction I already had to so much German literature, of the increasing menace of the rise of Nazism in Germany. That rise, however, passed over Powell's head as he became increasingly intoxicated with German *Kultur*—and this despite the fact that the scholarships he gained enabled him, as an undergraduate, to make numerous forays into Germany. His awakening only came when the Nazi regime was already well ensconced; then, when the Nazi gangsters fell out, and Rohm and other homosexual Brownshirt leaders were slaughtered, suddenly he woke up to the naked brutality of the regime. Powell was in Germany during the time when the Nazis were already espousing racialist doctrines and sadistically acting upon them. All this the young Powell ignored. It was not the Nazi execution of Social Democrats or their persecution of the Jews that shattered Powell's confidence in Germany; the precipitate was the assault upon the homosexual leadership. In characteristically histrionic tones he wrote of his dismay:

> I can still remember today how I sat for hours in a state of shock, shock which you experience when around you you see the

debris of a beautiful abode in which you have lived for a long time. ... So it had all been illusion, all fantasy, all a self-created myth. Music, philosophy, poetry, science and the language itself—everything was demolished, broken to bits on the cliffs of a monstrous reality. The spiritual homeland had not been a spiritual homeland after all. ... Overnight my spiritual homeland had disappeared and I was left only with my geographical homeland.

This is the language of a bereaved lover, not that of a disenchanted ideologue. Today bisexuality can be shrugged off, and the youthful homosexual activity of a politician can, fortunately, attract no serious public opprobrium—as has been well-demonstrated in the case of Michael Portillo. But Powell was of another generation, brought up when a different and more oppressive *zeitgeist* prevailed, and with laws in place reflecting the most severe interpretations of the prohibitions of Leviticus. If official doctrine was defied, guilt and inhibition could be the consequence for the sinner; original sin was not an abstract doctrine but a reality for so many. Powell defiantly made a bid to jettison his guilt to free himself from God's injunctions which were so much in conflict with his private lifestyle and yearnings. As a young man he became a declared and committed atheist, and doubtless affirmed his disbelief with his customary display of dazzling logic. But disbelief and faith are not necessarily merely cerebral creatures; one can trace Powell's oscillations between godlessness and belief in the formative influences of his early familial life. For Powell was not born into a kingdom but, as his admiring biographer Roy Lewis tells us, into a family which was "a republic of three persons". And within that republic, all his biographers agree, there was an intense alliance between the young Enoch and his school-teacher mother. The father played a decidedly lesser role, leaving his wife to shape the gifted child into a mental athlete; and to perform her task, the mother gave up teaching and made the child her single pupil.

Predictable consequences flowed from such an austere and intense family unit in which loyalty was not ceded to the father and the foundations of which rested upon a coalition of mother and child. The narcissism of the child can be excessively corroborated by the admiring mother and then, insufficiently mortified by a strong containing father, the child can be left to grow up permeated by a haughty grandiosity. This trait, although often successfully borne by Powell's formidable intellect, was nevertheless one of the least engaging elements in his make-up, and was a severe handicap throughout his political career. The elimination of the father in the early years of the child from any claim to priority can lead, in adolescence and later, to a pronounced bias against father-asserting philosophies or religions perceived as surrogates. God the Father was clearly not tolerable to Powell as a young man and in his atheism he denied Him priority, as his own father had been denied.

But God the Son was to prove another matter entirely. The isolation of the only child growing up in a literary, non-gregarious family, over-valuing the word and seemingly deficient in human relationships outside the books, could not be sustained. The atheist must walk and die in his own footsteps, his eternity linked to his work and his children, and although Powell once said: "Unless one is alone one is unimportant," he lacked the resource to maintain that position. He turned to, and identified himself with, his Saviour, ready to emulate his Redeemer and to sacrifice himself for what he believed to be the true word. The political sophisticates who were astonished by Powell's renunciation in 1974 of his safe seat and power base in Wolverhampton, rather than fight under what he believed to be Heath's false banner, did not understand their man. He was acting out his needs; and lacking, as ever, subtlety or pretence, he made this explicit to those attuned to listen.

After briefly announcing his decision not to participate in what he described as "a fraudulent election" he remained silent for two weeks, except for one public intervention and that was his little-noticed sermon entitled *The meaning of sacrifice: the road to Calvary*. Powell went, with masochistic relish, on his way, enjoying every moment at the stations of his cross. To those who accused him of being a Judas, he retorted, with full justification, that he received no reward for his services. His critics misunderstood his role; his mimesis was no fringe part in the drama. His grandiosity, always teetering on the edge of omnipotence, insisted he was the central figure and as such he endured his political crucifixion. But it cannot be doubted that he went to his cross bearing not only the sins of the world but bearing his own sins, seeking redemption from his own guilts.[28] And they were the guilts of a man who could never forgive himself, that, unlike the Son, the Messiah Jesus with whom he identified, he was not a celibate; he loathed his own body, he had failed in his spiritual quest, he was not disembodied and was unable to declare to his followers *Noli me tangere*.

The resultant squeamishness of the "sinner" sometimes took a bizarre turn. On one easily forgotten journey, when travelling by train to give a lecture at York University, I was seated in my uncrowded compartment when the vacant seat next to mine was determinedly grabbed by a woman who chirpily and proudly introduced herself with a reminder that we had previously met at an Oxford symposium; to my dismay, this uninvited fellow-traveller was Mary Whitehouse, the scavenging propagandist who found filth in every human embrace. For some two hours, until her stop was mercifully reached, in a breathless monologue, her vanity oozing out of every pore, she regaled me with tales of her triumphs over her sex-sodden opponents in the BBC. And when she told me of the brave helpers who, when she was derided and traduced, supported her earliest campaigning, the glow of an orgasm suffused her cheeks as she recalled the never-failing encouragement and guidance she had received from her hero: Enoch Powell. They indeed had much in common; both feared the vigour of sexuality—she would censor its manifestations and he would control its most fearful expression: the prolific birth-rate of the blacks.

But the emphasis Powell ever placed on birth-rates should not be seen simply as an avoidance tactic, one to draw attention away from his prurient envious preoccupations with the blacks' sexual vigour; his constant citation of birth-rate statistics, ever attempting to distance births from conceptions, was no mere feint and should not be interpreted simply as a smokescreen. On the contrary, there is a fundamental interconnectedness between the alarums he deliberately set off and his own tragic entrapment, his incapacity to experience the vagina as an object of desire; for him it was a threat: it was the dangerous exit through which, in a terrible ordeal, he had been compelled to pass on his emergence from the womb. All Powell's non-white immigration "numbers" speeches tell how he was overwhelmed by an anxiety which sprang not, as he claimed, from his cold meticulous mathematics but from another far more menacing source: in his obsession with birth he provides us, as he converts his private anxieties to public anxieties, with an exotic case study of a man vainly struggling to overcome the trauma of his own parturition, for the obsessional birth preoccupations of Powell tell us of his desperate efforts to cage and contain anxieties. Mindful that the word "anxieties" has Sanskrit roots signifying an association with narrowness or restriction, Freud, in identifying the primal source of our anxieties made the connection between fear and the very act of birth.[29]

For all of us there is one travail, replete with anxiety, that is inescapable; being born is the trauma that all are fated to endure. Freud considered that it was the act of being born, when the biological helplessness of the infant is proclaimed, when the inner world of the womb is replaced by an unknown external environment, when the organism is flooded by amounts of excitation beyond its capacity to master, that induces what Freud named as "primary anxiety"; this is the common root of all the anxieties that afflict us later in life.

Painful or traumatic events have to be endured by most of us over our life-cycle; these are the times when the primal anxiety of the birth trauma is ever evoked. The ability to contain the panic and fear that can arise in later life is dependent upon the severity of the initial trauma—whether it was a difficult birth, perhaps because of the size of the baby—and, above all, by the quality of the caring reassurance that the totally disoriented babe needs when, as a screaming wailing neonate, he is initiated into the external world. The biological determinants may be intractable but how we are then received will decide whether or not the load of anxieties we are carrying is to be lightened. A warm mothering mother, with soothing affection, lullabying and loving, may quell the terrors of a babe so painfully expelled into a new and seemingly totally hostile world; enfolded and cradled within a mother's arms, held securely in a softly-lit room, feeling the heat of the mother's body, rocked gently to and fro, the babe softens its screaming as the sensitive holding mother evokes for her child the reminiscence of its earliest intra-uterine state. No such mimetic exercise, bringing much-needed solace, will be performed by an unempathic mother deficient in communication skills; for such a child as hers, no lost Eden is recaptured. Perforce, we cannot know what the particular early circumstances of his birth and rearing were that so left Powell loaded with the fears of the pressures and shortage of breath which constitute the most menacing and terrifying aspects of the birth process; but it is clear that burden was his fate. Every tabloid and almost all popular magazines have astrologists telling millions of their eager readers, on the basis of their birth day, how to face their destiny in the coming month; astrology, with all its nonsense, is the first doctrine of the birth trauma, teaching in half-truths that the entire being and fate of man is determined by what occurs at the very moment of birth. The astrologers are, of course, absurd when they say that what occurs in those crucial moments can be discovered by the reading of the stars. Yet although their claims are obviously fanciful, the validity of the belief in the determining influence on every individual of his own particular parturition is rational. It is unsurprising, given the terrors of birth, that many psychoanalysts in one form or another have proposed that later traumas, such as the shock experience of being weaned, or that the accompanying awareness in the Oedipal phase that castration would be the price to be paid if we pursue our incestuous desires, have the benign purpose of absorbing, as it were, some of the original threatening primary anxiety affect precipitated at birth. Powell, however, did not, could not, so loosen the grip of his birth trauma as appears to take place in normative development; he sought to extirpate the personal terrors the trauma of birth had brought upon him by displacing them into the public weal. By alarmist jeremiads, by warning the world in apocalyptic terms of coming disasters, he strove to relieve himself of the fears possessing him by unloading them on to the body politic of Britain.

The consequence was not always dire. His brilliant colleague, Iain Macleod who, but for his premature death would undoubtedly have become a Conservative prime minister, once remarked: "Poor Enoch, driven mad by the remorselessness of his own logic." But that logic, even although often echoing the reverberations of his birth trauma, could sometimes be applied devastatingly and constructively; nowhere is that to be seen more clearly than in his contribution to the debates on Britain's possession of nuclear armaments. All the doomsday forebodings that ever haunted him were woven into his powerful arguments against Britain depending for defence upon the nuclear bomb. Those of us who campaigned for nuclear disarmament had no more eloquent ally than Enoch Powell. His eloquence may have been suspect, charged as it was with reminiscences of the death threats endured by him as a neonate when, fighting for his life and gasping, he struggled out of the womb, but the logic of his argument was impeccable. To his party's considerable displeasure he insistently mocked the government's "nuclear assumption"—that the West might resort to nuclear weapons if NATO was faring badly in a war against the countries of the Warsaw Pact. He argued that the nuclear deterrent "about which we hear so much, is a pretend deterrent, in which nobody seriously believes ... Even if Russian troops were in barges about to invade Britain, we would still not commit national suicide by initiating a nuclear exchange, but would rather say: 'No, let us fight it out as best we can. If we lose, at least we shall not have destroyed the basis of our future resurgence'".[30]

When, with others, I had spoken against the bomb on marches, on plinths, and on many a platform with Bertrand Russell, never did any of us more vividly conjure up to our listeners the threat facing us of total annihilation than did Enoch Powell. The primal anxieties ever enveloping the man were being displaced upon apocalyptic warnings against the folly of imagining national security could be gained by the acquisition of yet more fiendish nuclear weaponry.

But the invasion of his private dilemmas into his political discourse, although charging his pronouncements with an élan rarely to be found in the cue-prompted recitations of today's wary politicians, more usually led to disastrous judgments. His squeamish aversion to the joys of genitality, his fear of returning to the site from which his primal anxiety sprang, brought about the inevitable corollary— the idealization of a pure sexless mother fantasized as a virgin to whom, without the agonies or traumas of birth, he had been born, the product of an immaculate conception. The morbid intensive relationship between Powell and his mother ensured the smudging of any link with the father; his arrival was, as in the Greek myths this one-time professor of Greek taught, the birth of the Hero. And it was with that endowment in heroic stances he role-played his defence of his supreme mother surrogates, first the British Empire and later Britain.

Always, with all the issues in which he became involved, as in the immigration debates, he portrayed himself as the defender of his motherland. So it was that once he, belatedly, grasped that entry into the European Community was not merely a commercial transaction but had political unification as its ultimate goal, the notion of his motherland being usurped by foreign elements was found to be intolerable; and no-one fought with greater stamina against Heath and those of us supporting entry into Europe than Powell. He believed he was rescuing his mother from a fate worse than death. When he lost his fight he taunted the British with having enjoyed the "rape" of their "national and parliamentary independence".[31]

When he so depicted our entry into Europe he was moved by the same determinants as those which moved him, years before, to resist independence being accorded to India. Then the British Empire as such had been his mother surrogate and, gripped by the irrational passions that always accompanied his attachment to such constructs, his political judgment deserted him: he put forward to Churchill the crazy plan to take and hold India with ten divisions. Powell could not bear to see his beloved Empire, epitomized as India, wrenched from him. His behavioural pattern found expression in his romantic imperialism; when he wrote of his sojourn in India, his language was of a love-sick swain: "India claimed me almost from the first moment there. I started to love and learn personally. I bought and read omnivorously anything about India I could lay hands on." There are more than shades of his own instructing teacher-mother as he learns from India and practises his Urdu among Indian villages. His love, of course, was blind; he could not initially face the reality of the situation.

Yet this sometimes astonishing man, one who teetered on the edge between madness and divinatory insights, a paranoid who could wildly allege[32] that "enemies of this country" had infiltrated the Home Office and were "conducting our immigration policy", and who could, in his anti-Americanism, make bizarre claims that the CIA was behind the IRA's assassination of Mountbatten and attempted assassination of Thatcher, fitfully possessed a rare capacity to face reality. And when he had at last mourned through his loss of India, he saw the situation as it really was. Using an explicit psychoanalytical insight he freed himself from his fixation on India and Empire, writing:[33] "So the psychoanalysis through which lies the cure for Britain's sickness has to be twofold; first, we must identify and overcome the mythology of the late Victorian Empire; then, we must penetrate to deeper levels and eradicate the fixation with India from our sub-conscious." But this attempt, at one remove, to examine his own motivation, is incomplete. It gave him the intellectual courage to discard his whole concept of a world role for Britain but then, when he began to re-think Britain's national status, he still remained locked into his compelling need for some mother surrogate. The boundless passion he had bestowed on the British

Empire was now concentrated upon Britain itself, and from then on he was to devote a lifetime to defending his motherland with a xenophobic fervour. And, unforgivably, it was with that same fervour that in his rabble-rousing "rivers of blood" speech he whipped up, as never before, obscene racialist prejudices against Britain's hapless non-white immigrant communities; self-indulgently, with a pitiless disregard of the consequences, the anxiety-ridden man spread his contagion.

As age advances, our threshold of tolerance so often diminishes and our worst characteristics become enlarged; age is certainly no guarantee that detachment is gained and our anxieties distanced. As he moved to the end of his parliamentary career, Powell's trajectory continued on his destructive course; inevitably it led, before the Commons days of us both were over, to our being in fierce combat once again. Like a moth around a flame, he was programmed by his primal anxiety to be lured into the *in vitro* birth controversy. In 1984, to the astonishment and bewilderment of most, Powell, having drawn in the ballot the right to introduce a Private Member's Bill, announced his intention to introduce one which would ensure that *in vitro* fertilization, and research into improvements in the techniques of fertilization, would be severely restricted. The Bill was greeted with acclaim by the fundamentalist lobbies. But Powell's move was nevertheless perplexing to them—as it was to the rest of the House—for his religion had subtleties and flavours far removed from the vulgarities of these lobbies; he had no history of a formal association with them, and such little contribution as he had made when what is now known pejoratively as permissive legislation was passing through the House, would certainly not have been approved by them. Instead, he had supported me in the lobbies when I organized the final end of capital punishment, and also when I had extinguished the criminality of private adult homosexual conduct. The House, wondering why he should voluntarily and unnecessarily throw himself into the tumult of the controversy, therefore cynically concluded that he was wooed by political opportunism. It was a shallow conclusion.

It was true that he was a septuagenarian politician whose frenetic physical activities and ceaseless speech-making displayed the politician's usual manic denial of the ageing process. It was clear that with a wish to fight yet again in his Northern Ireland seat, his age disadvantaged him. As an outsider in Ulster he had an uneasy relationship with his constituency where, as was later proved to be the case, his majority was more than precarious, depending as much on past divisions in the Catholic vote as upon the Unionist voters; and he was undoubtedly well aware that he could sink at any time in the treacherous bogs of Irish politics. To be the champion, therefore, of the movement against *in vitro* fertilization afforded him a singular opportunity to gain support from both his Catholic electorate and those stricken with Ulster's primitive brand of Presbyterianism.

Yet to attribute such motivations to Powell, a man who had so determinedly thrown away his safe Wolverhampton seat, is to misunderstand him. Though it is often difficult for his conduct to be understood by equivocating mean politicians who judge others as themselves, Powell gave the explanation for his intervention honestly and without trimmings: he said that his "instinct" determined his stance. He made no claim to be moved by religious conviction or by reason. Repeatedly he declared, when defending his intention to stop effective-embryo research, that his was a "gut reaction"; certainly it was not an intellectual response—but I, of course, would identify the bodily response as being a few inches away from the gut. It is predictable that the less sexually robust feel *in vitro* fertilization as a subversion of their own virility. Macho man, overdetermined in his bid to assert his maleness, finds the suggestion that he may be dispensable terrifying. Powell's anguish over the black population growth, as over embryo research, reveals the same psycho-pathology.

Powell's Bill endangered years of effort on my part; I have recounted fully elsewhere[34] the prolonged parliamentary battles I had, to draw the attention of a lazy House and a reluctant government to the need, within a framework that had taken account of the ethical, social, and legal aspects involved, to encourage, not fear, the availability of recombinant DNA, and to facilitate further research into *in vitro* fertilization and embryo transplants. The doctors and scientists had within their grasp wondrous possibilities; the desperate needs of the infertile could perhaps be met, the anguish of miscarriages relieved, and some terrible inherited diseases conquered. Step by step in my endeavours I had to overcome the resistances of those influenced by the fundamentalist anti-abortion lobbies never prepared to appreciate that abortion was concerned with the destruction of life and *in vitro* fertilization with its creation.

What became most evident in the ensuing debates surrounding Powell's Bill was Powell's commitment to the irrational which he unabashedly and fluently claimed was the moving agent of his course. Given the nature of his fundamentalist allies, it was therefore inevitable that the debates became musty, soaked in the vocabulary of medievalists. In and out of Parliament we conducted no pristine colloquy; rather, we witnessed the re-enactment of the old struggle between religious zealots and science. The physicist of the skies, Galileo, daring, by his advocacy of a heliocentric cosmology, to obliterate the distinction between the celestial and territorial, was condemned as a heretic by the Pope. The Catholic Church ensnared Galileo by charging him with "necessitating" God, for he was possessed of unforgivable hubris by imaginatively usurping God's place and telling Him how He must have created the universe. Huxley, in his famed debate with Bishop Wilberforce, recalling the sage when defending Darwin against the onslaught of the churches, asked who could number the earnest and ancient seekers for truth from the days of Galileo until his times, whose lives had been embittered by the mistaken zeal of bibliolators. And Freud was later to endure the self-same prejudices compelling him to refrain from publishing some of his works in Catholic Vienna; exploring the psyche was seen as soul-searching, a monopoly to be preserved by the Catholic Church. Enoch Powell, by threatening the medical community as he did with the stigma of criminality if they dared in future to pursue their embryo research, was aligning himself with a long and dishonourable tradition.

In the Commons in 1984 Powell had no difficulty in steamrollering his Bill through its second reading and committee stages. He had at his disposal not only his own eloquence but also a huge majority; the anti-abortionist fundamentalist lobby, unsurpassed in its passion and, more relevantly, in its organizational skills, marshalled its forces: and MPs, out of conviction, religious affiliation, or electoral opportunism, obeyed its whip. A generation before, Labour benches were often packed as we pushed through in the 1960s the social reforms which we believed would create a more civilized Britain; but by the '80s, Thatcherite attitudes had already infected the newly-arrived and younger Labour MPs. Preoccupied with devising economic programmes that would enable them to claim an ability to bring the greater wealth desired by a materialist Britain, too often they considered debates about more profound human needs as peripheral to the central argument as to how to shower yet more consumer goods on the electorate. Within such an ambience, with opposition so muted, when Powell brought his intact, unamended Bill to its final report stage in the Commons, he had the right to assume there were no serious hurdles in play that could deny him his victory.

But I had other thoughts. On the fateful day allocated in the Commons for the completion of the report stage of Powell's Bill, I arrived armed with a load of Law Reports on a dozen or more cases relating to road traffic offences. I had noted that a minor technical Bill, which slightly amended the rule relating to the production of motor-car licences, was due to precede the consideration of Powell's Bill. It was a very little Bill, approved of by government and the opposition alike as well as the motoring lobbies. No-one had ever expressed any objection to its form or intention. It was anticipated that its passage was a formality taking up little more than five minutes to pass through the Commons before the House proceeded to consider Powell's Bill. But it was that seemingly irrelevant Bill that afforded me an opportunity to sabotage Powell's dangerous attempt to criminalize the much-needed medical research. Many years before, as a newly-qualified and impecunious young solicitor just starting up my own practice, I had welcomed work farmed out to me at two guineas a case by the over-burdened local prosecution office; during my first 12 months of practice, by conducting the prosecution of scores of traffic offences, I had been well-schooled and was able to draw upon that experience when, in a filibuster, I spelt out my reservations about the innocent Traffic Bill. I spoke non-stop, literally for hours, making the longest speech in the whole of my parliamentary life. The fretting Deputy Speaker, despite pleas from Powell's supporters, could not halt me since I was, with the material in my hands, too experienced a parliamentarian to stray from the rules of order. When Powell's Bill was finally reached, I had put down an amendment to his Bill which the procedural rules required to be called first and, having dallied with that amendment, despite Powell intervening to indicate his readiness to accept it—as he tried desperately to save his Bill—my supporting colleagues had no difficulty in consuming such little parliamentary time as was left to his Bill. The Bill ran out of time, and thus fell. My pact of animosity with Powell was well and truly sealed.

In some ways Powell's failed Bill was to be a watershed; tardily, liberal and medical opinion, alerted by the threats to benign scientific advancement that his Bill had advertised, gradually organized itself to meet the challenge of the fundamentalists. And when, in 2008, after many a battle, alarums came from the Catholic prelates that scientists, unless stopped, would now create Frankenstein's monsters, a better-informed public opinion and Parliament rejected their extravagances, and a new Human Fertilisation and Embryo Act was put in place. Within a responsible framework geneticists, in the interests of mankind, can now engage in genetic engineering without fear of the law. Posthumously, Enoch Powell has finally been defeated.

But in his lifetime, Powell himself never accepted defeat. Unto his last days, stricken with Parkinson's disease, still he heroically fought back, determined to affirm, despite *in vitro* fertilization, the exclusiveness of the virgin birth. Rejected by his electorate and marooned in bitter retirement, he continued to wage the battle away from Westminster, finding the ideal terrain in the Jewish Palestine of the first century.

Squandering his formidable intellect and his masterful command of Greek, he turned, obsessively, to a prolonged and detailed scrutiny of the New Testament and set out to upset the belief of the overwhelming majority of scholars that Mark's gospel was the first, and that it was upon that gospel that Matthew and Luke drew; this was utterly unacceptable to Powell for in Mark's gospel Jesus appears on the scene fully grown, and if its priority was accepted, then the annunciation and virgin birth recounted in the gospels of Matthew and Luke—but not in the writings of Paul, John and the rest of the writers of the New Testament—would be relegated to the realm of fanciful and mythological additions.[35]

With Powell, in his political stances always perilously near messianic identification, it was an essential need for this extraordinarily mother-bound man to erase a human sire and to assert the divinity of a Jesus fathered by no-one except God; sex and intercourse were thus banished from the tale, and the holy mother was to remain virginal, a state which unconsciously Powell doubtless wished upon his own mother.

It was indeed a tragedy that Powell, the great parliamentarian, should have ended his last years entangled in such a bizarre exercise;

but it was the price he paid for having wrestled so unsuccessfully to come to terms with his own sexuality. He always reminded me of the Cathars, the courageous 13th century heretics of the Languedoc who, to become *"parfait"*, advocated celibacy and suicide, both ideals negating the physical side of our nature. Powell's yearnings were congruent with those of the Cathars. On television he had once declared his real desire was not to be a politician but to be a monk; but he had failed to achieve celibacy, and not having achieved suicide, he felt guilty in living, more than once expressing his dismay that, unlike many of his comrades, he had survived the war. Such life-negating, not life-enhancing, moods enveloped his politics, making them dangerous yet seductive. In the end he himself became entrapped by them; his last work, *The Evolution of the Gospels*, obsessive and manic, has an intellectual framework only fitfully able to contain near-madness. And so he was to die, not in glory but with a whimper.

***

The financial need in my adolescent years to earn my keep as a factory-worker freed me from the rigours of a set course at a university; as an auto-didact I alone was the arbiter deciding who I would worship at my pantheon. Now, in the last months of my life, not all of those adolescent gods are still in place; many, found wanting, have been discarded. An old man, so often disenchanted, wisely suspects all heroes; but still, alongside the shrines to Freud, Marx, and Nietzsche, I make my obeisances to the man, founder of the modern Conservative Party, twice prime minister of Britain, who was the greatest and most outrageous racist to ever grace the House of Commons: Benjamin Disraeli.

His racism was grand, overt, not sneaky; it was never wrapped up, as was Enoch Powell's, in a confection to hide its content. As he climbed up the greasy pole he, like all over-ambitious politicians, made his self-serving compromises and skilfully practised his mendacities, but in his assertion of racism, he never trimmed; it was his holy credo, never to be defiled. In our politically correct post-Holocaust days we flinch as repeatedly he declaims a racial doctrine as hierarchical and racist as Noah's; nothing dented his belief in the paramount importance of race. Near the end of his days he said to a Jewish boy who had been presented to him: "You and I belong to a race which can do everything but fail." He was instructing the lad, even as he taught the nation when unabashedly he wrote: "Progress and reaction are but words to mystify the millions. They mean nothing, they are nothing, they are phrases and not facts. All is race. In the structure, the decay, and the development of the various families of man, the vicissitudes of history find their main solution."[36]

My generation, traumatized by our witnessing the apotheosis of Aryanism, celebrated as it was by the suffocation of hundreds of thousands of Jewish children in the German gas chambers, recoil as Disraeli insists on his advantage in belonging to a "pure" race, unlike the mongrels resident in Britain. A provocative passage from his novel *Contarini Fleming*[37] tells its own tale as he mocks the descendants of a:

> troop of Norman knights whose fathers were wreckers, Baltic pirates. ... Was then this mixed population of Saxons and Normans, among whom he had first seen the light, of purer blood than he? Oh no, he was descended in a direct line from one of the oldest races in the world, from that rigidly separate and unmixed Burgeoning race who had developed a high civilisation at a time when the inhabitants of England were going half-naked and eating acorns in their woods.

Today, endorsing Disraeli's uncompromising racialism would doubtless be widely regarded as scandalous. When Nobel laureate James Watson, one of the world's leading scientists, even dared to venture, in 2007, that:

> there is no firm reason to anticipate that the intellectual capacities of people geographically separated in their evolution should prove to have evolved identically. Our wanting to reserve equal powers of reason as some universal heritage of humanity will not be enough to make it so.[38]

he was universally condemned, as he was for his comment that:

> I am exceedingly gloomy about the prospect of Africa. ... All our social policies are based on the fact that their intelligence is the same as ours—whereas all the testing says not really.[39]

So outraged was the Federation of American Scientists that it declared Watson was choosing "to use his unique stature to promote personal prejudices that are racist, vicious and unsupported by science". This intemperate condemnation by the American scientists tells us more of the unexpurgated guilt felt by a nation built upon the enslavement of millions of captured African blacks than the interpretations that can be placed on the 20th century discovery of so many of the secrets of the human genome. We shall not, however, wipe out the malignant consequences of Noah's curse by denial, by an insistence that race is a social construct and devoid of any biological determinants; such extravagant hostility to any scrutiny of differentiation between peoples, as is the stance of too many liberals over-anxious to display their anti-racialist credentials, in fact does a disservice to those the potential victims of racism. It leads to too great a deference being given to multi-culturalism, to an over-valuation of the benefits of plurality, and gives respectability to the ghettoization of our cities. This, in the end, is to the disadvantage of non-white citizens who, by self-exclusion, invite hostility and lose so many of the benefits available to those in the host community.

Similar *faux* liberal mind-sets have led too many 20th century critiques of Disraeli to impertinently attempt to exonerate him from the charge of racialism; fundamentally, such would-be apologists claim that his ostentatious racialism is not authentic; variously they suggest it was a pose, an over-compensative defence against anti-Semitism, a carapace, or, as told in more sophisticated presentations, the by-product of an attempted existential resolution of a man in search of an identity. Isaiah Berlin, the renowned Oxford historian of ideas, a man with whom I enjoyed dining but whose excessively charitable judgments on men who we both knew was, I found, often to be awry, entitled his essay on Disraeli *Search for Identity*.[40] The over-civilized fellow of All Souls found that Disraeli boasted of his Jewish origins almost too insistently and mentioned them in and out of season at risk to his political career". Berlin cannot bring himself to accept that Disraeli's pride in his race was genuine, that his advertised beliefs that he belonged to a superior people was anything but an affectation, one assumed "in order to feel that he was dealing on equal terms with the leaders of his family's adopted country, which he so profoundly venerated".

I find Berlin's contention droll; the notion that Disraeli of all people lacked a confident identity, that he was "a brilliant performer" and "an actor who became one with his own act" who was "taken in by his own inventions" is a fanciful construction. No man lacking fundamental conviction would have dared to face a hostile House of Commons in the terms in which Disraeli did as he flaunted his racialist doctrine. In the decades I spent in the Commons there were many occasions when my reforming zeal brought me into conflict with majority opinion in the House and there were times, when expressing an individual and unpopular view, I found myself howled down. But I wonder at the breath-taking *chutzpah* of Disraeli when, without any support from his own party, he urged that Jews should be admitted to Parliament since it was the least that could be done to repay the debt due to them for if they had not crucified Christ, the Honourable Members would not have been redeemed. It was a disconcerting theme, deliberately calculated to turn on its head the conventional assumptions of the anti-Semitic Christian; and it was a theme Disraeli persistently pursued in his novels. Speaking through the beautiful Jewess portrayed in *Tancred*,[41] the question is put:

> Now tell me; suppose the Jews had not prevailed upon the Romans to crucify Jesus, what would have become of the Atonement ... the holy race supplied the victim and the immolators. What other race could have been entrusted with such a consummation? Was not Abraham prepared to sacrifice even his son? And with such a doctrine, that embraces all space and time; nay more, chaos and eternity; with divine persons for the agents and the redemption of the whole family of man for the subject; you can mix up the miserable persecution of a single race! ... Persecutors! Why, if you believe what you profess, you should kneel to us! You raise statues to the hero who saves the country. We have saved the human race, and you persecute us for doing it.

Disraeli's challenging assertion is made by an extraordinary intact man, not one fumbling with his selfhood; he is revelling in the superiority which he profoundly believes membership of his race has bestowed upon him. Because, as he more than once retorted to malicious enquirers of his origins, he sprang from the same race as the Apostles, he had the right, as did the Jewess, to demand that others made their genuflections to Jewry; for it was the Hebrews who had provided:[42]

> a sacrificial Mediator with Jehovah, that expiatory intercessor born from the Chosen House of the Chosen People, yet blending in His inexplicable nature the divine essence with a human element, appointed before all time, and purifying, by His atoning blood, the myriads that preceded and the myriads that will follow us, without distinction of creed or clime.

Only a man comfortable in his own skin could have dared, whatever the consequences to his political advancement, to have declared his racialist mantra to the Christian world so arrogantly and abrasively. For a man to possess confidence of this order, he needs to be at ease with his own sexuality. Enoch Powell's destructive racialism, as we have proposed, stemmed to a considerable degree from his wracked, guilt-ridden sexuality; the homosexual components of Disraeli's disposition were certainly no less than Powell's but how marvellously he accepted them and then put them at his service in his political manifestos and novels. The beautiful young aristocrats, products of Eton and Cambridge, seduced by Disraeli, swooned gracefully as under his leadership of the Young England group in the Commons they subverted the government; and in his early novels, all autobiographical, we continually find lingering references to Greek and Roman male friendships. In *Vivian Grey, The Young Duke, Contarini Fleming, Alroy, Henrietta Temple* and *Venetia*, the male heroes often look like girls, often are dandies, ever getting tangled with handsome young men and frequently put into homoerotic situations, spending hours in Turkish baths or dressing in female costumes. In *Venetia* Disraeli makes open references to Byron's Thyrza's verses, love poems addressed to a boy, and his Byronic hero remarks on two figures of the classical world whose same-sex experiences were well-known: "I think of the Ancients ... Alcibiades and Alexander the Great are my favourites. They were young, beautiful, and conquerors; a great combination."

Unlike the Enoch Powells of this world, he was not frightened of his homosexual component. Teasingly, he titillated his male readers as, covertly, he told of the homoerotic escapades of his handsome young Anglo-Saxon heroes; he knew that those familiar with classical literature would complicitly understand what he was conveying, while those unschooled in such literary convention and unburdened by insight or guilt would innocently bask in the erotic resonances of his florid, languorous prose. Always, in his politics and his novels, it was Disraeli who was in control, ever an exploiter and never a victim of his temperament.

When, in my teens, I avidly first read Disraeli's novels, his paeans of praise for the benefits his racial heritage had bestowed upon him never jarred on me for they were corroborations of what I had been taught by my Talmudic grandfather and which would have been upheld by Disraeli's strictly Orthodox grandfather. When the boy Benjamin walked from his home in Bloomsbury to his grandparents in Kensington he received not only extra pocket money from his grandfather; the precocious boy could not have failed to return home without an increased awareness of the religious observances practised by his synagogue-attending grandfather—to the distaste of his snobbish wife—. Young Ben, while well-exposed to Christian belief in his early attendance at a school run by a Nonconformist parson and later at a Unitarian boarding institution, continued to receive weekly private lessons in Hebrew from a Jewish religious tutor until he was 12 years old; he was preparing for his bar mitzvah, the initiation ceremony that requires a Jewish boy at 13 to publicly recite in Hebrew, at the synagogue, a section of the Law and so enter into Jewish Manhood.

But as he approached the crucial 13th birthday, young Ben was abruptly left in a religious limbo; his family no longer had a synagogue in which to celebrate the rite. Ben's unworldly dreamy bibliophile father, Isaac, indifferent to the claims of any institutionalized religion and free from the constraints of his recently deceased religious father, had bitterly quarrelled with his synagogue, refusing to pay a fine levied on him because of his defiance of repeated requests that he take on duties as a warden, a duty which the Ascamot, the laws of the congregation, prescribed should be rotated among the membership.

The breakdown between the synagogue and Isaac was the opportunity for Isaac's close friend.

Notes

1. *Proverbs*, ch. 20, V. 1.
2. *The Book of Psalms*, ch. 80, V. 8–11.
3. Scruton, R. in *The New Statesman*, 5th February 2007.
4. *The Gospel According to St. John*, ch. 2, V. 1–11.
5. *The Gospel According to St. Luke*, ch. 22, V. 20.
6. *Genesis*, ch. 9, V. 20–27.
7. Alter, R. *The Five Books of Moses, op. cit.*
8. *The Fourth Book of Moses, called Numbers*, ch. 12, V. 1–15.
9. *The Song of Solomon*, ch. 1, V. 5–6.
10. *The Book of the Prophet Jeremiah*, ch. 13, V. 23.
11. Brichto, S. *The People's Bible: Book of Genesis, op. cit.*
12. *Babylonian Talmud, Sanhedrin, 17a.*
13. Alter, R. *The Five Books of Moses, op. cit.*
14. Braude, B. *Ham and Noah: Sexuality, Servitudism and Ethnicity,* University of Yale, 2003.
15. Freud, S. *The Ego and the Id,* SE, Vol. IX.
16. Fenichel, O. *The Psychoanalytic Theory of Neurosis,* Routledge & Kegan Paul, 1946.
17. Abse, L. *The Bi-Sexuality of Daniel Defoe,* ch. 10, Karnac Books, 2006.
18. *Genesis*, ch. 9, V. 1.
19. Chasseguet-Smirgel, J. *Creativity and Perversion, op. cit.*
20. *Genesis*, ch. 1, V. 2–7.
21. *Genesis*, ch. 1, V. 11–12.
22. Goldenburg, D.M. *The Curse of Ham: Race and Slavery in Early Judaism, Christianity and Islam,* Princeton University Press, 2003.
23. Ferenczi, S. *Thalassa, A Theory of Genitality,* Karnac Books, 1989.
24. Nettle, D. *Personality: What makes you the way you are,* Oxford University Press, 2008.
25. *Hansard 799:290,* quoted in Heffer, S., *Like the Roman: The Life of Enoch Powell,* Weidenfeld & Nicolson, 1998.
26. Heffer, S. *Like the Roman, ibid.*
27. Heffer, S. *Like the Roman, ibid.*
28. Abse, L. *Fellatio, Masochism, Politics and Love,* Robson Books, 2000.
29. Freud, S. *Beyond the Pleasure Principle,* SE. Vol. xviii; Fenichel, O., *The Psychoanalytical Theory of Neuroses,* Routledge & Kegan Paul, 1971; Rank, O., *The Trauma of Birth,* Kegan Paul, 1929.
30. Powell, E.
31. Interview with Robin Day, BBC Radio 4, 21st October 1974.
32. *The Observer,* 21st June 1992.
33. Powell, E. in *The Spectator,* 13th September 1968.

34. Abse, L. *The Politics of In Vitro Fertilisation in Britain*, essay in *In Vitro Fertilisation*, ed. Fischel, S., IRL Press, 1986; Abse, L., *Margaret, Daughter of Beatrice*, Jonathan Cape, 1989.
35. Powell, E. *The Evolution of the Gospels*, Yale University Press, 1994.
36. Disraeli, B.
37. Disraeli, B. *Contarini Fleming*, 1832.
38. Watson, J. *Avoiding Boring People*, Oxford University Press, 2007.
39. Watson, J. *The Sunday Times*, October 2007.
40. Berlin, I. *Against the Current: Essays in the History of Ideas*, Oxford University Press, 1981.
41. Disraeli, B. *Tancred*, 1847.
42. Disraeli, B. *Tancred, op. cit.*

INDEX

Abishag
  story 154
  the lure of incest 127–160
Abraham, Karl 64–65, 142
  biological father 64
  condonation 65
  thesis 142
Al Aynsley-Green 118
Al chate prayer 6
Alexandrian priest Arius 76
Almighty's commandment 131
Akhenaton
  code 140
  condonation of deviances 145
  creed 39
  downfall 143
  entourage 143
  expositions 143
  ideal 39
  monolatry 147
  Moses and Monotheism 142
  reign 136
  religious innovations 142
Ambivalent antagonism 181
American Pentecostals 68
American Urie Brofenbrenner 93
Amnon's transgressive desire 149
Amsterdam synagogue 2
Anaphrodisical calm 158
Anatomy of Melancholy 159
Ancient Israel, queen of 145
Anglican Church 47
Anna, Maria 27
Annunciation 79
Anti-abortion lobbies 194
Anti-Americanism 192
Anti-Christianity diatribes 130
Anti-discrimination 178
Anti-discriminatory measures 182
Anti-monotheistic brigade 38
Anti-segregation legislation 178
Anti-Semitism 200

INDEX

Apocalyptic warnings 183
Apocrypha 151
Arianism 78
Aryanism, apotheosis of 199
Assmann, Jan 141
Assyrian 136
Athanasian Creed 77, 79
Australian Aborigines 8
Aton
    believer 139
    feminine dimensions of 139
Axe symbolizing domination 10

Babylonian
    gods 10
    Talmud 171
Bacon, Alice 100
Barenboim 30
Barenboim, Daniel 30
Beethoven's A-minor string
    quartet 29
Bible-reading Nonconformist
    Wales 66
Biblical
    canon 144
    creation story 53
    emphases 166
    historical accounts 42
    scholar Robert Eisenmann 73
    scholars 171
Bipedal hominid 16
Birmingham racialists 184
Bisexual mixture 50
Boers of South Africa 177
Book of Common Prayer 154
Bormann, Martin 70
Brahms, Johannes 53
    adult private life 54
    asexual relationships 54
Braude, Benjamin 171
Breasted, James 136
Breeches 50

Britain's children's laws 113, 117
British National Party
    in London's Barking and
        Dagenham districts 169
British political history 182
Brown, Gordon 97, 121

Callaghan, Jim 116–117
Camden children's officer 109–110
Cardiff Labour Party 146
Cardiff's fish market 130
Carmel, Mount 38
Catholic
    conscience 103
    doctrine 54
    dogma 44
    prejudice 102
    Vienna 195
Catholic and Eastern Orthodox
    Christianity 73
Catholic Church 44, 176, 195
    anathematises 77
    orthodoxies 77
Cecilia, Saint 32, 42
    rôle millennia 36
    soothing emollients 47
Celtic imagination 157
Character disorders 74
Chasseguet-Smirgel, Janine 175
Chatwin, Bruce 14
Cheders 67
Child murder 108
Children's Act 110, 118
    1975, 117
    2004, 118
Children's Plan, 10-year 122
Children's Protector 116
Child's sexual desire 108
Christendom 36, 41
Christendom's myth
    magic imaginative super-
        reality of 85

INDEX 209

Christian, Any 76
Christian
　anti-Semitism 81
　archaeologist 138
　doctrine 77, 80, 166
　Ebionite sects 72
　ethos 69
　Europe 83
　Gentile 85
　Gnostic sects 72
　humanists 46
　maiden 41
　pacifism 138
　philosophers 43
　renditions 140
　slave-traders of Europe 168
　theology 140
　verity 40
　wine 166
Christianity 39, 44, 72, 138–139
　Godhead 47
　in the Roman Empire 83
Christian Jews 41
　of Palestine 73
Christian theologians
　speculations 79
Christology Movement 78
Church Jubal 23
Clark, Kenneth 26
Clement of Alexandria 47
Code of Laws 133
Collective guilt 6
Consensus-seeking committees 145
Conservative Party 198
Council of Nicaea's
　condemnation 76
Counter-cultural assaults 118
Counter-reformation 42
Cretney, Stephen 104, 110
Criminal Law Review
　Committee 103
Cromwell's Puritans 23

Daniel, Prophet 152
　120 *Days of Sodom* 133
Darwin, Charles 7
　hypothesis 7
　romantic conclusion 14
Darwinian flourish 16
Das Judentum in der Musik,
　venomous anti-Semitic 58
David, King 122, 149, 160
　supporters 152
Deceased Wife's Sisters' Marriage
　Bill 155
De-colonization 180
Defeatism 51
Dehumanization 180
Demeter's happiness 98
Depat-Ponson 180
Depth-psychology 19
De-sexualization 26
Deutsch, Helen 99
　The Dialogue with Trypho the Jew 81
Dionysian 34
Discursive meditation on music
　and its origins 1
Dishonourable tradition 195
Disraeli, Benjamin 182
　uncompromising racialism 199
Divine Idea of wine 167
Divinity 43
Doom-laden tale 63
Douglas, Mary
　Catholic anthropologist 135
Dryden, John 34
Dürer, Albrecht 45
Dyadic relationship 65

East Prussian Kônigsberg 130
Egypt God's holy people 144
Egypt's polyandry 147
Egyptian 136
　lore 145
　polytheism 144

temptation 149
transgressions 145
gods 10, 39
Egyptian Empire, Akhenaton 138
Egyptophobia 144
Ehrenzweig, Anton 20
Eliot, T.S. 158
Embarkation 69
Embryo transplants 194
Erasmus's *Encomium Moriae* 45
Euphemistic quality 6
European Community 180
The Evolution of the Gospels 198
Exodus prohibition 134

Faux 200
Federation of American
    Scientists 200
Female soprano 50
Femmes fatales 157
Ferenczi, Sandor 111
    theory 182
Finer, Morris 122
    premature death 122
Finnish anthropologist 93
Frazer, J.G. 7

Gaitskell, Hugh 101
Gardiner, Gerald 104
Gardner, Howard 12
Genesis story 71
Gibbon 78
Glass, Philip 39
God in Trinity and Trinity 77
God of Samuel 150
Gorer, Geoffrey 94
Gospel of Matthew 73, 76
Gospels 43
Great advance in intellectuality 144
Great Covenant 86
Greek Church 41
Greek cosmogony Cronus 63

Greek mythology 79
    Persephone 97
Greek protagonists 34
Groddeck, Georg 112
Guilt-inducing memory 8

Hallucinatory wish-fulfilment 85
Ham's inferiority 182
Hanagid, Samuel 158
Harman, Harriet 120
Hartshorne, Charles 11
Hebraic scholar Robert Alter 129
Hebrew
    Adam 53
    Bible 37, 140, 145
    god 38
    quit Egypt 38
Hellenic Christian Jews of the
    Diaspora 73
Hellenic Diaspora 72
Henotheism 141
Henry VIII 154
Hermaphroditic ideal 49, 52
Heterosexual relationships 28
History of the Jews 3
Hitler, Adolf 51
Holy Ghost 74
Holy Writ 147
Hungarian Jew Sandor Ferenczi 181
Home Office's
    advisory committees 146
    traditional negative
        responses 110
Homosexual
    culture 150
    crimes 107
Human Fertilisation and Embryo
    Act 197
Hungarian Jew 111

Incestuous homosexuality 171
Indo-European languages 19

INDEX 211

Indo-Iranian gods 143
Infanticide Bill 102
Institute for Fiscal Studies 96
Inter-generational sex 159
   reminiscent 156
Inter-Testamental age 71
In vitro fertilization 194
IRA's assassination of
   Mountbatten 192
Ironic antithesis 52
Israel's unchallengeable
   orthodoxy 40

Jacob/Israel, significance of 86
Jacob's
   allegory 75
   engagement 74
   Oedipal struggle 68
   sexual life 68
   working life 68
   wrestling match 63–87
James, King 67
Jehovah's Witness 78
Jerusalem Temple 146
Jesus, Christ 44
   of Burgos 46
   virgin birth of 45
Jewish
   ancestor-father Abraham 84
   Biblical myths 69
   literature 71
   movement 130
   Palestine 197
Jewry's dietary laws 127
Jezebel
   prophets 38
   tale 38
Jew Matthew 69
Joachim, Josef 55
   Hungarian-Jewish violinist 57
Josipovici, Gabriel 149
Jubal 47

Bible story of 36
discursive meditation
   on music and its origins 1
frightening *shofar* 7
mortality 4
progenitor 4
sibling 4
stirring incitements 47
Jubilation 4
   original musical 21
Judaeo-Christian, Greek-
   speaking 70
Judaism 84
Judgment of Solomon 91–123

Karl Marx 83
Kashrut 134
Keller, Hans 19
Kiddush 165
Kierkegaard's insight 133
King James Bible 140
Kippur, Yom 81–82
Kramer, Jonathan 29
Ku Klux Klan lynching 177

Labour benches 195
Law Commission 104, 106–107
Leviticus 142
   injunctions 154
   prohibitions 145
Life-affirming philosophy 51
Lincoln, Abraham 178
Lodge politics 113
Lofty speculations 79
Lord Longford 103
Lord of Burgos 46
Luther's Protestantism 46

Macleod, Iain 190
Maderno, Stefano 36
Madrasas 67
Mahler's ninth symphony 29

212 INDEX

Maimonides 84, 128, 130
Male-female relationships 121
Mann, Thomas 51
Marian basilicas 46
Mariolatry 42, 138
   ethos 46
Mary, Virgin 42–45, 75, 139
   sexuality and her ultimate disembodiment 44
   Significance 43
Masochism 69
Masturbatory thrills 159
Matrimonial pranks, undignified 157
Medical Research Council 102
Messiah Jesus 183
Mother-child dyad 98
Matthew 80
   collator 71
Matthew's Gospel 74
Melancholy of impotence 53
Michael Portillo 186
Middle Eastern
   Jewish 68
   region 39
   tribes 169
Midrash Haggadah 1
Miriam's dancing 4
Mithen, Steven 19
Monotheism 22, 137
Monotheistic revolution 39
Morley, Iain 17
Mosaic
   doctrine 138, 140, 144
   prohibition 142
Moses and Monotheism 141
Moses, Hebrew 144
Moses, Paul J., otolaryngologist 49
Mozart 26
Multi-culturism 180, 200
Muslim perpetrators dark-skinned 183

Nakedness of Noah 165–203
National and parliamentary independence 192
National Council of the Unmarried Mother and her Child 122
National Health Service 102, 106
National Insurance Act 106
National Society for the Prevention of Cruelty to Children 94
Nazism 185
Neo-German movement 57–58
   revolutionary 58
   self-styled 57
Neo-German theories 57
New Testament 44, 69, 197
Nietzsche's admiration 51
Nimrod, King
   army 64
Noah's
   curse 179, 200
   curse in contemporary Britain 182
   nakedness 170
   story 174
Nobler motivation 180
Nonconformists 41
   teachers 165
Non-white immigrants 183

Obama, Barack, campaign 169
Obsessiveness 135
Oedipal
   conflicts 159
   dilemma 67, 76
   manifestations emerge 65
   phase 190
   rivalry 107
   struggle 78
Oedipus complex 64, 172–173
   negative 173
Oedipus Rex 107
Old Testament 43, 71

admonition 165
God of Justice of 13
scribes 170
woman 44
Oxford symposium 188

Parliamentary calendar 183
Paul's antagonism to sexuality 44
Peart, Fred 184
Pentateuch 64
Peripatetic synagogues 38
Persephone myth 97–98
Persian king 145
Personal responsibility 21
The Philosophy of Music 13
Pines, Malcolm 109
Plato's *Symposium* 48
Platonic speculations 79
Polymorphous perverse
    accompaniment 50
Polytheism 36, 42
Polytheistic encroachments 135
Pope Pius XII, 44, 102
Portuguese Mozambique,
    pre-independence 176
Post-Thatcher/Blair Britain 92
Powell, William 13
Powell, Enoch 182, 188, 190–191, 195
    commitment 195
    confidence in Germany 185
    dangerous attempt 196
    formidable intellect 187
    non-white immigration 188
    oscillations 186
    renunciation in 1974, 187
Pre-Oedipal stages 174
Primordial
    pain 52
    time 53
Pristine configuration 29
Prohibitory monotheism 37
Prophetess 37

Protestant communions 77
Protestantism 171
Psycho-dynamics of emotions 18
Psychological witness 115
Psychosomatic medicine 112

Queen of Sheba 169
Queen Tiy 142

Reaction-formation 174
Red Riding Hood 100
Regensburg
    Pilgrimage 45
    synagogue 45
Révész, Géza 12
Richard Dawkins' ilk 130
Roberts, Beatrice 106
Robertson-Smith, William 7
The Roman Catholic Church 73
Roman Catholic dogma 44
Rome's full approbation 102
Róneim, Géza 8
Rousseau, Jean-Jacques 17
Royal College of Art 158
Royal Commissions 94, 122
Russell, Bertrand 191
Russell, C.T. 78
Russian Jewish philosopher 80

Saint Justin 81
Samuel reality 149
San Giovanni Church of 47
Scarman, Leslie 104
Schematisation 172
Schori, Katherine 47
Schubert's C-major's string
    quintet 29
Scruton, Roger 167
Sebold, W.G. 14
    Freudian quote 15
Self-aggrandisement 52
Self-dramatisation 52

Septuagint 70
Sex-obsessed reporters 159
Sex-sodden opponents 188
Sexual
 associations 10
 excitement 25
 intercourse 51
 selection 16
 violences 20
Sexuality 46
Shofar 1–3, 5, 10
Sick psycho-dynamics 182
Siegmund and Sieglinde 50
Solomon
 Judgment 91–123
 renowned judgment 115
 wisdom of 119
Song for Saint Cecilia's Day 34
Stekel, Wilhelm 99
Strauss' *Der Rosenkavalier* 50
Superb resignation 58
Suspitosus cultus imaginum 45
Symbiotic relationship 115

Tchaikovsky 55
Temple's Holy of Holies God 85
Ten Commandments 37
Thalassa, A Theory of Genitality 181
Thatcher, Margaret 102,
 106–107, 177
Thatcherite society 107
The History of Human Marriage 93
The Home Office civil servants 117
The Origin of Music 32
The Royal Society for the
 Prevention of Cruelty to
 Animals 94
Theodor Reik 10
Thraldom 92
Totem and Taboo 8, 150
Trans-generational sex 151–152
Trinitarian doctrine 41

Tunbridge Wells 28
Tyrannical master 158

UK's Internet Watch Foundation 95
UNICEF report 113, 119
Unitarian boarding institution 203
United Kingdom ranks 95
United Nations Children's Fund 95
US Episcopal Church 47

Verdi's *Un Ballo in Maschera* 50
Verlikovsky, Emmanuel 142
Vitriolic recriminatory attacks 72

Wagner
 gaudy effects 57
 histrionics of 57
 imperious commands 51
 operas 50
 sado-masochistic idyll 51
Wagnerian fantasies 58
Warsaw Pact 191
Watson, James 199
Wegener, Phillip 18
Weigall, Arthur 138
Westermarck, Edvard 93
Western Christianity 23
Western civilization 167
Williams, Shirley 102–103
Wilson government 104
Winnicott, Donald 15
Wolverhampton South-West,
 Rt Hon Member for 184
Wolverhampton virility 184
Wolverhampton,
Wundt, Wilhelm 19

Yahweh's pantheon 9

Zeitgeist 146
Zion 135
Zwingli, Huldreich 23